Charlotte Mann Beaumont Oates

Miscellaneous Poems, Songs and Rhymes

Charlotte Mann Beaumont Oates

Miscellaneous Poems, Songs and Rhymes

ISBN/EAN: 9783744775298

Printed in Europe, USA, Canada, Australia, Japan

Cover: Foto ©Thomas Meinert / pixelio.de

More available books at **www.hansebooks.com**

MISCELLANEOUS

..POEMS,..

SONGS and RHYMES,

BY

CHARLOTTE OATES.

Entered at Stationers' Hall.

Bradford:
PRINTED BY J. S. TOOTHILL, 71, GODWIN STREET
1898

PREFACE.

It is with genuine pleasure, and some pride, that I am now able to accede to the wishes of my sympathetic readers, and present to them this collection of my poetical compositions in volume form. Many of the shorter ones have previously appeared in various journals, whilst others are now published for the first time; and I hope these may meet with that kindly reception which has hitherto been accorded my simple effusions.

I would here gratefully acknowledge the generous response I have had from all classes; and only hope this work will be found to merit the support it has received. My thanks are alike due to those appreciative readers who have encouraged me to bring out my poems in this compact form, and to the kind patrons who have enabled me, by their support, to do so.

If my numerous subscribers and readers have as much pleasure in accepting, as I have in presenting this volume the effort will not have been in vain.

CHARLOTTE OATES.

CONTENTS.

	PAGE
Dedication	1
Lulled to Rest	3
The Maiden's Dream	11
A Queen's Sacrifice	20

Pastoral Poems

A Peasant's Home	25
Signs of Spring	28
The Old Bridge	29
"Birdie's Dream	32
Lovely May	33
A Summer Shower	34
"My Home"	35
To a Diverted Mountain Stream	36
Summer Days	37
To a Bird	38
The Moorlands	38
The Afterglow	39
The Last Sigh of Summer	40
Eventide	41
Harold Park, Low Moor	42
Ode to the Moon	44
Moorland and Sea	45
Norwood Green	47
A December Rose	49
The Lunar Rainbow	50
The First Snow of Winter	51
Nature's Melodies	52
The Frozen Brooklet	53
Royds Hall	54
The Name in the Snow	55
Sabbath Bells	56
Winter	57
"The Days are all Alike"	58
The Snowdrop	59
The Mountaineer's Song	60
At Nature's Shrine	60
When the Evening Lamp is Lighted	62
Spring	64

The Nightingale	
"The First Rose of Summer	
"The Country Cottage Girl"	6
The West Wind	71
On Finding a Bird's Nest in the Garden	72
Moonlit Flowers	73
Daybreak	75
Twilight	76
Night	79
Autumn	79
Stars of Midnight	82
Compensations	83
A Wintry Sunset	84
To a Robin	85
The Old Sycamore Tree	85
The Beauties of Snow	87
Dead Leaves	89

Sea Songs and Oceans Ode

A greeting to the Sea	9
The Whispering Waves	91
The Return of the Fishing Fleet	92
A Farewell to an Old Lifeboat	94
To the Sea	95
The Captain to his Crew	96
The Disconsolate Heart	98
The Skipper to his Boat	10
"Sailing on the Sunlit Sea"	101
The Widow's Lament	102
The Rainbow	103
The Lifeboat Bell	104
The Wreck of the "Sirene" at Blackpool	106
Meditations	108
Fishermen's Wives	11

CONTENTS.

	PAGE
On the Resignation of Coxswain Bickerstaffe ..	111
A Sea-Side Sunset ..	112
The Ocean's Charm ..	114
A Sail at Sabbath Eve	116
The Lifeboat Coxswain to his Crew	118
"The Palace on the Sea"	119
Shells of the Ocean ..	120
A Poet's Wish	121
Solaced	124
On Leaving the Sea ..	125
"The Gallant Lifeboat Crew"	127
"That House by the Sea"	128
The Fleetwood Lifeboat Heroes	129
On seeing the Wrecked Battleship "Foudroyant"	131
The Fisher Brothers ..	132
A Dream of the Sea ..	133
A Secret of the Sea ..	136
A Sea-Side Reverie ..	137
The Rescue	139
The Blackpool Lifeboat Crew	141
Father's Boat	142
The Margate Lifeboat Disaster	143
The Veteran's Resolve ..	145
The Heroes of the Fylde	147
"Beautiful Blackpool" ..	149
"Music on the Water" ..	150
The Ocean Monarchs ..	152
Lost!	154
The Fairy Bark ..	155
On the Return of Dr. Nansen	159
The "Bradford" to the Rescue!	162
H.M.S. Atalanta ..	163
Song of the Homeward Bound	165
The Lifeboatman's Widow and Orphan	167
A Farewell to the Sea..	170

ELEGIAC EFFUSIONS:—

I am Weary, let me Rest"	172
In Memoriam: H.R.H. Princess Alice	174

	PAGE
On the Death of the Duke of Clarence	175
In Memoriam: The late Prince Imperial of France	177
"Gone, but never once Forgot"	181
In Memoriam: Lord Tennyson	182
The Mourning Mother ..	184
On the Death of a Nonagenarian	185
In Memory of a Philanthropist	187
On the Death of Madame Patey	188
In Memory of an Old Shrimper	189
Sacred Memories ..	190
In Memory of a Poet ..	192
To a Young Friend ..	194
In Memoriam: The Crews of the St. Annes and Southport Lifeboats ..	196
"Thy Will be Done" ..	197
"He is not Dead, He only Sleeps"	199
In Memory of a Lancashire Bard	200
"Our Janey"	202
His Best Reward ..	205
A Tribute to the Memory of the Rt. Hon. W. E. Gladstone..	207
Passing Hence	208
Consolation	209

CHRISTMAS CHIMES:—

Christmas	211
Christmas Eve	212
Christmas Morn ..	213
A Christmas Greeting..	213
How to spend Christmas ..	214
The Dying Year ..	216
To the New Year ..	217
A New-Year Greeting ..	218
Resolutions for the New New Year	219
Nellie's Christmas	220
A Christmas Gift ..	223
New Year's Eve ..	225

iii.

	PAGE
The Meeting of the Years	226
Hope with New Year's Dawn	227
New-Year Reflections	228
A Prayer for the New Year	230

RANDOM ME

Past and Present	233
Yorkshire Factory Girls	236
An Old Maid	237
"That Naughty Demon Drink!"	239
"Speak of a Man as you find Him"	240
The Country Cousin	242
"What must I Wear"	243
A Lady's Leap-Year Proposal	244
Pomp and Vanity	245
A Cynic's Opinion of the "New Woman"	248
The Same on the "New Man"	249
The Queen's Jubilee at Norwood Green	251
"Three Things"	252
Blackpool's Attractions	253
"Auntie"	255
The Cunning Mouse	256
A Grandfather's Advice	258

PROMISCUOUS PIECES

The Queen's Jubilee, 1887	261
Youth	264
Birthday Lines to an Absent Friend	267
"My Mother"	269
Obscure Heroism	270
The Ellis Memorial Clock Tower	272
"Part in Peace"	274
To My Father on His Seventieth Birthday	275
A Rustic Beauty	278
A Plea for the Miners	279
Hope	280
The Mother's Prayer	281
Troubled Hearts	284
Goodness brings its Own Reward	285

	PAGE
"I Heard Thee Sing"	287
To a Lady	288
Sabbath Day	290
"Waiting"	290
A Mother's Love	292
On the Death of a Favourite Dog	2
"Summer Time will Come Again"	294
The Aged	295
The Parting	296
Guardian Angels	29
On the Opening of the Forth Bridge	298
Moral Courage	300
"Faces"	300
To a Friend Leaving England	30
Birthday Lines to My Aged Mother	304
Birthday Wish to My Father	305
Happy Memories	306
A Pair of Lovers	308
nother Pair	311
The Patrican's Curse	313
Dreams	317
To a Young Lady on Her Twentyfirst Birthday	318
Dejected	320
Answered	322
A Silver Wedding Greeting	323
To an Afflicted One	324
Music	325
Black Diamonds	327
To a Writer of some Verses to the Authoress	329
To E.J.H. on her Seventeenth Birthday	330
A Mother's Lullaby	331
The Lover's Lay	332
The Flower Girl	334
To a Youth on Attaining His Majority	336
The Dying Child	337
Ode to the Poet Longfellow	338
United	340
"The Battle is Over"	341
The Maiden and Her Lute	342
Lines to an Infant	343
Retrospection	345

CONTENTS.

	PAGE
Farewell Lines to Departing Friends	347
The Evening Star	348
A Simple Truth	349
On the Opening of Harold Park	350
To Katie; on receiving Her Photo	352
The Blind	353
Remembrance	355
Words of Cheer	356
"Drifting Apart"	357
"I love to kiss that Faded Cheek	358
The Beggar Girl	360
"Brothers and Sisters"	361
The Lover's Lament	362
Grief	364
A Welcome Home	366
Old Friends	367
On the intended Demolition of Haworth Old Church	368
Sorrow's Seal	371
The Blind Mother	371
Despondency	372
Pictures in the Fire	374
A Sonnet	375
A Marriage Ode	375
My Childhood's Home	377
The Old Man's Soliloquy	379
Merit Rewarded	380
The Horse	380
"I Dreamt She Died in Childhood"	381
The Italian Boy	383
Smiles and Tears	384
A Good Son	385
Old Letters	386
Not Forgotten	387
The Poet's Pleasure	389
Our Gallant Fire Brigades	390
On Seeing an Artist at Work	392
Sky-tints	392
Modern Society	393
To a Bride	396
An Optimistic Prophecy	397
Valediction	399

POEMS

BY

Charlotte Oates.

DEDICATION.

I dedicate,—
    This simple, unassuming Muse
      To all my dearest friends:
    Framed by Imagination wild,
      To Nature's throne it bends.
    I spread my Fancy's roving wings,
      And bade it freely play;
    It sped to dreamy realms, and brought
      Some gifts from far away.
    And then it took its wayward flight
      To depths of vision too;
    I caught these as it passed me by,
      And penn'd them here for you.
    I have not climbed Parnassus' height,
      And yet its balmy breeze,
    Has come in wafts across my path,
      And lightly left me these.
    If any simple lay of mine,

    Has either worth, or power
To charm the heart, or help to pass
    Away one dreary hour;—
Oh, then I have a rich reward,
    I've laboured not in vain;
Forgive, if I too oft have sung
    A melancholy strain.
If they will call a tear or smile,
    Or touch some tender heart,
Then my reward is double-fold—
    I've played my humble part.
If aught of classic lore were mine,
    They had been nobler far;
I could not brook that every one
    Should think they worthless are.
Both rhymes and poetry will be found,
    My earliest efforts make:
So take them all, my dearest friends,
    And keep them for my sake.

LULLED TO REST.

The time was evening, and the crimson sun
   Had dropt to rest behind the purple hill;
His weary round of labour he had done,
   And left the lovely valley calm and still:
Where flowers nestled in their grassy beds
When he had gone, they slept, with bended heads.

His glow still lingered on the tree-tops high,
   His kisses yet were warm upon the leaves:
A glorious light suffused the western sky,
   Shone down on acres rich with golden sheaves:
And everything was touched with amber light,
From lowland fen, to breezy mountain height.

It rested on the tow'r, with burnished vane,
   That crowned an ancient castellated hall;—
It glittered on each narrow window pane,
   That peeped, half hidden, from its ivied wall:
In whose dark shades the wild birds had their nest,
Beneath the battlements they loved to rest.

Within those walls, the youthful Harold dwelt:
   An invalid from childhood he had been;
Some quiet joy in living still he felt,
   His life was blameless, godly, and serene:
He watched the sky, as on his couch he lay,
He saw its splendour wax, then melt away.

He loved the sky, and noted every shade
   Pass o'er the mighty dome at close of day:
For as he watched the golden sunlight fade,
   He thought of one in Heaven far away;
His angel brother trod its hallow'd aisles,
In dreams he saw him, wreathed in sunny smiles.

For they had been companions here below,
   And Harold held his memory sacred still,
Rememb'ring how that brother soothed his brow,
   And tended him, when he was weak and ill:
Though strong of limb, discarded healthful play,
To sit beside young Harold, day by day.

But Death unwarned, had snatched him from his side,
    And left the weaker brother to repine,
Whose years now rolled in an unbroken tide,
    Marked by each one with slow and sure decline :
No wonder then, he heavenward turned his eyes,
To watch the mystic changes in the skies.

And yet he had a sister left to him,
    Whose joy it was to cheer his lonely lot;
Her rounded cheeks, and every supple limb,
    All plainly showed that sickness knew her not ;
Her eyes were bright their frames of darkest fringe,
Contrasted with her smooth cheeks carmine tinge.

A sweet young girl she was, her hair unbound
    Fell in dark curls, around her well-formed head :
And in her presence Harold ever found,
    A tranquil pleasure ; and the evening sped
On light'ning wings, when she was by his side. —
That favoured sister long had been his pride.

In peace that eve he watched the lucent sky,
    Its clouds with crimson edges paler grow ;
And mused alone, with meditative eye,
    Yet sweet contentment rested on his brow ;
His face was pale, and noble, and his hair,
About it hung in wavy clusters fair.

His thoughts reverted to some long past scene,
    Into his mind a mournful feeling came,
Of what he was and what he might have been,
    Had he been gifted with a stronger frame :
Half sad regrets,—all he had left undone, —
And yearnings vague for life that was to come.

His Maker he had ever loved and praised,
    In tender years the Word Divine had burst
Upon his soul, and he had often raised
    The golden chalice to his lips athirst :
To drink the Saviour's all-redeeming blood ;
And broken bread of Jesus Christ the good.

The glow-light died, and then the dusk-time came ;
    Its solemn shadows filled the spacious room :
The fine old pictures, each in massive frame,
    In deep recess, grew dimmer in the gloom ;

LULLED TO REST.

The waning light was yet more sombre made
By window hangings rich, of olive shade.
Their heavy folds made all subdued and dim, –
   The tapestry, the oaken cabinets old,—
The statuary, seemed all obscure and grim,
   And gems of art in chaste designs of gold.
Grew indistinct, as night came stealing on,
And dropt its silent tokens one by one.
In semi-darkness Harold still reclined,
   When whispers broke his contemplative mood;
A smile o'erspread his features so refined,
   To see his sister Elsie near him stood;
For she had softly entered at the door,
Unseen by him, had crossed the spacious floor.
"'Tis growing dark, shall I bring thee a light,"
   The maiden said, but Harold answered "no," -
"I feel most happy in the calm twilight,
   But bide with me, I would not have thee go;
I feel so well to-night, so with me stay;
And wilt thou get thine harp, and sing and play?"
"Come close to me, and raise my cushioned head.
   And sing the songs thou know'st I love the best:"
"I will, if thou wouldst wish me," Elsie said,—
   'Twas her delight to grant his mild request:
She took her harp, and drew beside him there,
A richly carved and antiquated chair.
To him his sister ever had been kind,
   And to that brother who was ta'en away;
And since he died, her love was all enshrined
   In Harold, he grew dearer day by day:
Then near the window in the fading light.
Her sweet voice broke the silence of the night.
The moon was rising, and began to make
   The room grow lighter, as its tranquil ray
Fell on the frescoes, and the fine mosaic,
   Till all seemed purer 'neath its sovereign sway:
Its light beamed in, to intercept the gloom,—
A gleam of glory in the dusky room.
She sang to him, at first so soft and low,
   As wild birds' warble when they see the light:

To higher strains then she began to flow;
   (Her voice was clear and flute-like in its height,)
And as she trilled, her sweet voice gathered power,—
She was the fair enchantress of the hour.

And all the while she gently touched the strings
   Of her loved harp, and slumb'ring chords awoke;
In Harold's heart revived the feeble springs,
   He felt her power, what though he never spoke:
His soul was soothed, the lyrest held the charm,
Upon his spirit fell a holy calm.

While at his feet, beside his couch she played,
   The pale moon kissed her with its golden light;
To Harold, as he lay back in the shade,
   She looked like some fair picture, warm and bright;
In moonlight pale, her graceful form appeared,
In strong relief against the background weird.

Outside the mullioned windows, fair flowers grew,—
   Amongst the ivy twined their tendrils sweet;
As through the panes the moon their shadows threw,
   There fell a golden tracery at her feet:
And when the zephyrs 'mong the leaflets strayed,
The lovely fretwork trembled while they played.

A stream of light from the ascending moon,
   Then reached his face, so pensive and so calm,—
Shone on his ample robe of rich maroon,
   Whose cumbrous folds wrapt his recumbent form:
He through the window upward gazed afar,
His dreamy eyes were fixed on one bright star.

So far away, 'twas but a silvery speck—
   A little spangle in that boundless space,—
A priceless gem, which mutely seemed to beck,
   As down it smiled so sweetly on his face:
Its quivering light was dimmed, but did not wane,
In passing through the night-dew on the pane.

He'd seen it kindled 'neath its Maker's hand,
   In realms of peace and silence far on high;
He wondered if it knew the " Better Land,"
   Across the grave, beyond its native sky;
'Twas all unsolved, he only knew its light
Enhanced the beauty of the summer night.

When Elsie paused, she met his thoughtful gaze,
   That spoke his thanks, ere he one word had said;
Enough for her, she had no need of praise,
   For gratitude in his mild orbs she read:
A faint sweet smile his gentle face enwreathed,
"Thanks, sister mine," at length he softly breathed.

"Sublime, dear Elsie, is that gift of thine,
   Since thy soft music broke the silence first,
My heart has thrilled, and rapture sweet is mine;
   It felt like nectar to a soul athirst:
One favour more I yet must ask of thee,
Sing our loved childhood's hymn,—"Come unto me."

She sang the hymn, with sympathetic voice,
   It was the one their mother used to sing
When they were children, and 'twas Harold's choice,
   A wealth of comfort those sweet words could bring;
Though simple, and can boast no lofty strain,
Yet Harold loved it, with its brief refrain.

She sang it slowly, and the music shone
   Into his soul, and shed a stream of light;
A tender pathos flowed through every tone,
   The space around him filled with visions bright;
And forms that had their being within his brain,
Came with the cadence of the soft refrain.

And when she paused, a slumbrous silence fell
   Upon the room, and everything around:
And Harold lay, as if beneath a spell,
   So pale and passive, in the peace profound:
The solemn moon was shining clear and bright,
And softly fell the "footsteps of the night."

The pendant candelabra yet was dark,
   In every nook there lurked a shadow dim;
And there was nought the passing hour to mark,—
   The hush was deep, there came no sound from him;
He prostrate lay, his heavy eyelids closed,
And Elsie saw that sweetly he reposed.

And then she sang the touching hymn again,
   Then paused once more, and weary felt and lone:
The stillness grew oppressive unto pain;
   With steady light the moon in splendour shone,—

Upon the couch it threw its ghastly beam,
Where Harold smiled, as in a blissful dream.
The night had come, and things looked gaunt and drear,
   She wished the hush to gently melt away,
And softly said in loving tones of cheer.
   " Have I again to sing to thee and play,
Or art thou tired, and dost thou wish to rest ? "
No muscle stirred,—no thoughts his face exprest.
She left her harp, and stole up to his side,
   Said, " Harold speak, for thy dear sister's sake; "
Still no response, then louder still she cried
   In fear and desperation, " Harold wake ! "
He answered not, she stroked his fair young head,
And touched his cheek, then found that he was dead !

She knelt beside him with a startled wail,
   Upon his neck her head in grief she bowed :
Then in a moment Memory raised the veil,
   That hid the past, and all his virtues showed ;—
His finest traits to her were then laid bare,
His faults and failings all dissolved in air.
Till then she knew not how much Death had ta'en,—
   How good and noble to the last was he ;
She cried, " Oh ! Harold wake but once again,
   Oft-times impatient I have been with thee ;
Speak, if but once, to say thou dost forgive,
Oh ! had I asked thee whilst thou still didst live."

No answer came, for cold and still he lay,
   To seek forgiveness then, was all in vain :
She asked too late, the soul had passed away.
   Those pallid lips would never speak again :
No more he felt his sister's fond embrace,
For white as marble was that lifeless face.

In tearless anguish in the dusk she knelt,
   Upon the floor her flowing drapery spread :
In that first hour of poignant grief, she felt
   Remorse come near, while looking on the dead :
Her trifling faults to him had been but few,
Yet they to her as heavy burdens grew.

She wished in vain she had the power to make
   Her peace with him, but he was past recall ;

LULLED TO REST.

In vain she asked that brother to awake,
    Upon her ear his voice no more would fall;
In vain she pleaded for one single word,
    He lifeless lay, and neither spoke nor heard.
She cried, "why wert thou ta'en away so soon,
    Without a single farewell word or look?
Thy face is cold and ghastly 'neath the moon,
    Teach me, oh God, this sorrow how to brook:
I cannot yet while grief swells in my breast,
Say meekly, "Jesus all is for the best."
From off the soul earth's trammels now were flung
    The flower was plucked before the heat of day;
His life for long upon one hinge had hung,
    But He who gave can surely take away?
And Death's more painful pangs had stung him not,—
Serene his transit to a fairer spot.
The tired one had gone to rest at last,
    He being aweary, found life's hill too steep:
In early years the yoke from him was cast,
    He passed away while in a dreamless sleep:
Why should we grieve at all for deaths like his?—
The soul unfettered, found its lasting bliss.
And it was meet that he should pass away
    While list'ning to his sister's music sweet,
Into the Regions of Eternal day,
    Where pain is not, but all is bliss complete:
His sister's voice, his last glad sound while here,
The Saviour's words had soothed his dying ear.
And when his soul had soared on mystic wing,
    And in its freedom passed the starlit dome;
His angel brother There the first would sing,
    And bid him welcome to the Heavenly Home;—
His voice would greet him, in that Sainted Land,
And Jesus place him with the angel band.
And all that once had seemed to him obscure,
    Would be unfolded as he entered There;
The angels in their vesture white and pure,
    With wreaths, and crowns, all glorified and fair:
The Throne of God, on heights of love supreme,
And Jesus near it, in a hallowed gleam.

And sweeter far, than aught he heard on earth,
  Would be the music that would charm his ear,
In Paradise, when he had found new birth,
  Where angels claimed, and crowned their brother
And took him all their wonders to behold,   [dear;—
And gave to him a precious harp of gold.

THE MAIDEN'S DREAM.

"Oh! Mother, hark, the roaring wind,
   Hear how the raging blast
Tears in gusts around the house,—
   And rain is falling fast!"
"Child, its every piercing wail
   Brings nought but woe to me;
To-night in such a furious gale—
   God help all those at sea!"

"Hark! Mother, what a dismal howl
   Sweeps through the chimney wide;
I *do* wish Father was at home,
   And sat here by my side:"
"My child, that is a useless wish,
   When he is far from thee;
But oh, on such a night as this,
   God help all those at sea!"

"'Tis bedtime Maggie, go to rest—
   Repose thy youthful head,
And pray that ere the morning breaks
   The tempest may have fled."
Beside the bed, a white-clad form
   Soon bowed on bended knee;
Her voice was heard amid the storm
   "God bless all those at sea."

Her prayer was earnest, and sincere,
   As humbly kneeling there,
She sought, with supplicating voice,
   Kind Heaven to hear her prayer:
She pleaded long, her faith was strong,
   As e'er a child's could be;
And often came the words among
   "Protect all those at sea."

And then she laid her down to rest,
  And quailed not at the storm;
For soon upon her senses fell
  Repose, so sweet and calm.
While Morpheus held her in its power
  All through the darksome night;
The mother watched each dreary hour
  Pass on, and yearned for light.

She paced the room, nor could she sleep—
  All night she kept awake;
For with the fury of the wind,
  The cottage seemed to shake:
The window rattled in its frame—
  A frail and trembling mass;
Like pelting sand, the driven rain
  Beat hard against the glass.

The thunder, with a threat'ning voice,
  Was mutt'ring midst the storm;
The wild wind blew in fitful gusts,
  Then waxed a moment calm:
She opened then the cottage door,
  And peered into the night;
The leaves rushed in, along the floor,
  Escaped the tempest's might.

She paused and listened to the sounds
  Within the vale below;
The beck, that bounded o'er the stones
  With rapid, rushing flow;
The wind had travelled to the wood,
  And moaned like restless seas,—
Had left the spot where then she stood,
  And racked the distant trees.

But only to return again—
  'Twas but a moment's peace,
Another moment saw the storm
  Of wind and rain increase.
The thunder with a vengeance fierce,
  In fury shook on high;
And clouds, too dense for stars to pierce,
  Rolled on the midnight sky.

THE MAIDEN'S DREAM.

She closed once more the cottage door
    Against the driving blast,
Against the leaden hail and rain,
    Then streaming down so fast.
The corner clock, with measured tick,
    Was all the sound within ;
The candle, with its drooping wick,
    Was burning,—faint and dim.

The clock gave out each passing hour,
    But still she could not rest ;
The more she listened to the gale,
    The more she felt opprest.
As, through the night, 'mid wind and sleet,
    The light'ning played in glee,
She often would the words repeat—
    "God help all those at sea!"

And once she went, with light in hand,
    To where the maiden lay,
Unconscious of the storm, she dwelt
    In Dreamland far away :
She softly kissed the fair young face
    That in calm slumber smiled ;
And murmured as she left the place,
    "Sleep on, sweet trusting child,"—

"The tempest now is nought to thee,
    But makes thee sleep the more ;
The wind has soothed thee fast asleep—
    And lulled thee with its roar.
But how thy father will be tossed
    Upon the billows free ;
Oh! if to-night he should be lost, —
    God help all those at sea!"

When morn at last began to dawn—
    The tempest to abate
She crossed the threshold once again,
    And went towards the gate ;
She gazed around, the air was chill,
    Then looking up she said,
"Thank God! it is His holy will,
    The storm at last has fled."

"The rain has ceased, the wind has hushed,
 The clouds have drifted far;
And lo! above my head there beams
 The gentle morning star!
It seemeth like a hopeful ray,
 Its paling, trembling light;
Now waning, as the morning grey
 Is wrestling with the night.

"I see the outline of the hills,
 As lighter grows the day,
Their barren ridges meet the sky,
 In distance far away.
And far beyond the mountain chain,
 There rolls the mighty sea:
And one I love sails on the main,
 Lord watch him there for me!"

Then looking down the vale she said,—
 "Has all here braved the storm?
No! where is that familiar tree?
 I miss its noble form.
Ah, it is changed, the ash tree old,
 That graced the meadow there,
Now prostrate lies, that seemed so bold,
 And all its roots are bare."

"Oh, Mother, come and sit by me"—
 'Twas Maggie's gentle voice:—
"The storm has hushed, the morn is calm,
 Does not your heart rejoice?"—
"It would my child, did I but know
 That Father's ship was in;
To think he's on the ocean now,
 Still gives me fears for him."

"Oh Mother, I have had a dream,
 Its deep, mysterious power,
Has held my senses in its thrall,
 Through many a weary hour.
I felt so happy when I woke
 From that strange thrilling dream:
The voice of Mercy in it spoke
 But must I tell its theme?"

"Yes child, relate thy dream to me,
  My gentle Maggie, do;
And I will sit beside thy bed,
  'Twill give me comfort too;
For night has gone, the tempest passed,
  The East is in a glow;
The lovely sun now shines at last,
  Upon the mountain's brow!"

"Well Mother dear, I closed my eyes,
  With many haunting fears;
The roaring wind, and pattering rain
  Were sounding in my ears;
But when I fell asleep, the noise
  Of wild wind, and of rain,
Were then to me the booming voice,
  Of billows on the main."

"I thought I saw a raging sea,
  With waves that leapt so high,
Their snowy crests gleamed white as ghosts,
  Against the midnight sky.
At first a silvery mist hung o'er,
  The offing far away,—
For I was stood upon the shore,
  And felt the fresh'ning spray."

"I heard the waters' thunder loud
  Their boom against the rock;
The echo in the cavern cell,
  Their fury seemed to mock.
The hail and rain were falling fast,
  The sky was low and dark—
When midst the storm I saw a mast,
  And then a storm-tost bark."

"It was my father's ship I saw
  Upon the surging sea;
It rocked and pitched upon the waves,
  Each mast bent like a tree;
And oft 'twas nearly lost to sight,
  The billows rose so high;
Then once again I saw its height,
  Loom black against the sky."

"The sails had broken from the yards,
    And flapp'd all wet and torn;
I saw them flutt'ring in the wind,
    The ship before it borne.
Then in a mist of silvery spray,
    The vessel would be lost,
But still it bounded on its way,
    Amid the tempest tost."

"Then with a weird phosphoric glow,
    The waters glittered bright:
As with a flame, from stem to stern,
    The ship was all alight:
Hugg'd in the waves' impulsive clasp,
    Amid the dancing foam;
It bravely struggled in the blast
    As it was steered for home"

"Then all at once a dark'ning cloud
    Came drooping o'er the sea,
It seemed to hang above the ship,
    And spread its edge o'er me:
'Twas purple black, and cast a gloom
    Upon the ocean's breast;
But still I heard the billows boom,
    And saw each foaming crest."

"And then a veil of vapour bright,
    Ascended from the deep;
In curling wreaths, it rose above,
    From where the sea-shells sleep.
It settled in that cloud so drear,
    Suspended o'er the main;
And left the restless waters clear,—
    The ship appeared more plain."

"It looked so white against the cloud,
    While darker seemed the sky;
And then above my father's ship,
    At last it rested high:
It smaller grew, but more intense;
    'Twas like a radiant light,
As thro' the depth of darkness dense,
    It shone so strangely bright."

THE MAIDEN'S DREAM.

"And then, dear Mother, as I gazed,
   The white mist took a form;
I think I see it even now,
   Distinct amid the storm.
For graceful fingers, one by one,
   Developed in the sky;
Until a perfect hand there shone,
   Above the waters high."

"At first 'twas faint, and indistinct,
   But soon grew more defined:
Until at last it seemed to me
   'Twas Mercy's hand so kind!
I knew that Heaven had sent it there,
   To guide the vessel's course;
The thought that He had heard my prayer,
   Rose up, with all its force."

"For there I saw my father's ship
   Careening on the deep;
While high above it was that hand,
   As if a guard 'twould keep:
And as the vessel tossed among
   The wild waves mid the storm,
This mystic token moved along—
   The dark sky showed its form:"

"Right o'er the toiling ship it kept,
   A true protecting hand—
As if to lead it o'er the sea
   In safety, to the land:
A silvery halo round it gleamed,
   Of vapour, soft and bright;
And as it moved along, it seemed
   To leave a streak of light."

"And all the while, I heard the wild
   Pulsation of the sea,
'Twas beating on the barren shore,
   And rushing up to me:
And then I heard a rustling noise,
   Beside me in the gloom—
Then whispered low a mystic voice—
   "I'll guide him safely home!"

"The words awoke me from my dream,
  And gave my heart a thrill;
And now I find the storm is o'er,
  The morn is calm and still;
And, Mother dear, I feel full well,
  That vision came to me,
To bid us both our fears despel,
  For Father on the sea:"

"A loving deed, by Him above,
  Revealed to me in sleep;
'Twas Mercy's hand, He sent in love,
  To light the desert deep;
I trust that Father soon will come,
  To join us once again—
That God will send him safely home,
  From off the mighty main."

"Now I will rise, my heart is glad,
  That dream was full of cheer;
For hope that now dwells in my heart,
  Has chased away all fear."
"My child, thy words have comfort brought,
  I too will trust thy dream;
And cherish every happy thought,
  Suggested by its theme."

. . .

The time wore on, then came a day,
  The sun was bright and warm,
The latticed window open wide,
  The air was full of balm.
A gentle, soothing, whispering breeze,
  Defused the scent of flowers;
And lisped among the garden trees,
  That twined in rustic bowers.

The white-winged clouds, of silvery sheen,
  So softly rolled on high,
Upon a ground of azure blue-
  A fair and sunny sky.

Without, an air serene and calm,
  The flowers all in bloom;
Within, a peaceful fireside warm—
  An English cottage home.

The mother and the gentle girl,
  Were quietly sitting there;
A hopeful smile lit Maggie's face,
  Her mother's told of care.
The little captive singing bird
  Was pouring out its song;
What though unheeded, and unheard,
  Throughout the whole day long.

"Hark! Mother, 'tis the garden gate,
  I hear its rattling sound;
And now I hear a step approach,—
  A firm tread on the ground:"
And looking through the window bright,
  They saw a well known form;
"Oh joy!" cried Maggie in delight
  "'Tis Father coming home!"

Dressed in a garb of navy blue,
  Came he they loved so well;
He raised the latch, and there beheld
  His wife, and winsome girl!
With happy hearts, relieved from care,
  They kissed his sunburnt face;
With loving words, united there,
  The three with fond embrace.

That night, when Maggie went to bed,
  Before she sought her rest
When kneeling at her evening prayers
  Her Maker's name she blest;
Poured out her grateful thanks alone,
  Before the Throne Above;
To Him who sent her father home,
  In pity, and in love.

A QUEEN'S SACRIFICE.

There stood in a gorgeous palace old,
   A royal lady divinely fair :
A crown superb of the purest gold,
   Lay on the coils of her glossy hair ;
Her purple vesture proclaimed her birth,
Amongst the highest she ranked on earth.

And though she ruled o'er a wide domain,
   And swayed the sceptre upon the throne,
Upon her face was a look of pain,
   As there in luxury all alone,
She sat and mused ; as the sunlight fair
Gleamed on her robes, and her jewels rare.

The necklace rich on her shoulders white,
   The bracelets coiled on her lovely arms,
All set with diamonds, that flashed with light,
   But seemed to heighten her outward charms :
A single glance at her brow serene,
Revealed the noble, and high-souled queen.

A queen? ah yes! but withal there beat
   A woman's heart in that regal breast ;
A truer, nor tenderer one, ne'er yet
   Graced royal crown, or a noble's crest ;
Of womanly virtues although possessed,
Why did she languish, as one depressed ?

A paper lay in her dimpled hand,
   That held a plea for the honest poor ;
Her suffering sex in her much-loved Land,
   To whom was open no friendly door :
It showed how needed for such when ill,
Was a place of rest, with the surgeon's skill.

Her aid was sought, and her heart was moved,
   In anguished, pitying tones she cried ;
" My Kingdom's poor, I have ever loved,
   To mind their welfare has been my pride ;
But oh! they know not, what though a queen,
How low in wealth I have always been.

"They think their Sovereign rich indeed,
　　And crave the help that I fain would give.
Must these, my sisters then, vainly plead?
　　Whilst I in luxury still must live?
They need a refuge that must be free,
The pains of women assuaged must be.

"Can I, a mother, sit here in ease,
　　And hear the plaints of the sore distrest?
Nor try their suffering to appease,
　　Nor find them shelter, and skill, and rest?
This breast would cover a heart of steel,
If I were deaf to their sad appeal!

"They deem me wealthy, but little know,
　　I am but rich in a yoke of care;
There's many a richer with uncrowned brow,
　　That does not a nation's burdens bear:
The gaudy trappings of pomp and state,
Are naught but trammels, nor make me great.—

"The gems I wear are my only wealth,
　　And these my offering now must be;
Shall suffering women ne'er gain lost health,
　　That costly gems may be worn by me?
These jewels bright that my arms adorn,
May purchase life for the lowly born!

"My courts be rid of a useless band,
　　Half my attendants but be retained;
No gem shall shimmer upon this hand,
　　Thereby the good that I seek be gained;
I keep the sceptre, nor yield the crown,
Those being my birthright, I still must own.

"Self-love and vanity hence shall go,
　　Nor find a refuge again in me;
Each conquered, flee like a vanquished foe,
　　A bloodless victory mine shall be;
The power I hold, and by right divine,
Shall through my vast dominions shine!"

She wrenched the diamonds from off her wrist,
　　They danced in beauty before her eyes;
That dim were then with a tender mist,
　　Where Pity sat in her sweetest guise;

The queen's heart ached for her subjects sake,
Her warmest sympathies were awake.

She quickly summoned her courtiers near,
   Whom she commanded with stately mien:
"Take these, my jewels, I held most dear,
   They never again shall deck your queen:
Go take them hence, as my gift of love,
Surrended freely my heart to prove.

"And mark! whatever the price they bring,
   Devoted be to the women's home;
And never a debt to it shall cling,
   Endowed 'twill be for the years to come:
God's hallowed blessing rest on the spot,
His poor by me shall be ne'er forgot."

Amazed the courtiers stood, yet they
   Dared but obey, at their queen's command:
The royal mandate none could gainsay,
   The deed was signed, by her own fair hand:
All meekly bowed to the queen's decree,
Revered and blest from their hearts was she.

The rich sun set in its ruby gown,
   On stately stairways, of marble white;
On ornate pillars, and walls, streamed down
   Erewhile, the glorious orb of night:
On downy pillow kissed by its beams,
The good queen smiled in her happy dreams.

    *   *   *   *   *   *   *

A year passed by; then she stood one day
   Within the "home" of her tender care:
Where those in mortal affliction lay,
   Whose faint hearts brightened, to see her there:
And while she sat by the couch of pain,
Their faltering faith was revived again.

She softly glided from ward to ward,
   O'er forms recumbent she gently bent:
She soothed the sufferers' lot so hard,
   And comfort offered where e'er she went:
An angel spirit in woman's guise,
Shone from the depths of her splendid eyes.

A QUEEN'S SACRIFICE.

In simple raiment, devoid of state,
    She viewed the structure her wealth had raised:
The sacrifice she had made was great.
    Her noble efforts were prized and praised:
Though boundless good had her action wrought,
Yet never a word of thanks she sought.

Anon she stooped o'er a lowly bed,
    Where lay a woman by pain opprest:
Through long affliction had drooped her head,
    And oft she yearned for the promised rest:
Their hands were clasped, as if loth to part,
Compassion melted the loved queen's heart

The patient sufferer's soul was thrilled,
    While by her queen's, was her hand caressed;
Her long tried heart for the moment filled,
    With reverent love, that was unexprest:
Her homage flowed in a voiceless prayer,
But for her queen she had not been there.

Her deepest feelings were not to seek,
    For oh! the gaze of those grateful eyes;
They beamed the thanks that she could not speak,
    And made the tears of the good queen rise:
That look had pierced to her inmost soul,
'Twas 'graved on memory's choicest scroll.

A world of feeling was there exprest,
    A wealth of love for the good received;—
Of gratitude for the needed rest.
    Through all the ills that were being relieved:
For hope's bright rainbow appeared o'erhead,
And threw its light o'er the sufferer's bed.

They felt a moment as equals there,
    Their souls had met in that mutual gaze:
The queen's and peasant's illumined were,
    By nature's subtle, magnetic rays:
For human sympathy far can reach,
And levelling pain can lessons teach.

The wasted lineaments fain had smiled,
    Though racked by pain was the prostrate form:
'Twas like a mother's to helpless child,
    That touch of sympathy, true and warm:

A quiver passed o'er her face, and showed
The fervid font of her heart o'erflowed.

And lo! a tear from her eyes dropt down
    Upon the sovereign's hand so fair;
Like some bright jewel from regal crown,
    It glistened, and trembled a moment there:
As clear as crystal, so pure and bright,
It gemmed the beautiful wrist so white.

The good queen saw it, and cried "behold!
    There gleams a gem on my wrist once more:
A liquid jewel of worth untold,
    And one more precious I never wore;
A diamond sparkles, and trembles here,
Of purest water,—a woman's tear!—

"Who says my jewels to me are lost?
    I see their value before me here;
Dissolved, condensed, at the dearest cost,
    They've ta'en the form of a beauteous tear!
I am happier far than I were of old,
When decked in gems that were hard and cold.

"This grateful tear, that thou couldst not stem,
    Is my reward that my God has given;
A beautiful, crystal, priceless gem,
    Dropt by a soul on its way to Heaven:
My sweetest recompense this shall be,
Baptized henceforth by this tear from thee.—

"'Tis consecrated, for herein sleeps
    The essence sweet of the purest love:
Such tears as these, which a torn heart weeps,
    Conveys a message from Him Above;—
God's blessing comes in its liquid sheen—
Falls on the hand of the happiest queen."

True words! at peace with her God above,
    Through her good deeds was His love revealed;
She had lost her jewels, but won His love,
    And by that tear was the compact sealed:
For each one lost, she could not forget,
A priceless gem in her soul was set.

Pastoral Poems.

A PEASANT'S HOME.

Give me the little family group,
   Where piety and love
Reign all supreme, though poor the cot,
When these pervade the humblest spot,
   'Tis blest by Him above.

When parents and their children all
   In bonds of love unite :
And all a true affection feel,
And labour for each other's weal,—
   Then hearts, and homes are bright.

When wreaths of fondest love entwine
   Around their tender hearts :
That makes them cling to home so dear,
A sacred feeling binds them near,
   And homely joy imparts.

   .   .   .   .

The wintry sunshine glinted through
   The cottage window bright ;
Then sunk so calmly in the west,
And seemed to bid the workers rest
   Awhile,—for it was night.

So weary with his honest toil,
   The cotter seeks his home ;
The children for their father wait,
They hear the clinking garden-gate,
   And smile to see him come.

Within the little rustic cot,—
   Where all is clean and neat,—
The grandsire has the warmest nook,
And on his face there beams a look
   With happiness replete.

The sturdy son comes whistling home,
    From field-work far away;
The little circle is complete,
The boys and girls their parents meet,
    To end the happy day.

The gentle mother minds her babe,
    With fond devoted care,
The eldest daughter has her place,—
A graceful girl, with comely face,
    And neatly braided hair.

The peat-fire sheds a ruddy glow
    Upon the cottage wall;
The frugal little board is spread,
They eat their well-earned daily bread,—
    Then offer thanks for all.

The pussy too, is sitting there,
    She blinks and purs away;
And courts the warm domestic hearth,
Among the children's joyous mirth,
    To watch her kittens play.

Outside, the night is bleak and cold,
    The stars are glitt'ring bright;
The frost-wind, wailing at the door,
In gusts, from off the heath-clad moor—
    Attends the wintry night.

Within the cot, the peasants rest,
    The happy evening long;
The old fire-side is bright and warm,
And music lends its soft'ning charm,
    To their enliv'ning song.

Oh, music! chast'ning every joy,
    A noble art divine:—
That draws together soul to soul,
And o'er the feelings has control,—
    While kneeling at its shrine.

Its influence on the human heart,
    Is soothing and refin'd;

It cheers the poor man's leisure hours,
Bestrews his path of toil with flowers,
   And elevates his mind.

Sweet plaintive strains, that find the heart,
   Resound within that cot;
'Tis not a master's finished touch,
And yet the simple airs are such,
   That will not be forgot.

The mother plying there her work,
   Oft pauses as she feels
The thrilling pathos of the strain,
And asks to hear it o'er again,
   As to her heart it steals.

The old man feels its soft'ning power,
   As with his locks so white,
He sits there, in the corner chair;
And see his cheek, a tear is there—
   So tremulous and bright!

It brings up recollections old,
   Of days when he was young;—
The melodies that he has taught,
Arouses every lofty thought,
   To hear them sweetly sung.

Their better nature seems to wake,
   At music glad and sweet;
Oh! blessings on these peasants' lot,
Content, and happy in their cot,
   The hours so softly fleet.

"A peasant's home," how sweet the name,
   When it is such as this;
Bound heart to heart, by sacred ties
Of love, how fast the evening flies,
   So full of tranquil bliss!

The soul of music swelling forth,
   From that poor humble place;
Where happy voices all unite
In songs, that make the household bright,
   And grander spots would grace.

The working man reclining there,
   A father true is he;
He yields his soul to music's spell,
And clings to those he loves so well,
   His children round his knee.

It cheers him for the morrow's toil,
   To hear these glad'ning sounds;
The cares and hardships of the day,
'Neath this enchantment pass away,
   And peaceful joy abounds.

See! now at last the time has come
   For slumber, peace, and rest;
The baby long has been asleep,
And laid its little dimpled cheek,
   Upon its mother's breast.

Now all is hushed,—the fire is low
   With but a flickering light;
Behold! the father kneeling there,
He offers up an evening prayer,—
   Then each one says, "Good-night."

SIGNS OF SPRING.

There's a sweeter swell in the robin's song,
   And a deeper red on his ruffled breast;
   He has day-dreams bright of a downy nest,
Of the mate he'll charm as the days grow long.

And when to the throstle's song we list,
   There's a richer ring in his plaintive notes;
   While on the breath of the breeze there floats,
Prophetic symbols, consigned in mist.

There are tender buds on the sapful tree,
   And signs appear through the yielding earth,
   Of latent life, and of mystic birth,—
An index sweet of the things to be.

Before we even have ceased to hear
  The merry sound of the hunter's horn,
  Two wee white lambs in the flock are born,—
Their tremulous bleating greets the ear.

Eve's sun-rays linger on mountain crest,
  Of lengthening days 'tis a token fair;
  While the midges dance in the genial air,
'Neath the amber glow of the radiant west.

Life essence dwells in the sunshine warm,
  That tempts the bees from their wintry hives;
  All nature stirs, from its trance revives,
And the daisy blooms with a spring-like charm.

The white-tailed conies at early morn,
  Begin to sport by the brown copse bare;
  A presage bright for the youthful year,
Rich with the wealth of its hopes new-born.

As through the desolate meads we pass,
  In pasture's bleached to the dull grey-green
  Of shrivelled herbage, e'en now is seen
Bright emerald blades of the new spring grass.

There's a brighter sheen in the glistening brook,
  And a hopeful tone in its brisker flow;
  Unfettered now by the ice and snow,
It blithely babbles by grassy nook.

The year is young, but it seems replete
  With welcome signs of an early spring;
  May summer days in their fulness bring,
The fruitage rich of a promise sweet.

THE OLD BRIDGE.

My favourite haunt; I love to stray,
  Upon a balmy summer's day
  By this old bridge, that spans the brook:
A beautiful sequester'd nook.

In this lone spot I oft have stood
And gazed into the silent wood,
The noble trees of varied hue
Point to the sky so deeply blue:
The honeysuckle, and wild rose,
Bloom here alone in sweet repose:
In solitude as oft I stray,
The fragrance of the new-mown hay
Fills all the air so rich and sweet,
Within this shady, cool retreat.
In pensive mood I linger long,
And listen to the wild-birds' song—
The wren, the linnet, and the thrush,
Among the thicket and the bush:
Each warbles forth its plaintive lay,
To while the summer hours away.
By this old bridge I love to roam,
So near my little cottage home;
And lean upon its moss-grown wall,
Above the silvery waterfall,
To watch the lazy waters run,
That glisten brightly in the sun;
And gurgle on with rippling sound,
Enliv'ning all the woods around:
While leaves upon its surface float,
Each like some little fairy boat,
And when the evening softly fades,
The twilight gathers in its shades:
The little wild-birds cease to trill,—
The valley sleeps, so calm and still.

Then in its wintry aspect grand,
On this old bridge I love to stand:
Its massive walls adorned by age,
Defy the storm in all its rage:
And weather still the driving blast,
As boldly now as in the past.
And tufts of silken grass so green,
Peep out from every open seam.
The ivy in a creeping spray,
Clings to its walls so damp and grey.
I court it in a nobler form,

Amid the grandeur of the storm,
And in the snow, so beauteous, when
Each stone is like a crystal gem
The hoar-frost hangs from every edge,
Like silvery fringe upon each ledge;
When snow envelopes all the scene,
And 'neath it sleeps the vale so green;
The whole presents a lovely sight,—
When every thing is touched with white
The streamlet frozen in a mass,
Arrests my footsteps as I pass.
The beauteous sight mine eyes allure,
Those blocks of solid ice so pure;
Sweet Nature's artist been at work,
And sculptured from a marble rock :—
Had chiselled temples it would seem,
From out a liquid, running stream !
So wonderful and deft its hand,
Designs translucent caverns grand,
And shielded by the ice and snow,
A warmer current glides below
The tiny ice-bergs, pure and white—
So fair, and crystallized, and bright ;
Like polar seas in miniature,
But far too lovely to endure,
They 'neath the sunlight melt so fast,
Too frail, too beautiful to last !

I love to wander by the wood,
On this old bridge, when foaming flood
The waters, as I lean me o'er,
And listen to their hollow roar ;
No longer frost-bound on they flow,
In swollen torrents rush below :—
Beneath the archway they resound,
Like Ocean's voice as on they bound,
It seems as if with one accord,
They are responding to a word,
That Nature speaks, or gives a sign,
That they have slumbered now their tin
An unseen messenger on wing,
Had loosened every little spring;

The drifts of snow dissolve away,
Beneath the sun's warm genial ray.
The little water-courses run,
And shimmer brightly in the sun.

What inward ecstasy is mine !
As here in silence I recline ;
On this old bridge, my favourite place,
And nature's countless beauties trace.
In winter drear, and summer green,—
And all the shades that come between.
Amid the storm, and when 'tis calm,
This old bridge has a lingering charm.

"BIRDIE'S DREAM."

In the solemn hush of midnight,
    When the stars so softly shone ;
Once I heard a little minstrel,
    When I thought I was alone.

Everything was steeped in silence,
    Darkness filled my chamber small ;
When the stillness deep was broken
    By a little birdie's call.

On the rose-tree, perched at midnight,
    Close beside my window bars ;
Pretty birdie woke from sleeping,—
    Trilled a moment to the stars.

Had the little wild-bird, dreaming
    Happy thoughts, it could not keep,—
And a sudden gush of gladness
    Made it murmur in its sleep ?

Oft since then I've heard it twitter,
    To my room its music floats ;
In the fulness of its gladness,
    Sweetly fall its silvery notes.

How I love it when I hear it!
  Tho' its song too soon is o'er;
Just a warble, then it ceases—
  All is silent as before.

LOVELY MAY.

Behold she comes! with a smiling brow,
  The blithe and beautiful month of May;
Enrobed in blossoms, as white as snow,
  We trace her step through the woodland way.

Emerging fresh from the wintry gloom,
  Her dainty presence on every hand,
Flings radiant light into every home,—
  Her gifts she scatters o'er all the land.

The sweetest born of the glad new year,
  Nursed in the lap of the bounteous Spring;
She lifts her beautiful face so fair,
  Her voice is heard as the woodlands ring,

With sweet bird-music; rich notes ascend
  From cloisters wild, in the forest shades;—
The warblers' tenderest love-songs lend,
  A May-time glory to sunlit glades.

Thrice welcome May! with her wealth of flowers,
  That through the gossamer garb of morn,
Peep forth in beauty, or bathed by showers,
  Exhale perfumes that are hither borne.

Sweet bright-eyed May, how we love her face!
  Her glad'ning glance and her mirthful moods
She drapes the groves, and transforms with grace
  To emerald splendour the sylvan woods.

A taste of Heaven she gives to earth—
  Leaves beauty-spots on the path she treads;
One touch from her, and the buds have birth,
  A myriad flowerets lift their heads.

Our pulses quicken, for hope is rife,
   She brings the key to its fairy bowers:
And all are feeling the glow of life,
   Who breathe the scent of the new-born flowers.

Oh, lovely May! with her sunny brow.
   By Nature crowned, and her chaplet's gems
Are pure as fleeting, wee wild flowers low,
   Mid velvet verdure, uplift frail stems.

The nymph glides on with her garlands gay,
   Bestowing kisses on one and all;
Nor from the lowly she keeps away,
   All free for such do her favours fall.

Her touch transfigures, her smiles renew,—
   Invest the earth with a vernal charm;
The daisies drenched with the diamond dew,
   Like jewels flash in her sunlight warm.

Sweet Nature's handmaid, young joyous May!
   Her fair arcadian bowers we love;
Her pink-white blossoms, though frail, convey
   A hidden promise from One Above.

A SUMMER SHOWER.

O look at the rain, the heaven-sent rain,
Steeping the garden, the woodland, and plain;
See how each tree and each little flower,
Holds up its head at the life-giving shower!

What is so sweet as the freshening rain,
Bathing the face of sweet Nature again?
See! how she smiles as her daisy-decked brow,
Is replete with the raindrops that gleam on it now.

The flowers their petals outspread to the rain,
With thirst they were parched, yet new life they regain;
What can the sweet-briar in fragrance excel,
When sprinkled afresh with the rain, can ye tell?

We can but rejoice at the soft gentle rain,
That brightens the grass in the dust-covered lane ;
Nature's sweet elixir, purest and best,
Restoring her charms when she's sad and depressed.

"MY HOME."

My home, is but a lowly home,
   And yet I love it more
Than all the stately dwellings fine,
   That rise from shore to shore.
It cannot boast one costly thing,
   Or grand and outward show ;
But oh ! the love that dwells within,
   Far more than others know.

My home, it is a pleasant home,
   And full of love and bliss :
Oh ! what would many sad hearts give
   For such a home as this !
And many happy years I've passed
   Beneath its shelt'ring roof,
The pleasant hours I've spent within
   The homestead of my youth.

My home, it is a rural home,
   Beside the old green lane :
In summer, blooming flowers bright
   Festoon the window pane.
The rose-trees climb its mossy wall,
   And form a rustic bower,
In which I've often sat and dreamt
   Through many a sunny hour.

My home, it is a happy home,
   And where I live content ;
Our love is all united here,
   And in one channel bent.
Our cot o'erlooks lone fields and woods,
   And this is more to me
Than all the gay and busy throng,—
   Because I feel so free.

My home, it is a peaceful home,
  Where all is calm and still,—
All, save the warbling of the birds
  And rippling of the rill,
That flows into the old stone well
  With murm'ring music sweet.
The plane-tree throws its grateful shade
  Across the garden neat.

My home, it is a blissful home,
  Fond love is centered here;
And thanks I render for it all,—
  It is my daily prayer.
God gives me health and happiness,
  Contentment, peace, and love,—
These are the greatest blessings sent
  To us, from Heaven above.

TO A DIVERTED MOUNTAIN STREAM.

Beautiful water, thou knowst not thy bourn,
Free and unfettered, thou erstwhile hast torn
Down from the solitudes, sombre and wild,
Born of the moorland, their bright wayward child.

Life of the mountains! with rippling tone
Singing to virginal grandeur alone;
Bounding at random by moorland-rock side,
Here thou wert narrowing, there thou wert wide.

Flowing in purity, mountain-born spring,
Freedom thy birthright, sweet undefiled thing;
Wand'ring untrammelled where few feet have trod,
Nearer than us to the regions of God.

None but the shepherd, and grey agile sheep,
List to thy music while mounting the steep;
Knowing thy source, is amongst their delights.
Up on the breezes-kissed, dusky-browed heights.

Hither for ages thy pathway has been,
Down through lone peat-mosses, purple and green ;
Summer's sweet heather-bells, Winter's white shroud
Long hast thou mirrored the sunshine and cloud.

Down through the wilderness, streamlet till now,
All unmolested has man let thee flow,—
Wholly unfettered, thy glory complete,
Nursed in the lap of the heather so sweet.

Babbling along in thy natural glee,
Making thy track to the far-away sea ;
Longing to join it, nor dreaming that man,
Here would arrest thee, and alter thy plan.

Beautiful streamlet, but what has he done ?
Made thee a channel, in which thou shalt run !
Shackled thy movements, and altered thy course,
Put thee in service, and felt no remorse !—

Bound thee to flow in conventional form,—
Never to swerve at the call of the storm,—
Never to dance, nor diverge at thy will,—
Stray in thy windings, to sport with a rill.

Made thee to glide in a civilized way,
Straight 'tween two walls, with no prospect of play ;
Poor mountain rivulet ! I with a sigh,
Dropped for man's selfishness, bid thee good-bye.

SUMMER DAYS.

All Nature now with smiles enwreathed,
Looks on her work with tender gaze ;—
Breathes fragrance o'er these summer days,
Expands her blossoms all unsheathed ;
Reveals rich beauties just conceived,
To those who worship at her feet.
Benign her face with charms replete ;
Enchanting are the songs she's breathed,
Naught can surpass these dreamy days !

But far too soon they pass us by,
Like all earth's things each flower decays :
You grow to love them, then they die ;
Enjoy them now, ere they are past—
Sweet summer days, too fair to last !

TO A BIRD.

BIRDIE, where art thou ?—
   Dost thou know where ?
Perched on that message-line,
   High in the air.
Singing so charmingly
   Up on the wire ;
Trilling and warbling,
   Higher and higher.
What if the telegram
   Flying along,
Twines with its sentences
   Thy little song ?
Rods are vibrating,
   Words quiver down
To the fine gentlemen,
   Far in the town.
When they receive them,
   What will they say,
If with their business,
   Mingles thy lay ?
Sweet little minstrel,
   Strange things combine ;
Science and Nature,
   Often entwine !

THE MOORLANDS.

ON the dreary northern moorlands,
   Stretching out so wide and far ;
There it is I love to linger,
   Where no human dwellings are.

When the piercing wind is blowing,
   And the sky is dark and drear,
Let me wander on the moorlands,
   Where no kindred form is near:—
Wander where the waving heather,
   Sweet and wild, has there its home,
Looking in the sad'ning autumn,
   Rich with bronze and purple bloom.
On the wide expansive moorland,
   There as far as eye can see,
All is barren, save the heather,
   And the hardy bilberry.
Tinged with russet, sombre-shaded,
   Grand and solemn, vast and bleak,
All among the haunts of wild-birds
   Is the spot my footsteps seek.
Oh, 'tis there I love to wander,
   Where few human feet have trod;
Far from man, I feel not lonely,—
   Feeling nearer unto God!

THE AFTERGLOW.

How lovely is the opening morn,
When gorgeous colours flush the east;
Then, over fields of yellow corn,
   The brilliant orb of day
Shoots forth a gleam of golden light;
And as our dreams take flight at dawn,
So melts beneath the sunshine bright,
   The purple mist away.

Yet what appears more beauteous still,
Is when it sinks away to rest,
And slowly drops behind the hill,
   When white with purest snow:
And what to me is sweeter far,
The glorious light that comes between
The daylight and the evening star—
   The transient afterglow.

'Tis even so with life ; we know
That childhood is both sweet and fair ;
And rosy as the morning's glow,
    That teems with fresh'ning balm :
When Truth and Innocence are theirs—
These little sisters who are twins :
The noontide's heat, man's prime and cares
    And age, the twilight calm.

'Tis hallowed as that evening time—
Reflections of a well-spent life :
When beauteous locks, like snow and rime,
    Lie on the ample brow.
When Heaven seems near, and earth seems cold,
Life's light is chastened and subdued :
Its sun has set, and we behold
    The peaceful afterglow !

And thus, the verdant spring is sweet,
When blossoms fling their scent around :
Its advent we rejoice to greet,—
    The promise of the year.
But when fulfilled, and on the trees,
The luscious fruit hangs rich and ripe ;
The autumn's mellow beauties these,
    Can spring with it compare ?

When Time the thoughtful brow has prest,
And left his impress there, life's work
Is done ; and evening's twilight rest
    Sweet mem'ries can bestow :
It owns a charm which youth may crave,
A splendour all unknown before :
Age softens, as it nears the grave,—
    'Tis life's sweet afterglow.

THE LAST SIGH OF SUMMER.

I HEARD the last sigh of the summer,
    As it swept through the burnished leaves,
And over the silvery streamlet,
    Then it died 'mong the golden sheaves.

I heard the last rustle of summer,
   As softly it glided away—
The trail of its beautiful garments,
   As it passed by the jasmine spray.

I felt the sweet spirit of summer,
   It breathed in the scent-laden breeze:
The song of the birds in the woodlands,
   The music that played in the trees.

It stole through the fast-fading garden,
   And threw its sweet kisses around;
On fruit that was hanging in clusters,
   On woodbine that trailed on the ground.

It lingered awhile with the flow'rets,
   And murmured in tones of regret;
Their faces were drooping and tearful—
   The roses and sweet mignonette.

It seemed as if loth to resign them—
   To leave them alone in the cold;
In the hard cruel grasp of the winter,
   Whose fingers are shrivelled and old.

I heard the last voice of the summer,
   As it whispered its fond farewell;
Then dying away in the distance,
   It hushed in the charm-haunted dell.

I saw the last smile of the summer,
   It spread o'er the heathery hill;
And peered through the mist in the valley,
   Where Nature sat gloomy and still.

It dreamily beamed on the landscape,
   Whose foliage soon would be dead;
And then when the darkness o'ershadowed,—
   I felt that the summer had fled.

EVENTIDE.

I LOVE to walk at eventide,
   Beside the placid river;
And watch the boats upon its tide,
   And see the aspen quiver—

Quiver in the evening breeze,
   That comes from off the stream,
Whose brink reflects the aspen trees,
   Beneath the sun's last beam.

I love to rove at eventide,
   Down in the grassy meadows;
And see the cattle as they bide,
   Among the cooling shadows.
I love to roam by marshy swamps,
   So thick with bending reeds;
And see afar the gipsies' camps,
   In green and rushy meads.

'Tis sweet to walk at eventide,
   Where golden grain is growing;
When song-birds in the bushes hide,
   And winds are gently blowing:—
Waving the rich corn to and fro,
   When evening's sun is setting—
The shadows length'ning as I go,
   All earthly cares forgetting.

But sweeter far at eventide,
   I love the lonely wood;
To quietly 'mong the brackens glide,
   And mark each closing bud.
To hear the night-birds' shriek on high,
   And nightingale so sweet;
Warbling his notes unto the sky,
   Within his wild retreat.

HAROLD PARK, LOW MOOR.

Well! can this really be the place
   That I in childhood used to know,
Where 'mong the bare black hills of shale,
   Nought but the golden gorse would grow?

It is the same, but oh ! how changed,
    For verdure now crowns every spot :
The wild and barren moor of old,
    We now may seek, but find it not.

A thoughtful fairy might have been
    And touched it with her magic wand,
For ornamental lakelets clear,
    Now drain what once was swampy land.

The broad expanse of water there,
    All wavy, like a mimic tide :
Upon its rippling surface bright,
    Such dainty boats now gaily glide.

And lovely flowers now deck the sward,
    Arranged with true artistic skill :
While variegated foliage bright,
    Adorns each verdant slope and hill.

Here, toiling ones, when work is o'er,
    May find repose in shady bowers :
And have their senses charmed the while,
    With music, and the scent of flowers ;

And in the summer sail the lake,
    To court the breeze, or warm sunlight :
In winter test its crust of ice,
    With all a skater's fond delight.

But what is treasured most of all,
    This polished granite column here—
A fit memorial fount to one
    Whose honoured name is graven there.

That name is blest, thro' him that sleeps,
    The ruggéd waste has been refined :
In everything around we see
    His generous hand, and noble mind.

When on the shifting sands of time,
    He left behind a golden mark
Which fadeth not ; for this fair spot,
    Now bears the name of " Harold Park."

ODE TO THE MOON.

O GENTLE Moon, sweet guardian of the night,
Pour down on earth thy flood of lustrous light:
Illuminate the firmament on high,
And fill with light the blue o'erarching sky.
Shed on these plains thy soft and dusky ray,
Let thy rich light the darkness chase away.
Smile down, sweet Moon, upon this world of ours,
Bathe these wild valleys all bedecked with flowers,
With thy sweet light, so placid and so clear—
Thy mellow rays that are so welcome here.
O'er Nature's face thy faithful vigil keep,
Watch o'er each little flow'ret while asleep.
Shed on this earth thy glory from afar,
Outshine in splendour every little star.
Smile on, fair Moon, I love thy streaming light,
Serenely soft; so sad, and pale, yet bright.
The fleecy clouds so swiftly pass thee by—
Obscure thee for a moment from the eye:
And all is changed again from light to shade,
Till once more thou appearest o'er the glade:
Unfettered from the clouds, thou seemst to shine
More dignified and lovely every time!
O beauteous Orb! thou full and splendid Moon,
Gem of the heavens, and to earth a boon:
Cast down on us thy tranquil, soothing light,
From the ethereal regions calm and bright.
Thou wanderer in the far celestial sphere,
O brightly beam upon us mortals here.
Shed thy soft light from vale to mountain steep,
And keep thy watch o'er thousands while they sleep.
O silvery Moon! thou source of light on high,
A halo round thee in the midnight sky:
And far removed from meaner things on earth,
With stars thy kindred, yet of smaller worth:
Thy courtiers, through heavens' boundless plain:
A moment seen, now lost, then seen again;
The silvery clouds come quietly floating by,
Like massive icebergs sail the azure sky.

But thou the brightest, richest gem of all,
O let on earth thy beams so softly fall.
A mystery to man, and ever will,
We try to solve thee, yet are baffled still.
We only know this planet thou dost light
At given periods, with thy beams so bright.
On slumber smilest, beauteous and sublime,
As glorious now as in the olden time.
In peace and unmolested silence, thou
Dost move, and flingest glory here below.
A Being so high and holy guides thy course,
We know not whence thy splendour has its source:
Thy mild bright orb reveals to us at least,
Thy path through the meridian from the east,
Describes a semicircle to the west,
Where peacefully thou sinkest to thy rest.
An unseen Hand Divine controls thy sphere.
I love thy sacred light so calm and clear:
Queen of the night! o'erlooking wood and dell,
Solemn and grand—ah, more than words can tell!

MOORLAND AND SEA.

It was a bright September,
   In golden harvest time,
I sought the lonely moorlands—
   The heath was in its prime.

Their beautiful proportions
   Rose high above the sea;
And stretched in solemn grandeur,
   Expansive, wild, and free.

As they for generations
   Have been, so are they now;
As known to our forefathers
   Each purple-tinted brow.

They're yet as God hath made them,
   So rugged and sublime;
And still in all their glory
   Defy the stroke of time.

Man's hand has ne'er molested
  Each undulating steep,
Where heather blooms unheeded,
  And bilberry bushes creep.

And when the bright Aurora,
  Flings ope' the gates of morn,
Each dewy head receiveth
  The first faint flush of dawn.

And when the sun at evening
  Slopes down into the west,
It kisses last the moorlands,
  Before it sinks to rest.

I plucked a sprig of heather,
  So rich in purple bloom,
And took it from its birthplace
  To my sweet woodland home:

Where flowers bloom in fragrance,
  Unknown to heather bells,
And grow in wild profusion
  In verdant shady dells.

But soon I left my homestead,
  And sought the bright seaside,
Where I in peace might wander,
  And watch the restless tide.

There's beauty in its waters,
  Subject to no control:
The music that it murmurs
  Is soothing to my soul.

A mighty moving mystery,
  As if a spirit chaste,
Breathed in the crested billows,
  Of that wild surging waste.

Of unconquerable waters,
  Obeying not man's will:
But calmed it once when Jesus
  Said softly, "*Peace, be still.*"

As 'twas in ages olden,
   'Tis yet, as fresh as free;
So will it roll for ever—
   As long as time shall be.

I took the sprig of heather
   I'd brought from far away,
And bathed it in the ocean
   That tossed with snowy spray

A voice then in a whisper
   Said softly unto me:
"It is as if the moorlands
   Had bowed to kiss the sea!"

NORWOOD GREEN.

A RURAL village, quaint and old,
Stands in the north of England bold,
Among the hills so rich and green,
Where shining waters wind between.
A sweeter spot can ne'er be found,
Where fresh and verdant dales abound;
And watered thus by many a stream,
The valleys are a deep dark green,
Where sweet wild flowers love to grow,
Among the long grass nestle low;
And in the thickly wooded steeps,
The ivy round the oak tree creeps.
A beautiful, romantic spot,
With here and there a low thatched cot
Built on a slope of cultured green
Gives life and beauty to the scene.
The strawberry plants with runners creep,
And blossom on the sunny steep;
Each cot, some peasant's much-loved home
Where lovely flowers brightly bloom,
And gaily deck the window pane
That peeps into the old green lane.

The honeysuckle 'round the bower
Is twined among the sweet-pea flower.
The rustic owns his humble cot,
And well-trimmed, pretty garden plot.
The village is a peaceful nook,
So still, by meadow, wood, and brook,
That ripples on so gay and free,
And dances in its very glee.
No noise disturbs the meads so still
Save one, from yonder old grey mill,
Its water-wheel goes splashing round,
With reg'lar, rumbling, drowsy sound.
The stream, with rural bridge across,
Its walls bedecked with softest moss.
The little school stands on the hill—
The village green, so quiet and still :
A simple, unpretending place,
Old Time has left on it a trace :
And there upon the Sabbath day,
The little children wend their way.
Such is the spot my father loved,
In youth where he so oft hath roved :
That house in ruins and forlorn,
The very place where he was born!
Where he was reared, and lived in youth,
Beneath that ancient, green-grown roof.
The hillock where he oft hath played
Beneath the oak tree's spreading shade.
Old tree, if thou to me could'st speak,
And tell the tale that I would seek :
Ye scenes of all his early youth,
If ye could tell to me the truth :
Could this green turf a tale reveal,
'Twould tell me of his early weal—
The place that knew him as a boy,
The scene of all his youthful joy.
Their tide of memory back would flow,
And tell a tale of years ago.
The hearts that knew him then are gone,
His house is desolate and lone.
The hands that him in youth caressed
Are in the churchyard, laid at rest ;

And many in this country spot
  Have passed away, and are forgot;
Have lived their uneventful time,
  Some died in years—some in their prime;
They in the out-world were not seen,
  But lived content upon the " Green."
The little churchyard now contains
  Their mortal clay that still remains.
Nought but a tablet now is seen
  To tell the stranger they have been,
With but the simple words inscribed,
  To tell that they have lived and died:
And even those that knew them best
  Have ceased to weep for those at rest.

A DECEMBER ROSE.

[*On a solitary rose being found blooming in December on a little girl's grave*].

When Winter's hand lay icy cold
  Upon the woodlands and the hills,
And in his grasp the streams were locked,
  And mute were little wayside rills,—
The old graveyard was lone and drear
  Upon that dark December day;
The Frost King touched the withered leaves,
  And glittered on the tombstones grey.

I wandered in, I know not why,
  In listless mood I love to tread
And meditate, where silence guards
  The cheerless precincts of the dead.
I came upon a little grave,
  Wherein there lay a sleeping child;
I stood entranced, for there, behold!
  A lovely rose upon me smiled.

A beauteous red December rose,
  Whose perfume filled the frosty air;
It bloomed alone, amidst decay,
  For all around was bleak and bare.

It blushed that I had found it dared
   In winter-time itself reveal:
And through those petals sweet, I felt
   The child's own soul to mine appeal.

It bravely bore the biting frost,
   And seemed to me a sacred thing,
To show that from the deepest gloom
   Of death and winter, life can spring!

An emblem of the child's pure soul,
   And of its love, and faith, and trust:
The flower it loved in life must needs
   Grow there, above its mortal dust.

'Twas life in death, and seemed to be
   All that a little child would crave,
Whose life was brief, whose death was sweet
   As that loved flower upon its grave.

A symbol of immortal life—
   The hope that puts to flight all fears:
Clear crystal drops stood on that rose:
   If angels weep, those were their tears!

That precious flower a sign may be,
   Which they have sent to us in love,
To tell us that her spirit now
   Lives fair as it with them above.

Or is it that the winter rose
   From Paradise was dropt below
From off her crown, to let us know
   That they have decked that darling's brow:

THE LUNAR RAINBOW.

Lo! this evening there appeareth
   In the starry, moonlit sky,
A beautiful, mysterious token,
   Spanning a vast cloud on high.

Lovely is the bow by daylight,
    But a sweeter sight by far
Is that mighty lunar rainbow,
    Bright as every silv'ry star.

Can it be the faintest shadow
    Of that bright arch far above ;
O'er the shining, golden portals,
    Leading to the Throne of Love ?

Know we not, and in not knowing
    Feel God's greatness doublefold ;
There it is, in strange, sad splendour
    For His people to behold.

THE FIRST SNOW OF WINTER.

All is silent this morning, no footsteps I hear—
There's a brighter reflection, so sparkling and clear
I look through the window, my heart gives a thrill,
For the first snow of winter lies thick on the hill.

How lovely the sight of the snow-wreaths around
A spotless white cover spread over the ground;
With feelings enraptured, my heart all aglow,
I gaze on the beautiful, heaven-born snow.

The sight of the snow recollections has brought,
How I watched it when young, with this innocent thought.
" Is it the angels in Heaven that fling
Soft feathers to earth from each beautiful wing?

When fresh from the region above us, the snow,
Too pure it would seem, for us mortals below ;
A carpet of crystal, by angels outspread,
Too chaste is the drift to pollute with our tread.

Yes, fair is the sight of the snow to mine eyes,
As it gleams in its splendour 'neath sunshiny skies
Untrodden, untainted, it lies on the hills ;
Then melts and commingles with mountain-born rills.

But what is the sight of the snow to the poor?
Who shiver, half famished, half clad, at the door;
To such, the cold season of snow-flakes and rime,
Is a pitiless, cruel, unmerciful time!

To those that are poor let us offer our aid,
And lighten the burdens that on them are laid;
A gift will enliven their homes we may know,
And help them to bear with the winter's first snow.

Our Father in Heaven, looks down from above,
And rewardeth good deeds with His blessing and love:
To give will relieve, and make glad the reciever,—
But happier far is the heart of the giver!

NATURE'S MELODIES.

I hear her songs in babbling rills,
But grander far to me than these:
   Is that deep strain,
    With sweet refrain,—
The music of the wind-swept trees!

The mighty monarchs swing their arms,
Reverberate like breaking seas;
   The sweetest sound
    In Nature found —
The music of the wind-tost trees!

Anon she chants a low response,
As if her child she fain would please:
   A soothing tone,
    Sweet, when alone,—
The music of the wind-kissed trees!

Oh! drowsy lisp of rustling leaves,
As they are playing with the breeze;
   That lulling song
    I've loved for long
The music of the whispering trees!

For when I hear those plaintive chords,
My memory back to childhood flees:
    That dream-time floats
    In those soft notes,—
The music of the wind-stirred trees!

Wild forest music! wafted here,
Its beauteous source its lover sees;
    Through branch and bough,
    Come anthems low,—
The music of the wind-swayed trees.

Blest Nature's sweet melodious voice,
I mark each change through all degrees;
    To her I cling,
    And 'neath her wing
I hear her music in the trees!

THE FROZEN BROOKLET.

Little brooklet why hast thou
On this morning ceased to flow?
Dost thou wait a gleam of sun
To kiss thee, ere I see thee run?

Pretty little crystal stream,
Waiting for a warmer beam;
And I miss thy music sweet,—
Like a heart forgot to beat.

Frost-bound brooklet, thou would'st say,
"I slumber till a milder day,—
Then, my little silvery song
Will be heard the woods among."

Rest thee, water, rest in sleep,
By the lovely snowy steep;
Rest in peace and beauty thou,
Till smiling nature bids thee flow.

ROYDS HALL.

I LOVE to look on thee ! Though grey-grown by time,
Yet seemest thou still in thy beauty and prime :
Looking serene in the moonlight so calm,
And tall trees around seem to heighten thy charm :
Nestling among all those stately old trees,
That whisper soft music when stirred by the breeze.
Herein a fair maiden who loved thee was born,
Her sweet childish presence thy halls did adorn :
Along with her brother, a bright noble boy,
This home of their childhood were wont to enjoy.
Oh, oft have I gazed in the silence of night,
Upon thy bold structure, with windows alight :
And thought of long centuries all passed away,
How hands that have built thee are gone to decay.
Though ancient thou art, yet I honour thee more,
Thou recallest the past, the old days that are o'er :
Since then in thy glory, thou firmly hast stood.
Surrounded by acres of pasture and wood.
The house of the manor so long hast thou been,
The pride of the country so fertile and green.
Two cent'ries and more thou hast smiled on the spot.
Where strife, and the turmoil of labour are not :
O'erlooking the parks, that extend far and wide,
Away to a distance on every side.
On an eminence stood, in the midst of thy ground,
Where the rabbit and leveret so joyously bound
In their antics and gambols so full of delight,
At dawn of the morning and dusk of the night :
In solitude oft have I watched them at play,
Beside the wild wood at the close of the day.
Nearly hid by the trees, I can see thee, Old Hall,
With thy evergreens high, and thy ivy-clad wall :
Thou seemest to guard the wild woodland and hill,
And lovely green valley, so lonely and still.
And all is so tranquil, no sound to be heard,
Save the bay of the dogs in thy spacious court-yard :
That echoes around as so loudly they bark,
Or the ring of thy bell that resounds in the dark.

A venerable link with past ages art thou,
We for thy antiquity cherish thee now;
The panels of oak in thy old-fashioned hall,
Accord with thy massive and time-honoured wall.
E'en once a tribunal, where scenes have occurred,—
The sentence in justice, thy old rooms have heard;
Bucolic offenders approached thee with awe,
Obeying the summons for breaking the law.
Grand solid old mansion! with nail-studded door,
Thou storms hast defied, and wilt brave many more;
Thou'lt smile on those hills to the South and the West,
When I in my grave shall be sleeping at rest!

THE NAME IN THE SNOW.

My dear young friend, thou has written thy name
On this beautiful white and spotless mound
    Of fair untrodden snow;
So pure and chaste, and without a stain:
It is traced in characters clear and round,
    That all may see it now.

And may thy name in years to come
Be traced as pure on a clear white page
    Of Life's mysterious book:
When thy days on earth are nearly done,
Then may'st thou in thy mellow age
    With honour backward look,

On the name thou hast left, as unsullied as this
Thou has marked by the path in the snow so white,
    And yet unlike it too;
Not dissolve in the earth, as when warm sunbeams kiss
The snow-name, and take all its characters bright
    For ever from our view.

And tho' to the dust shall thy body be placed,—
Shall sink like the snow to the depths of the earth,
    No more to meet our sight;
But may the name thou hast carefully traced
Be left behind as a proof of its worth—
    A pure and constant light.

SABBATH BELLS.

Hark! the Sabbath bells are ringing,
   Silvery sweet upon the air;
Welcome invitations flinging
   Round the village everywhere.

Oh! what memories awaken,
   With those pealing village bells;
Hearts and home that now forsaken,
   As the music softly swells,—

Come before me as I listen,
   Fresh as if 'twere yesterday:
Till my eyes with teardrops glisten,
   Called by scenes long passed away.

I have heard them oft in childhood,
   And the past comes back again:
When I first within the wild-wood
   Listened to their sweet refrain.

Why should solemn thoughts come stealing
   At those sounds of peace and love?
Striking on some latent feeling,
   Stirring thoughts of Heaven above.

Fancy sees the white-haired preacher
   Standing in God's house of prayer:
Sent by Him, a holy teacher,
   Speaking words of comfort there.

He, with earnest voice impressive,
   Pointing through the darkness, light:
Shewing us to be submissive—
   Teaching words of truth and right.

I can see the old and weary,
   Stooping 'neath the weight of years;
Treading in life's path so dreary,
   Going to church to kneel at prayers.

Then I see the young and careless,
    Youth and hope going hand in hand;
Moving with a step so fearless,
    Singing of the angel Land.

All are bowed with solemn feeling,
    When they hear the Gospel truth,
That the preacher is revealing,
    Pleading for old age and youth.

Such are visions floating o'er me,
    As I hear the Church bells ring;
Sweetest scenes will pass before me,
    That the Sabbath but can bring.

I love their soothing peal at even',—
    Ring away ye peaceful bells—
Speaking but of love and Heaven,
    Where in bliss the white soul dwells.

WINTER.

Who says Winter owns no beauties?
    To adorn its darkling days,
Bright attractions it possesses,
    In a hundred different ways.
Ever 'tis to us revealing
    Glories that were veiled before;
Nature shows us, though she's sleeping,
    Charms from out her boundless store;
Sets before us countless beauties,
    Crystal tears her sky now weeps;
Glittering frost-gems, virgin snow-drifts,
    While the tedium as she sleeps.
Who can see, unmoved, the splendours,
    Winter gives us in the dell?
Flowing cascades turned to crystals,
    Mute and shimmering as they fell!
E'en its fierceness owns a grandeur,
    While its skies in vengeance lower

In the storm-cloud is reflected,
   And revealed, a God-sent power.
To the poor and agëd only,
   Winter is a cruel time;
Shivering with its frost-breath hoary,
   Dreading all its snow and rime.
Such as these are ours to succour,
   All who can, our blessings share—
Make them feel that good old Winter
   Brings its joys, if well they fare.
Out-door pastimes, such as skating,
   Hearty youthful friends enjoy:
Then its moonlit, star-gemmed heavens,
   Offer charms without alloy.
And its long and cosy evenings,
   Are beloved, and never pall;
Study-time, or social gatherings,
   Bring delights to one and all.
Winter ever will be welcomed
   By the children, sweet and fair,
In its midst old Christmas hoary,
   Comes to crown the dying year.

"THE DAYS ARE ALL ALIKE."

There's no blossom on the black-thorn,
   There's no music in the rill;
But its waters are asleeping,
   With the blighting wintry chill.
There is snow upon the hilltops,
   And no leaves upon the tree;
And the days seem all alike, Mother
   They are all the same to me.

For my heart is sad and lonely,
   Yet I cannot tell you why;
But it seems asinking slowly,
   Like yond drooping, heavy sky.

For my life is dull and dreary,
    I have lost my lightsome glee ;
And the days seem all alike, Mother
    They are all the same to me.

The storm-cock in the distance
    Is complaining to the morn,
I can hear him whistle shrilly,
    On yonder old dead thorn.
And the bitter wind is sweeping
    Across the barren lea :
And the days seem all alike, Mother
    They are all the same to me.

Tho' I have not had a sorrow,
    And I have not had a care,
Yet the weight that presses on me,
    Seems more than I can bear.
And I long for you to cheer me,
    And to set my spirit free ;
For the days seem all alike, Mother—
    They are all the same to me.

THE SNOWDROP.

The land reposes, garbed in angel white,
A myriad snow-gems 'neath the noonday sun
Are scintilating ; few have yet begun
To liquify beneath the radiant light.
Thus while stern Winter's hand enzones the earth,
And Nature's shielded life-germ calmly sleeps :—
Lo! through the ground a pale-faced floweret peeps,
As white as if the snow had gi'en it birth !
Pure, silent courier of the coming Spring,
Uprising 'mong the gleaming crystals here ;
Its holy mission surely is to cheer,
For new-born hopes 'round those fair petals cling :
The lovely snowdrop from its cold white bed,
To give God's message, lifts its dainty head !

THE MOUNTAINEER'S SONG.

I would not leave my native hills
    For all the wealth the land can give :
They're more than all the world to me,
    Where I was born, I wish to live :
Secluded here, and be at rest,
    Nor mingle with the city's strife :
But climb my own, my native hills,
    And live a happy, peaceful life.

I would not leave my native hills
    For all the treasures you can bring :
Then let me mount their dusky steeps,
    Free as a bird upon the wing :
And tread their undulating heights,
    The heather springing 'neath my feet,
Where the freshening breath of heaven
    Oft waves that russet mantle sweet.

I would not leave my native hills
    When rich with autumn's purple glow,
Nor when their beauteous, radiant brows,
    Are crowned with purest crystal snow.
I love to see each noble ridge
    Rise boldly 'gainst the azure sky :
Then let me dwell upon the hills,—
    Where I have lived I wish to die.

AT NATURE'S SHRINE.

A reverence far too deep for words to tell,
I feel when I at lovely Nature's feet
Kneel humbly down : and unto her the while
Cast all my soul. Oh, glorious mother sweet
That erst has fostered me, her loving child :
In all her pristine beauty unto me
She stands revealed : and through all time remains
Inviolate : and yet freely she responds
With her own plaintive mellifluous voice
To those who worship at her peerless throne,
And love to hold communion with her soul.

Through sylvan glens and dim-lit forest aisles,
I hear her wondrous waves of music sweep
In anthems grand; then lisp in whispering tones
A soothing monody, that softly falls
Upon the senses like a gently sung
Sweet lullaby, unto her clinging child,
That loves to nestle 'gainst her throbbing breast,
And draws its nurture from her yielding soil.
Then while she holds me in her soft embrace,
There breaks from her some wild exultant strain :
In jubilation swell triumphant songs,
And rhapsodies ; in contact close she thus
Beguiles me with the witchery of her charms.
Anon in tortured, anguished tones she wails
In lamentation, when the troublous storm.
Disturbs her rest ; and rends and racks her soul
Unto its centre : as its withering power
Bows down her head, and shakes her to the heart ;
Thus with distorted visage she appears
To me more worshipful.
All those who kneel at Nature's hallow'd shrine,
Adore the Diety ; and methinks when we
Cling closely to her, we are nearer Heaven.
If I am sorrow-laden, I can throw
Myself upon thy mercy, Mother true ;
And rest my head in thy protecting arms,
And there pour forth into thy bending ear,
The pent-up anguish of a stricken heart ;
And find in thee more solace than a hard
And cruel, grasping, hollow world can give
Derive sweet succour from the soothing sound
Of purling streamlet, murmuring through the glade ;
Thus in thy lap, beneath the blackthorn bare,
Through which the cool and pure sweet evening breeze
Goes gently soughing, lulling me to rest,
I find true peace.
Through every season she some charm reveals
To those that love her. What can there surpass
The hope-bound beauties of her vernal spring ;
When from lethargic winter she bursts forth
In soft refulgence, decked with garlands green.

What in voluptuous splendour can approach
Her full-robed summer? when she sits enthroned
In rich luxuriance. Nor when in autumn she
With lowering pulse, a bright coronal wears
Of glowing tints, upon her pensive brow.
In winter when she rests and dreams, her form
Half hid in virgin vesture, angel white,
Set off with rich and sparkling crystal gems.
Her divers changes pass in mystic waves,
Obeying unsolved God-made laws, that gird
And govern all the universe. But she
Unto her devotees is never harsh
Nor yet unsympathetic.
Howe'er her face denotes her passing mood
Divine she is, and to my soul appeals.
I feel that she a loving message brings
From her own God. Through her His spirit floats
O'er all the Universe. In various forms
She is the reflex of His changeful will:
She breathes to me in mellow'd tones sublime
Of His omnipotence. His spirit moves
In all her aspects: in her silvery mists
And rains benign, I trace His falling tears:
Depressed He is, and mourns, when heavy skies
Droop o'er our heads. Then in the tempest's wrath
We mark His frown: His anger doth appall
When thunder echoes 'mong the solemn hills;
And when His brow is cleared, the clouds disperse
And show beyond, the bright ethereal blue.
In sunlight fair is mirrowed all His smiles:
When day-beams on His children fall, we feel
His benison divine.

WHEN THE EVENING LAMP IS LIGHTED.

When the evening lamp is lighted,
   And our dear ones safe at home,
In one bond of love united,
   Welcome is the wintry gloom.

Happy are the hours of evening,
    Sweetest time of all the day;
When the thoughts of care and labour
    For a while are laid away.

Scene of many an artless pleasure,
    Is this simple home of ours;
Memory owes a priceless treasure
    To some long past evening hours.
Sacred is the dear old hearthstone,
    Where we learn each other's worth;
'Tis a bright and faithful magnet,—
    Dearest spot to us on earth.

Loving hearts are filled with gladness,
    Mirth o'erflows in laughter sweet;
Oh! may never grief or sadness,
    Come within our loved retreat
Love cements the bright home circle,
    Hearts expand beneath its sway;
Like the trees that gather mosses,
    Grow they richer day by day.

Fancy is at daytime hidden,
    But when lamplight hours draw nigh
'Tis unchained, and roams unbidden
    As the daylight leaves the sky;
It is free to wander hither,
    Charm us, with its winsome wiles
And a book our sole companion,
    Oft the evening time beguiles.

Then we court the gentler Muses;
    And a silvery halo clings
'Round the light that lore defuses,
    Making gems of meanest things.
Thus the craving soul is feasted
    With a sumptuous, sweet repast;
And upon our happy circle,
    Thus a potent spell is cast.

When our evening lamp is lighted,
    It reveals a treasured home;
To the weary one benighted,
    'Tis a landmark in the gloom.

Strife and discord ne'er invade us,
　These we count our bitter foes;
But the soul of peace surrounds us
　With a sweet and calm repose.

SPRING.

Spring has come, with all its beauty
　Fast unfolding every day—
Come with all its lovely freshness—
　Nature in her new array.

Mark each tiny bud unclosing
　From its pretty velvet case:
Brought forth by the hand of Nature,
　Each to its appointed place.

Peeping shyly at the daylight,
　Half afraid to come at first,
Then when they are fully wakened,
　Forth in all their beauty burst.

Nature dons her garb for summer—
　All things seem so lively now;
Note the pretty meadow flowers,
　We can almost see them grow.

Tender shoots are now appearing
　From the earth where they have hid:
Where for long they have been sleeping,
　Coming forth when they are bid.

First the pure and lowly snowdrop,
　Ventures forth the Spring to meet:
Next the primrose and the daisy,
　Then the daffodil so sweet.

And when they are bathed with dewdrops,
　How they glisten, pearly bright!
In the fresh and early morning,
　And the cooler shades of night.

See the fair and flowery meadows,
    Brightly clad in verdure gay;
Nature smiles in all her gladness,
    Now that winter's passed away.

Hark! the little lambs are bleating
    In the pasture by the stream;
With each other they are playing—
    'Neath the sun's reviving beam.

All the neighbouring woods are ringing
    With the little wild-birds' song;
From each tiny throat comes trilling
    Notes of music all day long.

First, the homely robin-redbreast
    Sings so sweetly to his mate;
For we gave them crumbs in winter,
    When they perched upon the gate.

Then we hear the plaintive cuckoo,
    With its loud peculiar call:
Then the thrush, the wren, and linnet
    Singing to each other all;

And the gentle lark, ascending,
    Sings its varied, tuneful lay;
To the skies its song 'tis pouring,
    As it soars from earth away.

Joyous song-birds imitating
    Trying which can warble best;
Never weary of rehearsing
    Never take one day of rest.

Let us greet the lovely Spring-time;
    Nature looks so bright and fair;
Sweetest flowers and scented blossoms,
    Fragrance laden on the air.

We can trace the good Creator;
    He has spread with lavish hand
Given new life to the drooping,
    Scattered beauty o'er the land.

Welcome, welcome, happy Spring-tide;
  Sweetest time of all the year;
Rich in variegated foliage,—
  Beautiful beyond compare.

THE NIGHTINGALE.

Beautiful warbler, singing in glee,
Perched on the bough of yon wide spreading tree;
Trilling a song from thy little throat,
Gushing with music, its every note.
Songster of midnight, beautiful bird,
Through the wild glen is thy melody heard;
Soon as the moon takes her path through the sky,
Commences thy singing, so plaintive and high;
When darkness descends, and the farm-yard is still,
And silence reigns over the valley and hill.
The birds of the wood are asleep and at rest,
'Tis now that thou lovest to warble the best.
Unmolested and free there to tune a sweet lay,
Preferring the silence of night to the day.
Beautiful bird, in thy lonely retreat,
Pouring forth melody charming and sweet.
Queen of the songsters, sweet Nightingale,
Reigning supremely in the dark vale.
Now imitating the lark, or the thrush,
Untutored and free, and thy melodies gush,
In cadences sweet, at once thrilling and high,
With rich mellow notes that swell forth to the sky;
Then dropping so suddenly low and yet clear,
That falls in a whisper so sweet to the ear.
Again it drifts into a melancholy strain,
So piercing and wild, then is silent again.
Though mocking the other birds' every call,
Thine own silvery music surpasses them all.
Thy song is far sweeter to me than the rest,
Thou wild nightingale, with thy dusky brown breast.
Sweet serenader, when we are asleep,
Bidding them all to be joyous that weep.

Thy sweet thrilling song putting sorrow to flight,
And cheering the lonesome, deep silence of night.
I love thee, sweet birdie, for singing alone.
When woodlands, and valleys, and hills are thine own.
Other birds love to sing in the day,
When all the world shineth so bright and so gay;
Thou choosest the holy hushed stillness of night,
When all the world round thee is peaceful and quiet.
Delighting to sing amidst solitude free,
With no one to hear thee, and no one to see:
None but the Master, who dwelleth on High,
Will hearken thee chanting thy praise to the sky:
Sweet little minstrel, in thy delight—
Singing thy beautiful hymn to the night.

"THE FIRST ROSE OF SUMMER."

'Tis the first rose of summer that dares to appear,
All suffused in the dew of an angel-dropt tear;
So modestly, timidly, it has displayed
Its virginal charms, in their freshness arrayed.

But soon 'twill discover that it was the first
To allow its fair petals from bondage to burst,
Nor must it then languish, but with us abide,
Till more of its sisters bloom there by its side.

We joyfully greet thee, thou dainty-lip'd rose;
It is cheering to see thy soft petals unclose:
Fair emblem of love! with romance ever bound,
And the essence of hope in thy bosom is found.

This message from Heaven thou truly dost bring,
That summer has merged from the promise of spring;
The soul of it lies in thy beauty we see,
It breathes in the scent that thou bearest with thee.

How dar'st thou expand 'neath this weeping grey sky?
The sullen north-easter thou seem'st to defy,
So courage we find in thy loveliness dwells,
'Tis but the unwise one, at fate that rebels.

Stern Boreas will melt at this ravishing sight,
Thy exquisite beauty he'll seek not to blight;
Such trustful temerity can but disarm,
All vengeance will soften, he'll bow to thy charm.

Thou art faithful to Nature, thou beautiful flower,
She fulfills the commands of the All-seeing Power;
And obeying her dictates, to her ever true,
Thou comest in season, be skies grey or blue.

Oh! linger frail rose, till the sun shall appear,
To kiss thy young beauty, and dry up that tear;
And when his warm rays on thy white petals shine,
'Twill enhance the loved charms that by birthright are
    thine.

His smiles will disclose what we love in thee most,—
The splendours that none but the white rose can boast;
Unequalled in purity:—fit to adorn,
The breast of the noblest that ever were born!

God's delicate handiwork! lovingly drest
In nature's soft textures, the thought will suggest—
Oh, wert thou immortal! why canst thou not stay?
Why beauty and perfume should yield to decay?

This is thy brief mission, thou gem amongst flowers!
Thou harbinger sweet of the bright summer hours;
As there in thy depths are the jewel-drops seen,
O'er all in the garden, to reign as their queen!

"THE COUNTRY COTTAGE GIRL."

    They seek to lure me from my home,
      That I in London may abide;
    They'd have me change my simple life
      For one of indolence and pride;
    They know not, oh! they know not,
      The sacrifice t'would be;
    The dear ones in my cottage
      Are all in all to me.

The town is never tranquil,
  'Tis one perpetual whirl;
'Twould turn my brain!—Let me remain—
  A country Cottage Girl.

Yes, they would have me leave this home
  For yonder gay and splendid town;
They'd have me cast this cotton frock,
  And don me in a satin gown.
They take me for a dreamer,
  And think I long to go;
They cannot guess my feelings,
  My heart they'll never know:
I covet not their riches,
  The diamond or the pearl,
They tempt not me, I'd rather be—
  A humble Cottage Girl!

A child of freedom I am here,
  No tow'ring walls obstruct my view
Of yonder ever changing sky,
  And hills enwrapt in vapour blue;
A landscape clothed in beauty,
  Here lies before me far;
The black domes of the city,
  My view shall never bar:
The music of the forests,
  The streamlet's soothing purl;
Oh! grant me these, if you would please—
  A rustic Cottage Girl.

Are those who live in pomp and state
  The happiest ones upon this earth?
Ah no! a yoke of care and grief
  Oft burdens those of noble birth:
Some think such live for pleasure,
  It cannot well be so;
We know that rank is often
  An heritage of woe.
And those who own their titles,
  The Countess and the Earl,—
Of high degree,—may envy me—
  The lowly Cottage Girl.

The tiara, and the royal crown,
 Oft-times must weary heads adorn;
And aching temples throb beneath
 The flashing gems so proudly worn.
If I had wealth and fortune,
 But bound to join the strife,
And give up for the city,
 My peaceful country life,
I could not then be happy,
 My wealth from me I'd hurl:—
The world ignore, and be once more—
 A careless Cottage Girl!

They fain would show their gems of art,
 And let me see their wondrous sights;
They'd take me through the festive halls
 Illumined with electric lights:
They vainly seek to make me,
 In these my youthful days,
An artificial lady,
 With studied, formal ways;—
To lounge within a carriage,
 My fingers idly twirl,
Would suit not me, I'd rather be—
 An active Cottage Girl!

They say my face is bright with bloom,
 But from these cheeks would fade the rose,
Were I to breathe the ball-room air,
 And not till dawn seek my repose;
They tell me I might marry
 A man with purple blood;
What care I for the colour?
 His *heart* may not be good;
Give me my faithful Gilbert,
 Though but a village churl;
He'll happy make, and ne'er forsake—
 His little Cottage Girl.

Their costly treasures they may take,
 I still will draw from Nature's store;
I mark her every changing mood,
 And read her tokens o'er and o'er.

   The ruby and the sapphire,
     May facinate the eye;
But they are matched in splendour,
     By hues that deck the sky;
Yet when the works of nature,
     I gladly would unfurl:
The London born, would laugh to scorn—
     The simple Cottage Girl.

No murmur of the world's unrest,
     These woodland solitudes comes near ;
The breezes in sweet undertones,
     Their secret plaints breathe in my ear ;
I ne'er was made to dazzle,
     I ne'er was made to charm ;
Unto my high-born sisters
     I freely give the palm ;
I *will* not be a lady,
     Bedecked with many a curl ;
My lot is best, God's love hath blest—
     A country Cottage Girl!

THE WEST WIND.

O Westerly Wind, of thee I would sing,
Bringing a health-giving scent on thy wing :
From over the moors, and from off the sea,
Blowing thy fresh sweet breath to me.

O frolicsome wind from over the hill,
Rising and falling, and coming at will ;
Wafting the smell of the gorse and the broom, [home.
Where sweet heather blooms, and wild-birds have their

From off the moorland upon thy wing,
Thou bearest the fragrance of heather and whin ;
Purple and golden, they blossom so wild,
And known to none but the mountain child.

O Westerly Wind, with boisterous glee,
From off the Atlantic thou'rt blowing to me ;
Thou hast cross'd the deep, and kiss'd the spray,
And brought the ozone from far away.

O Westerly Wind, so bracing and free,
Bringing the smell of the wild briny sea;
Zephyrus! I love to feel thee blow,
Bringing a freshening healthful glow.

O Westerly Wind, what music is thine—
Æolian harps that are sweetly in chime;
Now thou art racking the boughs of the trees,
Then dropping again to a murmuring breeze.

O Westerly Wind, could I follow thy flight—
Be borne on thy wings through the day and the night;
Over the moorland, over the sea—
What would I give but to travel with thee!

ON FINDING A BIRD'S NEST IN THE GARDEN.

They say that "love doth love beget,"
   It seemeth so to me;
A little bird I love so well,
Has built its pretty downy nest,
   Upon the garden tree.

Does it, too, bear a love for me,
   That makes it come so near?
Why did it leave the woods and meads,
And build its home so close to mine,
   To rear its nestlings here?

It seems as if it knew full well
   That I would be its friend;
That I would shield its home from harm,
Protect it from the ruthless hand,—
   Its little ones defend.

Then I will not betray the trust
   It doth repose in me;
But watch it with a tender care,—
The precious gift that it has placed
   For me, upon this tree.

What made it build its little nest
  So near my cottage door?
It must have been a link of love,
It knew that it would welcome be,
  Which makes me love it more.

Who taught it how to weave its nest
  With moss and silvery thread?
And bits of our discarded floss
Are twined among this withered grass,
  To make a soft warm bed.

It is a loving Being on High,
  A mighty guiding power,
Who gives it instinct for it all,
And bids it when to soar and sing,
  And sleep at midnight hour.

And when I see the little birds
  In beauty take their flight,
And soar on wings towards the sky,
My kindest wish shall follow them,
  When they are from my sight.

And they'll away to yonder wood,
  Their happy songs to sing:
Soon they will leave the parent home,
O'er vale and mountain as they soar,
  Seek freedom on the wing.

MOONLIT FLOWERS.

  Moon of the summer night,
  Soft and subdued thy light,
  Kissing the roses white,
    The while they sleep.

  Roses so rich and fair,
  Filling the evening air,
  While ye are slumb'ring there,
    With perfume sweet.

Softly the summer breeze,
Speaks to the moonlit trees,
Plays with the cream-white leaves
   Where dew-drops gleam.

Only to look at them!
Trembles each liquid gem,
Poised on the mossy stem,
   So crystal clear.

Down in the fair rose bower,
Drooping its head still lower,
Blushes the sweet-pea flower,
   And clasps the rose.

With clinging tendrils fine,
Lovingly they entwine,
Dew-jewelled flowers of mine,
   This summer night.

After the sunshine warm,
Bathed in their nightly balm,
Wearing a fresher charm,
   Beneath the moon.

Transient gifts from Heaven!
Scenting the breath of even;
Would that to each were given
   Perpetual life!

Taking its own sweet will,
Straying along the sill,
Into my chamber still,
   Peeps one white rose.

Into the shadows deep,
Hither it fain would creep,
Bowing its head in sleep,
   Against the pane.

Rose of a summer's day,
Born but to fade away;
Frailer than mortal clay,
   And lacks the soul.

Whispers this dreaming rose
Wrapt in its calm repose,
" Time for the eyes to close,
    Good night, good night!"

DAYBREAK.

I STRAYED along the meadows,
  When day began to dawn:—
As from the face of nature,
  A curtain was being drawn.
It moved away so slowly,
  And then disclosed to view,
Sweet nature just awakened,
  Commencing life anew.
Like jewels were the dewdrops,
  Upon each blade of grass,
Those glinting gems were trembling,
  To wait each zephyr pass.
So lovely and transparent,
  They beaded every spray,
And clung to every flowerct
  I passed upon the way.
The world as yet was sleeping,
  The village all was still;
The scene was sad and lonely,
  The morn was cold and chill,
The mists were fast dispelling,
  The sky was clear and grey;
A fresh'ning breeze was blowing,
  To usher in the day.
And by-and-by a birdie
  Began to greet the morn,
I heard it chirp and twitter,
  Upon the leafy thorn:
It seemed to waken others,
  In meadows all around;
They called unto each other,
  With sweet and merry sound.
And as I lingered longer,
  The sun began to rise;—

A light so soft and rosy
   O'erspread the eastern skies :—
And then a ball of crimson
   Appeared upon the scene ;
It shone upon the hill tops,
   And o'er the meadows green,—
Till Phœbus, bright and glorious,
   Illumined heaven and earth,
And nature roused from slumber,
   Was full of life and mirth.
The flowers op'ed their petals,
   So softly one by one,
And smiled, amid the dewdrops,
   To greet the morning sun.
The little bees so busy,
   Came near with humming sound,
And gathered sweetest nectar
   From flowers all around.
Then came two village rustics,
   The hour of toil had come :
I bade good-bye to Fancy,
   And went towards my home.
They broke my meditation—
   The village was awake :
I hastened to my duties—
   I'd watched the morning break.
And all was life and gladness
   Amongst the fields of corn ;
The birds were singing sweetly
   Their carols to the morn.
I turned and left the meadows,
   When morn was in its prime ;
I'd seen another instance
   Of God's own hand divine.

TWILIGHT.

I took a walk at twilight,
   That loved and peaceful hour,
When dew is softly falling
   Upon each drooping flower.

The day and night were meeting ;
   Each moment 'neath my gaze
The vale was growing dimmer,
   Enwrapped in purple haze.
All steeped in solemn silence,
   Was tranquil, calm, and still ;
I saw the distant village,
   And church upon the hill,
With spire pointing upwards
   Against the dusky sky ;
And as I gazed upon it,
   My bosom heaved a sigh.
For there my little brother,
   Who died a lisping child,
Within that churchyard sleepeth,
   Safe from a world defiled.
There others of my kindred,
   Are quietly laid at rest ;
The sun's last rays had kissed them,
   When sinking in the west.
I felt alone with Nature ;
   The busy world was still,
And all was sad and lonely,
   The birds had ceased to trill.
The murmuring little brooklet
   Went singing through the glade,
'Twas all that broke the silence
   The music that it made
Then from that old church tower
   I heard the chiming bell ;
So sweet and undulating,
   As zephyrs rose and fell ;—
Its soothing sound came floating
   In waves upon the air ;
Then all again was silent,
   And Nature looked so fair.
The western skies were glowing
   With mellow amber light ;
The day was softly waning,
   And mingling with the night.
The moon came slowly rising,
   When vanished had the sun,

And shone with chastened splendour—
　The day its course had run.
I saw the stars come peeping
　Into the evening sky—
They one by one so brightly,
　Lit up the heavens on high.
Then in the far-off village,
　The lights began to shine :
But in this spot secluded.
　'Twas but the Hand Divine
That hung those lamps in Heaven,
　And placed them at His will,
To light this glen sequestered,
　That slept so lone and still.
The day was gently dying,
　A lull was over all—
A hush came over Nature,
　To wait the darkness fall.
The dim grey light grew fainter,
　The night was stealing on ;
I stood alone in silence—
　The day-sounds all were gone.
I watched the mystic changes
　Come over Nature's face :
The daylight had departed,
　And moonlight filled its place.
The trees in stately grandeur,
　So tall and noble stood,
And formed a sombre background —
　A dark and silent wood.
I worship my Creator
　When viewing scenes like this :
I seem to feel His presence,
　The hours are full of bliss :
Him through His works I worship,
　I know His subtile power,
And feel so near my Maker
　At twilight's restful hour.
Subdued, and calm, and holy,
　It holds a charm for me :
It seems to whisper softly,—
　" Now let thy fancy free."

NIGHT.

The day is done, and Night descends,
   And spreads its shelt'ring wing ;
It wraps the earth beneath its folds,
   And sweet repose doth bring.
The mist descends mysteriously,
   And makes the grasses weep ;
'Tis Nature's veil thrown over all,
   That it may quietly sleep.

Night has come, and darkness falls
   While Somnus holds his sway ;
Tranquillity sinks over all,
   Until another day.
The western light so softly glows
   Upon the silence deep ;
The breath of heaven gently blows
   And lulls the flowers to sleep.

All is hushed, and silence reigns,
   O'er all the land around,
Save the nightingale's sweet strains,
   To break the peace profound.
'Tis Nature in her solemn mood
   The silence of the night,
When stars look down so sad and calm,
   And beam with twinkling light.

All is peace, and Nature sleeps,
   Beneath the moonlight pale ;
Repose is on the mountain steeps,
   And in the lonesome vale.
The night was sent by God Above
   And ordained for the best ;
He, in His love and mercy, bids
   Us sleep, and be at rest.

AUTUMN.

Golden harvest time is past,
Soon will blow the wintry blast,
   Autumn winds are sighing ;

Shorter grows the light of day,
Summer's flowers have passed away.
　　All its foliage dying.
Bright-hued leafage now we see
Ripe upon the forest tree,
　　Quiv'ring, rich and mellow.
Changing is the woodland scene,
All that once was fresh and green,
　　Turning red and yellow.

Nature now has lost its bloom,
All things blighted, tinged with gloom,
　　Gone is Summer's gladness;
Earthward fall the leaves away,
Where was life in now decay,
　　Wrapped in dreamy sadness.

Stubble fields bereft of corn,
Looking barren and forlorn
　　In the lonely gloaming.
We might weave a russet wreath
Of the scattered leaves beneath
　　Trees no longer blooming.

We are trampling 'neath our feet
Nature's leafy carpet sweet,—
　　On the ground reposing.
Peaceful Autumn, pensive, still,
Waits for Winter's touch to chill,
　　Now her reign is closing.

Fruit is garnered; on the steep,
Web-entangled brambles creep,
　　Autumn's fragrance flinging;
Yet some wild blackberries grow,
On those bushes trailing low,
　　To the thorn-tree clinging.

Birds that trilled in Summer time,
Go to seek a warmer clime,
　　O'er the wave retreating;—
They that sung so sweetly here,
Leave us till another year,
　　With the Autumn fleeting.

Mournful season of the year,
Withered herbage, brown and sere;
    Winter near advancing;
Ling'ring flowers no perfume shed,
Only nuts and berries red,
    Through the thicket glancing.

And a hazy veil hangs round,
Drooping slowly to the ground,
    In the swampy valleys;
All the fields look long and grey,
At the closing Autumn day,
    As the twilight tarries.

Keen east wind around us creeps,
See! the low'ring sky now weeps,
    Summer's thirst 'tis quenching;
Raindrops make in yonder pool
Eddies in the water cool,
    Woods and meadows drenching.

Wild Æolus tunes his lays,
Mourning o'er the bygone days,
    With a sad repining:—
Its sweet requeim chanting low,
For the Autumn's hectic glow,
    Shows the year's declining.

Nature heaves a weary sigh,
Now her Summer charms must die,
    To her couch she's creeping;
Of all vernal beauty shorn
Is the garb she long has worn,
    She unrobes for sleeping.

How the swollen stream is sped!
O'er its clear and stony bed,
    Ever quickly flowing;
On, to meet the mighty sea,
Careless in its course so free,
    Whither it is going.

Wandering by grassy slopes,
Through the dingle and the copse
    And among the rushes;

Onward, babbling streamlet flow,
Sweetly murm'ring, and thy low
    Music seldom hushes.

Riv'let giving life and sound,
To the landscape all around,
    Where the ferns are growing:
Winding where the twigs entwine
By the pastures, where the kine
    Seek it, gently lowing.

Winter soon will wave his hand—
Cast his spell o'er all the land.
    Trees their boughs be baring:
While we stroll the woods among,
Nature's kneeling, for her long
    Winter's sleep preparing.

Autumn-time I love the best,
When all Nature sinks to rest,
    Varied tints revealing;
So from life, we too, must part,
Thus those tokens fill my heart,
    With a solemn feeling.

STARS OF MIDNIGHT.

Stars of midnight, softly shining,
    Would that ye could speak to me:—
Tell me of the far-off Heaven,
    All its love and mystery.

Stars of Heaven, can ye answer?
    Smiling sweetly in the sky;
Like the light of happy angels,
    Looking downward from on High.

Stars of Heaven, I am lonely,
    Standing on this desert earth;
Tell me of the great Jehovah,
    From Whose power ye had your birth.

Stars of midnight, brightly beaming,
  In your sweet celestial home:
How I long to come and join ye,
  Yearn to hear ye whisper "Come."

Stars of Heaven, all is stillness,
  In the space in which ye move;
Far above this world of trouble,
  All your path is truth and love.

Stars of Heaven, how ye glisten,
  O'er a thousand different places:
O'er a host of people moving,—
  Smile on their uplifted faces.

O ye stars in silent glory,
  Reflex of the Spirit-land;
Gems of beauty, like a studded
  Diadem, in my Father's hand!

O ye stars, in solemn splendour,
  How I love to see ye shine;
Now methinks my soul ye beckon,
  Upwards to your light divine.

Has one bright star left its sisters?
  It is gliding swiftly down;
Looking like a jewel falling,
  From that vast bespangled crown.

Star of Paradise, I wait thee,
  Coming from the Unknown Sphere;
Dost thou bear a message holy,
  Calling me away from here?

COMPENSATIONS.

When Summer's flowers are dead, and Winter's blast
Despoils the foliage, leaving black and bare
The trees and hedgerows; then white-jewelled fair
Coronals deck them, which are not surpassed
In lovliness. While those pure frost-flowers last,

All is transfigured: ice-pearled every spray
Glints glorified: and neath a rosy ray
In opal crystals every twig seems cast.
In vaporous frosts a feathery film depends
From every object; and yon vale below
Etherealizes: for each sprig and bough
Light, half-transparent tassels then suspends:
Entranced we gaze on glist'ning frost-gemmed bowers,
And wait the resurrection of the flowers.

A WINTRY SUNSET.

How splendidly the sun went down
    Behind yon snow-clad hill!
It tinged the clouds with fiery dye,
So calm and tranquil now they lie—
    And all is sad and still.

Around, above, where e'er I look,
    The scene is one of peace:
The far-off landscape draped in white,
As softly falls the veil of night,
    Its beauties still increase.

The garb of snow brings out in full
    The objects all around,
In bold relief: with tall bare trees
That stand out black, devoid of leaves,
    The distant hills are crowned.

That orb of crimson hue has sunk
    So softly in the west:—
Has shed its glory here below,
And kissed the pure crystal snow,
    Before it sunk to rest.

It glimmered brightly through the trees,
    And shot a parting ray:
First to the valleys bade good-bye,
Then smiled upon the moorlands high,
    And then it passed away.

Its disc has disappeared from view,
    And night has cast its pall ;
The dappled clouds retain their light,
Divinely beautiful the sight, —
    And peace reigns over all.

TO A ROBIN.

Come birdie, come hither, this winterly morn,
While hoar-frost is clinging to yonder bare thorn,
And shining so brightly on every bough,
The woodlands are clothed in a mantle of snow.
I hear thee lamenting upon the yew-tree,
Thou seemst to be chirping and calling for me ;
Then come to my window, and have thy repast,
Thy feathers are ruffled with bearing the blast.
Thou knowest me, birdie, obeying my call—
Thou'rt perching so near me upon the white wall.
How tame thou art, robin, the while thou art fed,
And taking for breakfast the crumbs of white bread.
Of all other birdies I love thee the best,
With sweet plaintive twitter, and bonny red breast.
Thou camest to my dwelling in summer so calm,
Nor dost thou forsake me amid winter's storm ;
Now I will befriend thee, for keeping so near.
So come, little birdie, and be not in fear :
And then, my sweet robin, the warm summer long—
I shall have my reward with thy beautiful song !

THE OLD SYCAMORE TREE.

I've dwelt beneath thy shelter, tree.
    For many long and happy years :
When I was young and merry, tree
    My heart untouched by worldly cares.

And since my sunny childhood, sweet,
   I've looked upon thee day by day;
And I have grown to love thee, tree,
   Thou sentinal, to guard my way.

Thou seemst to keep a watch, old tree,
   Upon this dear and lonely spot,—
To smile upon my pleasures here,
   Within my humble peaceful cot.

I've seen the little birdies, tree,
   Come perch upon thy top-most bough,
And trill a happy song to heaven,
   When in the west the sun was low.

Through every changing season, tree,
   Thy form has stood so staunch and bold;
Through Spring and Summer bright and warm,
   And through the Winter bleak and cold.

I've seen thee full of foliage, tree,
   And when thy every bough has been,
With fresh and sweetest blossoms filled
   Suspended 'mong thy leaves so green.

I've seen thee in the Autumn-time,
   Clad in thy russet dress so sweet;
When crisp and withered were thy leaves,
   And gently falling at my feet.

I've seen thee gaunt and bare, old tree,
   With all thy lovely verdure fled;
With snow upon thy branches, bent
   So like the aged, with hoary head.

Through many storms and tempests there
   Thy stately form has shielded me;
Nor ever bowed beneath their wrath
   Thou noble, fine, majestic tree!

I love to hear thy soughing low,
   I've listened to it o'er and o'er,—
So like the restless ocean-waves
   When they are surging on the shore.

I hear thee moaning in the night,
    When scathing winds are blowing high;
Or when the raindrops gently fall
    Upon thee, from the troubled sky.

This lay is in thy honour, tree,
    I've tuned it on a rustic reed;
Thou old familiar sycamore,
    Grand monarch thou of all the mead!

THE BEAUTIES OF SNOW.

Beautiful snow, falling around,
Silently, softly, on to the ground;
Falling in feathery flakes from on high,
Coming down from the thick and sombre-hued sky.
Falling so lightly from yond laden cloud,
Covering the earth with a pure white shroud;
Making the trees and the hedge-rows all white
Falling so softly from morning till night.
Coming so quietly, gently down,
Decking the hills with a crystal white crow;
Swaying the branches of each little shrub,
And on the tall trees in yonder lone wood;
Clothing the valleys in garments of white,
Beautiful snow so fair to the sight.
Stealing serenely and noiselessly down,
Wrapping the earth in its winterly gown.
Drifting in mounds so white and so fair,
Whereon is the trace of the fleet-footed hare.
Here looking like some little sylvan hall,
And there overhanging the old-fashioned wall;
Resembling miniature valleys and hills,
And embowering the limpid sparkling rills;

Then they burst forth in tiny and rustic cascades,
And ripple along through the beautiful glades,—
And the snow 'mong the branches and boughs of the trees,
Forms a lovely arcade, until stirred by the breeze.
Wreathed like fantastic garlands of white,—
Beautiful snow so airy and light;
Formed into fairy bowers and caves,
Wreathed into beautiful furrows and waves.
Clinging to railings in masses of white,
Beautiful snow, so sparkling and bright.

And when at last it has ceased to fall,
A solemn tranquility reigns over all;
The red sun sinks like a ball in the west,
And Nature reposes in night garments drest
All the land sleeps 'neath its coverlet white,
The daylight recedes and gives place to the night:
And the frosted flowers that figure the pane,
Are by Nature's own artist designed not in vain. [high,
Now the clouds have dispersed, and the moon shines on
'Mong the bright twinkling stars of the clear evening sky;
Shedding her sweet mellow light here below,—
Shines on the beautiful crystallized snow;
Making it sparkle like rich gems so bright.
Glitter and dance in the moonbeams so light.
Shines on the icicles drooping in clusters,
Making them look like beautiful lustres,
Pendent from rose-trees that climb to the eaves
Taking the place of the roses and leaves ;
And when they are kissed by the bright moonbeam,
Some like the richest emeralds seem;
Or diamonds, set amid pearls so white,
They glisten so lovely, transparently bright.
They dazzle resplendently, crystal and clear,
In the pale silver sheen they so beauteous appear ;
And the soft sad moonlight, so calm and serene,
Gives a sweet holy charm to the fair peaceful scene;
Beautiful snow, sent from Above—
Emblem of purity, light, and of love.

DEAD LEAVES.

Oh, russet leaves! ye seem to speak to me,
And tell in whispers what ye all have seen,
When ye were young, and flutter'd fresh and green,
And kissed the budding blossoms on the tree,
Whilst lisping songs, borne on the wand'ring wind.
Ye screened the ripe and luscious fruit from view,
And danced in sunlight; but ye paler grew
When all the fruit was garnered, ye declined.
More tanned and scorched became ye day by day,
And crispened in the Autumn's sunshine wan,
Till ye were dead; then softly earthward ye
All idly dropped; and now await decay,
Ye that were once the favoured shade for man,
Now withered lie, yet teach life's truth to me.

Sea Songs and Ocean Odes.

A GREETING TO THE SEA.

Beautiful, silvery, shining sea,
Dancing and rippling, ruffled and free!
Its waves sing a song to welcome me here,
As I gaze through the mist of a joyful tear.

The curves of its waters now burst on my view,
Reflecting the tint of the firmament blue;
My heart in its ecstacy throbs with delight,
As the fair ocean gleams like a far-off light.

Beautiful, boundless, billowy sea!
Noble, expansive, and smiling at me:
Bidding me welcome again to its shore—
Would that I now had to leave it no more.

Seen from afar, so fresh'ning and bright,
Peeping 'tween hillocks to gladden my sight;
Through ridges and tracks of golden sand,
Bright'ning the waste of barren brown land.

Since last I looked on thee, what storms must have crossed
Thy surface, now tranquil, with tempests have tossed;
Now peace has descended upon thy bright breast,
And soften'd the wrath of thy billows to rest.

The balm-bearing breath of the beautiful sea,
Is wafted so sweet o'er the mosses to me;
I'm coming, old ocean, to see thee again,
From over the heather, and sandy plain.

Beautiful, glist'ning, changing sea!
I come o'er the moorland to look upon thee:
Stupendous and mighty, come let us unite—
I languish to touch thy waters so bright.

I come to interpret the mystical song
Of thy murmuring waves that are flowing along;
Rolling and restless, controlled by a Hand
That lavishes beauty o'er ocean and land!

THE WHISPERING WAVES.

    In the twilight time of an autumn day,
    When the sunset colours had died away,
    And shadows weird on the waters lay,
        The whispering of the waves,

    Came sweet and low to my listening ear;
    I felt the soul of the sea was near;
    'Twas siren's music so soft and clear,
        The whispering waves, the whispering waves.

    Our fancy plays in the gloaming dim,
    The while we scan the horizon's rim,
    And listen to Nature's evening hymn,—
        The whispering of the waves.

    Out of the mist that seaward lies,
    Come nymphs, to revel 'neath twilight skies;
    They merrily dance, while fall and rise,
        The whispering waves, the whispering waves.

    The wordless songs of the sea-sprites free,
    Are melodies borne from the deep to me;
    I thus interpret the murmuring sea,—
        The whispering of the waves.—

    While mystic lights to the surface dart,
    They breathe of hope to the drooping heart;
    And oh! the charm that their songs impart,
        The whispering waves the whispering waves.

As unto me do the sleepless waves,
Fresh stories bring from the sea's dark caves,—
They tell of its heroes' far-off graves,
  The whispering of the waves.

Of deeds of valour they oft-times sing,
And how to faith must the tried heart cling;
A sense of peace to my soul they bring,
  The whispering waves, the whispering waves.

THE RETURN OF THE FISHING FLEET.

Night drooped upon the stilly wave,
  And wrapped the deep beneath its wing;
The gorgeous splendour of the day,
  Grew chastened, in the twilight dim.

The evening star hung o'er the deep,
  In solemn beauty, pure and bright;
And on the silent waters fell
  From far above, its silvery light.

The weary sun had sunk to rest,
  Upon the bosom of the deep;
The wind with murm'ring music soft,
  Had lulled the ocean sprites to sleep.

And from behind the old church tower,
  The moon had risen clear and bright;
And softly kissed the tranquil sea,
  And smiled upon the beach so white.

When o'er the silvery moonlit wave,
  So lightly sailed the fishing fleet;
Each coble with its crimson sails,
  And laden from the bounteous deep.

And on the shell-encrusted pier,
  A group of bonnie fishwives fair;
With wistful gaze, survey the sea,
  The night breeze playing with their hair.

And in the offing they discern
   All they had fondly wished to see:
As one by one, the little boats
   Come bounding o'er the waves so free.

They watch them near the harbour bar,
   In sheltered refuge, once again;—
Sail swiftly round the reef of rocks,
   And leave behind the open main.

With prows that cleave the waters bright,
   And outspread sails, they glide along;
The yawls and luggers, trimly rigged,
   And manned by sailors brave and strong.

A cheery shout rings through the air,
   To greet them as the strand they near;
The sails are furled, the anchors dropped,
   Beside the wave-washed wooden pier.

And in the soft and shady light,
   The trawling nets are hauled ashore:
Unburdened of their glitt'ring freight,
   The vessels lie at rest once more.

The crews have left, and lightly now,
   They ride at anchor in the bay;
And guarded by the gentle moon,
   That bathes them with its dusky ray.

Embellished names, in gold and blue,
   Are painted on each vessel's side;
His trusty boat the skipper loves,
   At once his fortune and his pride.

With cheery hearts, and weary hands,
   They seek the homes they love so well:
The merry fisher and his wife,
   In sweet contentment love to dwell.

A straw-thatched cottage — that is all,
   So lowly, yet as white as snow;
So near the sea, kissed by the spray
   Borne by the fresh'ning winds that blow.

Like marble cots, in moonlight pale,
   Their latticed windows all alight;
That speak of comfort all within—
   Of cosy firesides, warm and bright.

Deserted now the landing pier,
   For sweet "good-night" has echoed round;
The gates are closed, no footstep heard—
   The rippling waves the only sound.

And midnight soon sinks o'er the deep,
   Repose pervades the village street;
Thus we have seen the safe return,
   And mooring of the fishing fleet.

A FAREWELL TO AN OLD LIFEBOAT.

FAREWELL, poor old boat, we shall see thee no more,
For long hast thou been on our surge-beaten shore;
And well thou hast served in the years that are gone,
Thy record is noble, thy honour is won.
A friend thou hast been to the sons of the sea,
For eighty-one lives have been rescued thro' thee!
Thy gallant commander, thy mate on the wave,
He yet has a heart that is tender as brave;
Who knows, but he dropt on thy timbers a tear
When parting, like one from a friend on the bier?
For long have your fortunes been closely allied,
And each served the other when storm-tost and tried.
To years of good work the attachment is due,
You've been to each other both faithful and true
For twenty-one years. Now you're parted at last,
Who battled together with billow and blast.
For many a wreck ye have left the fair Fylde,
Returned with success, when the tempest was wild.
A cheer for thy coxswain, and all his brave crew;
Give honour to those to whom honour is due:
For landsmen are proud of such fellows as these,

Who never are daunted by roughest of seas,
And now let us call for the Fishermen's Band,
To greet the new boat, that is now on the strand;
May good luck attend on her future career,
I hope that the other will have her compeer.
Long life to the coxswain, and stout-hearted crew,
Farewell to the old boat, and welcome the new!

TO THE SEA.

Thunder, thunder mighty sea,
In thy peerless majesty,
Speaking as thy billows roll,
Appealing ever to the soul.
Always moving, always will,
Restless ocean, never still:
Commanding with imperious voice,
With an awful deafening noise:
Calling in the solemn gloom,
Hapless victims to their doom.
Soul of fierce despotic power,
Friend and foe in one brief hour.
Man to thee must ever bow,
Many, many moods hast thou:
Beautiful, and weird, and wild:
One day tranquil, calm, and mild,
Shining like a mirror bright,
Rippling in the fair sunlight.
Then as angry thou wilt be,
O thou changing, surging sea!
With thy mighty waves advancing,
And the seething white spray dancing
In their madden'd fury waking,
Rolling, roaring, bounding, breaking!
With thy broad'ning billows sweeping
Stately forward, booming, leaping:
With thy tossing foam-wreaths dashing,
And thy green-grey colors flashing.
Arch dissembler too, art thou,

Who would think to see thee now—
Laughing with defiant pride,
That those smiling waters hide,
Smould'ring passions laid at rest,
Underneath thy placid breast?
Thou, that only yesterday,
Summoned human lives away :
Many a fond heart was bereft,
When thy heaving billows cleft :—
Taking at one mighty sweep,
To thy yawning caverns deep,
Those who dared to cope with thee,—
O thou grasping, hungry sea!
Challenging with threat'ning roar,
All who cross from shore to shore.
With thine own mysterious light,
Beautiful thou art to-night.
All is thine that thou canst claim,
And looking on thee we exclaim—
"What wonders in thy waters lurk !
Thou art God's greatest, noblest work."

THE CAPTAIN TO HIS CREW.

Cheer up my men, cheer up my men,
  We've weathered the gale once more !
We'll boldly brave the bounding wave,
  As we steer for a distant shore.

The storm was fierce last night, my mates,
  The wildest I ever have known ;
We were nearly lost, as the good ship tost,
  And the sails to shreds were blown.

You know how we were tried my lads,
  It's a mercy we're spared to relate ;
How each one stood 'mid the foaming flood,
  And prepared for an awful fate.

But bravely you bore up, my lads,
  When Death seemed hovering near,
Each took his part with a cheerful heart,
  And never displayed a fear

Like a cannon's boom in the midnight gloom,
  The wind on the canvas prest;
Till it was all torn, yet we on were borne,
  By the gale from the wild sou'west.

The billows dashed, as the light'ning flashed,
  And the thunder rolled along,
And mingled its voice with the ocean's noise,
  In a loud tumultuous song!

It was flash for flash! and peal for peal!
  Oh! lads, 'twas a dreadful hour!
When the darting light showed the billows white,
  That reared with appalling power.

There's many a bright bright eye, my lads,
  That twinkled with merry light,
Now closed will be, in the cold dark sea—
  By the terrible gale last night.

Be merry while yet you may, my mates,
  For many a noble crew
Have passed away, who but yesterday
  Were as jolly, my hearties, as you.

Aye, many a manly heart I say,
  That beat full of hope and glee,
And honest pride, now lifeless hides
  Far down in the pitiless sea.

Then let's be thankful now my men,
  And let us be happy too;
"Hurrah!" I hear the sailors cheer;
  Long live my valiant crew!

Then here's a health to you, my men,
  And peace to the rolling main,
And here's to ninety days, my mates
  And good luck till we land again!

THE DISCONSOLATE HEART.

I stand beside the boundless sea,
Whose restless waves toss wild and free ;
The mist hangs round me like a pall,
The rumbling waters rise and fall.
The sky is grey, and cold, and drear,
I am alone, no form is near ;
The cheerless sky, and the ocean too,
And the mist alike, have a cold grey hue :
The sea-birds flap their snowy wings,
But their piercing cry no comfort brings.
My heart is sad, and their dismal screech
Is the only sound along the beach :—
But the voice of the sea, with its hollow roar,
As its swollen waves break on the shore :
And strings of seaweed here are spread,
Cast up from the ocean's deep dark bed.
The sea-star sprawls on the wet sands borne
When the tide was high, at the break of morn ;
And shoals of shell-fish around me lie,
'Mong heaps of seaweed brown and dry.
The limpet clings to the sea-worn rock,
Where the white sea-fowl in numbers flock.
Then scud along the surging deep,
Where the waters play, and dance, and leap.
The massive boulders far away,
Receive the ocean's feathery spray :
So green, and slimy, with the sea,
All rounded worn with the waves so free ;
And little spiral shells are there
Among the pebbles, white and fair ;
And wonders left by the out-gone tide
Are strewn around on every side ;
And many a pond like a miniature bay,
With tiny wavelets ripple and play.
I feel the smell of the briny sea,
So fresh and sweet it is borne to me ;
The wave-marks left on the soaking sand,
Are here before me where I stand ;

In curves fantastic they are seen,
Where but to-day the sea has been.
The soft breeze blows from the ocean drear,
I call aloud, there is none to hear :
The stormy petrels o'er me fly,
They heed not my despairing cry :
I call, but call for thee in vain—
My voice but echoes back again ;
The rocks and cliffs resound the more,
And echo back along the shore.
I call to thee across the main,
But the waters seem to mock my pain :
I call aloud unto the sea—
But the billows foam, and rave at me ;
And lash against the craggy steep,
Where creatures from the ocean creep :
The tufts of green in crevices grow,
And gently wave as the soft winds blow ;
I see the mark on its slippery side
That was left in the morn by the ebbing tide.
The murky sky, and the mournful sea,
Accord with the thoughts that arise in me :
And tell me thou hast gone to sleep,
While crossing o'er the mighty deep.
The sea has claimed thee for its own,
Thy spirit to the sky has flown.
The wild sea-fowls proclaim the same,
That in the fierce relentless main,
Thou art for ever lost to me—
Oh, why may I not rest with thee ?
Then comes a whisper from the deep,
As if its spirit wakes from sleep,
I seem to hear the wild waves say
" Arise, my child, and go thy way :
I have not yet a place for thee,
But one day thou shalt come to me."
I go, and leave this dull lone shore,
And these sad waves' tumultuous roar.
I seem to hear their wild refrain,
" Oh, go my child and work again ;
And waste not here thy still young life,
But go and mingle with the strife :

Repine not for the one now gone—
But go thy way, and still toil on."
I gaze once more upon the main,
I hear once more the sad refrain;
I leave, but still the wild waves say—
"Arise, and work while yet 'tis day!"

THE SKIPPER TO HIS BOAT.

A cheer for my boat, for my own faithful lassie,
    Full many an hour I have travelled with thee ;
We often have trusted our fortunes together,
    True mates we have been on the billowy sea.

With many a tempest we often have battled,
    When round and beneath us the elements roared ;
Thou hast brought me in safety again to the harbour,
    And now my brave lassie at anchor is moored.

Far on the lone sea we have been in the winter,
    Wearily toiling from morning till night;
Now still we are faithful, when kind friends surround us,
    And cling to each other in summer so bright.

I'm never so happy as when I am trimming
    Her beautiful sails, when we're out on the deep;
In the splendour of noontide, or glow of the evening,
    When Neptune is rocking the Syrens to sleep.

I see her so gallantly, gracefully riding,
    And swaying her wings at the breezes behest ;
She'll answer my hand when she'll answer no other,
    And bring her old master again to his rest.

Then hurrah ! for the lass that will always befriend me,
    My home on the ocean, the pride of my heart;
If we reach not the depths of the ocean together,
    I'll miss my old boatie, when ever we part.

"SAILING ON THE SUNLIT SEA."

Skies of azure, flecked with silver,
   Flossy clouds of vapour white;
Like the angels' flowing vesture,
   Glistening raiment, pure and bright;
Glorified with radiant sunshine,
   Half transparent some we see,
Floating o'er us, while we're gaily
   Sailing on the sunlit sea:—

Sailing, while those skies above us
   Give unto the sea's grey-green,
Tinges of the heavenly azure,
   And a dazzling silvery sheen.
Beautiful and calm the morning,
   Fair as aught on earth can be,
While with joyous hearts we're softly
   Sailing on the sunlit sea.

Sea-birds there are flitting near us,
   Poising o'er the wavelets calm;
With their quivering plumage gleaming,
   Whiter in the sunlight warm.
Sun-kissed sea-birds! hovering 'round us,
   Beautiful, and wild, and free!
Making circlets o'er the waters,—
   Sailing on the sunlit sea:—

Skimming near us, while the breezes,
   Lightly wafted, whisper low;
Bearing joyous songs to heaven
   From our vessel's stern and prow.
White-winged yachts bedeck the water,
   Graceful craft where-e'er they be;
Gliding, with their snowy pinions,
   Sailing on the sunlit sea.

See our vessel's transient way-marks,
   On the slumbrous surface shine;
In our wake are white foam-tracings
   Like a molten silver line;

Soon to be obliterated
  Like the worldly paths that we,
Trace in different shades, not always,
  Sailing on a sunlit sea.

Life is all around and 'neath us,
  Nature's here with noiseless tread;
Not a footfall breaks the silence,
  Peace below, and God o'erhead:—
Smiling through the silver sunlight,
  Ever keeping guard is He;
Watching o'er us, while we're gently
  Sailing on the sunlit sea.

THE WIDOW'S LAMENT.

When I hear the sad sea sobbing,
  It sounds like a dirge for the dead;
Its pulses unceasingly throbbing,
  Does it grieve for the Hearts that have fled?

It was there that the billows parted,
  And gathered my lad far below;
My Jimmie, the brave and true-hearted,
  In its dark stilly depths slumbers now.

And the waters wrap around him,
  For he lies neath the rippling wave;
The gems of the ocean surround him,
  As he sleeps in his deep silent grave.

His life was brief and cloudless,
  In the blossom of youth he hath died;
His form lies cold and shroudless—
  For his life ebbed away with the tide.

When the night and the morn were meeting,
  And the moonbeams still lingered so cold;
To the sky then his spirit was fleeting,
  As the sea did its victim enfold.

And I gaze with a restless yearning,
    On the turbulent, conquering sea;
While my bosom is beating and burning,
    For the soul that has vanished from me.

I can see the ship still rocking,
    As I look on the surging main,
That roars with a triumphant mocking,
    O'er its victims, all those it has slain.

Yet strange is this fascination,
    As I wander alone by its shore:
In my sorrow and desolation,
    Still I love to hearken its roar.

He rests on the bed of the ocean,
    And sleepeth the sleep of the brave:
Yet my heart overflows with emotion—
    When I think of my poor Jimmie's grave.

THE RAINBOW.

How beautiful the rainbow looks,
    Suspended o'er the deep;
Among the black and watery clouds,
With silver linings white as shrouds,
    That seem to want to weep.

How lovely, yet how strange it seems,
    Arched o'er the waves so free;
And smiling in the changing light,
With all its brilliant colours bright,
    Reflected in the sea!

That vivid arc of matchless hues,
    So transient and so clear,
Now reigns with triumph in the sky,
A few brief moments, ere the eye
    Will see it disappear.

And lo! another bow is there,
    With faintest violet rim;
Its 'semblance, but more undefined
With colours softened and refined
    A shadow vague and dim.

How lovely,— unperceived, they came
    Across the sky so dark:
Now they so softly fade away,
And melt among the clouds, till they
    Die out, and leave no mark.

Oh, welcome words of Holy Writ,
    They come before me now;
God's promise in that sacred Book,
I read his token as I look,
    Where He hath placed His bow.

THE LIFEBOAT BELL.

Come look at the gathering storm to-day
    And hear how the seabirds screech;
The roaring billows bound up and break
    Like thunder, upon the beach.
The wind has freshened, and veered a point,
    Increasing the water's swell;
Then hark! for lo! 'mid the storm there goes
    The clang of the Lifeboat Bell!

Oh! what does it mean? Look out at sea,
    A vessel drifts fast to wreck;
'Tis scarce discerned by the landsman's eye
    As waters wash o'er its deck:
Its hoisted signal appeals for help,
    The fishermen know too well;
The coxswain summons his crew, for hark!
    He's ringing the Lifeboat Bell!

With sea-trained eye he has watched that barque,
    So long on the great waves tost;
Now lifted high in their sportive glee,
    And then for a moment lost.

The shipwrecked strangers are baffled now,
   All quailed when the foremast fell ;
Could they but hear in their dire distress,
   The sound of the Lifeboat Bell !

All hearts are stirred by the startling sound.
   'Tis heard in the cottage home ;
The wives and mothers with anxious hearts,
   Rush out in the tempest's gloom ;
Their men are called to the treacherous sea,
   No mortal the storm can quell ;
And oh ! 'tis ever with heart-throbs wild
   They list' to the Lifeboat Bell.

The sea works havoc in storms like these,
   As thus in its great unrest,
It wages war with the sons it nursed
   And swayed on a peaceful breast.
Man's strength is tried with its forceful moods,
   But ne'er will his hand repel
Those storm-urged breakers, whose war notes dread
   Ring out with the Lifeboat Bell.

The wind has heightened, the clouds dropt low,
   The gale in its force swoops down ;
The boatmen dare it, their faces tanned,
   Storm-proof as their oilskins brown.
Those fluttering signs of their brother's woe,
   Enough to their staunch hearts tell ;
In wind and sleet they obey at once,
   The call of the Lifeboat Bell.

Nor long will the foundering barque ride on,
   No harbour of refuge near ;
And oh ! to them will the lifeboat crew,
   Take hope that will give them cheer.
Be quick ! brave hearts, for humanity's sake ;
   Your boat will their fears dispel ;
A score of fishermen now we see,
   Respond to the Lifeboat Bell.

From that imperative peal we know,
   If rung to the breakers' roar,
That work and peril, and dread suspense,
   Are rife on the sea-girt shore.

The hero fierce on the field of strife,
   In prowess can ne'er excel
Those valiant coastmen, who will dare
   To answer the Lifeboat Bell :—

Take hasty leave of their own dear kin,
   And then for a combat run :
That other fathers may be restored—
   The mother have back her son.
They carry their lives in their toiling hands;
   It may be their own death's knell
Is now being rung, yet for duty's sake,
   They fear not the Lifeboat Bell !

THE WRECK OF THE "SIRENE" AT BLACKPOOL,

—— OCTOBER 9th, 1892. ——

The Sirene sailed with the noonday's tide,
To proudly plough the Atlantic wide ;
In ballast, light, with her sails unfurled,
She started out for the great New World.

But when the vessel was under way,
A change appeared at the close of day ;
The clouds hung low in the evening sky,
At midnight's hour the wind shrieked high :

For lo ! a hurricane filled her sails,
Ere well in sight of the coast of Wales ;
Her course reversed, then she tacked again,
And tossed about on the troubled main.

All night she rode in the dreadful gale,
And vainly tried through the storm to sail,
But fiercer, louder, the west wind blew,
And baffled her brave Norwegian crew.

They lost control of their gallant barque,
As sails were torn by the storm-fiend dark,
And mighty billows around her boomed
Then each one felt that the ship was doomed.

The day wore on, and they sighted land,
And staightway made for the storm-washed strand :
They turned her head, they could do no more,
And let her drift to the wild lee-shore.

As nearer, and nearer, she swiftly drew,
A throng of faces appeared in view ;
The men stood up in her stern to wait
With throbbing hearts their impending fate.

The wind increased with the tide's full flow,
The Sirene rolled till her yards dipt low ;
And laboured on, with her lessening gear,
Through breakers white, to the crowded pier.

Hope buoyed the hearts of the crew, as each
Descried the thousands on Blackpool's beach ;
But sank, on seeing with blank despair,
No boat could live on the breakers there !

Then shouts went up, but they could not hear,
She headlong made for the wave-washed pier ;
A frantic rush, as its massive form,
Loomed helpless there, in the blinding storm.

She struck ! 'mid cries at the fearful scene,
The pier-deck shook, as the poor Sirene
Went bounding in—at the structure dashed—
And wrenched the girders, while timbers smashed !

An awful crash ! and a great rebound !
But willing helpers were gathered round ;
Each Norseman stood, with a seaman's nerve,
The while she reeled with a mighty swerve !

They saw their brothers, our boatmen brave,
Throw ropes to them o'er the yawning grave ;
Another heave, and she closer drew
A leap for life by the fainting crew !

So one by one they were got ashore,
'Mid thrilling cheers, and the sea's wild roar;
Another bang! then a desperate leap,
A life was snatched from the seething deep!

Thus each was saved from the foaming flood,
Till one alone on the taffrail stood;
A rope was thrown, and around him lashed,
They hauled him up, as the pier deck smashed!

And prayers were breathed by the people near,
As crew and rescuers left the pier,—
The hearts were moved of the anxious throng,
For cheers rang out as they passed along.

With beaming faces, their sufferings o'er,
The Norsemen greeted the folks on shore:
Then friendly shelter and succour found,
Through generous hearts, that were gathered round.

Like axe-felled tree, crashed each tow'ring mast!
All far and wide was the wreckage cast:
The Sirene, helpless, upon her side,
Was stranded there, in the swirling tide.

Forsaken thus, like a huge dead form:
And in the intervals of the storm,
Was heard the clang of the good ship's bell—
The waves were ringing the barque's death-knell!

Man, speak no more of thy vaunted power.
It answers not in the tempest-hour;
Thy works are frail, when the sea in wrath,
Obeys good Heaven, but naught on earth!

MEDITATIONS.

I sit within my rustic bower
  While Nature smiles around me here;
'Mid perfume rich from many a flower,
  The wild-bird's note salutes my ear.

From distant trees a low sweet song,
   Is borne upon the air to me;
Like murmuring waves, and makes me long
   To see once more the glorious sea!—

To look upon its throbbing breast,
   To hear its mighty pulses beat,
To see again each foaming crest,
   Its billows rolling at my feet!
Its tones reverberant in the storm
   Are always music sweet to me,
Or whispering wavelets, smooth and calm,
   It is the self-same grand old sea!

'Tis peerless in its strange unrest
   Shows Nature in her wildest form;
I long to be upon its breast,
   It bears for me a nameless charm.
My woodland glens I hold most dear,
   Their solitudes are wooed by me,
Yet tame their beauties all appear
   Compared with thee, thou surging sea!

The summer roses bloom to fade,
   The birds will seek a warmer clime,
The sea remains as it were made,
   No season knows, nor change with time.
I yearn to stand by it once more,
   Its grandeur it reveals to me;
As breezes soft play 'round my door—
   I long to-day to view the sea.

In fancy I can see thee now,
   Thy deep-toned voice sounds in my ear,
My own loved Sea! and on my brow
   I feel thy breath, so cool and clear;
But Fancy is a fickle maid,
   She flimsy fabrics weaves for me;
Delightful moment while she strayed!
   She would not keep me by the sea.

The sun sinks o'er the hill I see,
   To-night 'twill gild the rippling wave;
What silent raptures mine would be
   To watch it reach its liquid grave!

The cooing dove has sought her nest,
   While to the hive returns the bee;
I soon, like them, must seek my rest,
   And see in dreams my own loved sea!

FISHERMEN'S WIVES.

When your weary eyes close for a night of repose,
   When the wintry winds are blowing;
When you hearken the rain that is pelting the pane,
   And the streamlet that faster is flowing;
Do you think of the sea, what its fury will be,
Of the toiling and brave who are out on the wave,
   And ever in danger must be?
Then think of the lives of the fishermen's wives
   When their husbands are out on the sea!—

When those whom they love on the wild waters rove,
   In search for the treasures of ocean;
Then the roar of the wind fills each good woman's mind
   With throbbing and painful emotion.
To them a great storm seems a hideous form,
That is seeking to smite, in the depths of the night,
   Its victims, whoever they be;
Then pity the lives of these mothers and wives,
   When a tempest sweeps over the sea.

They bid them good-bye, with a sorrowful sigh,
   When the sea is so smooth and shining;—
So laughing and bright, with its varying light,
   No cause for the fishwives repining.
But the sea may betray, ere the close of the day,
Its billows may rise, and the cloud-covered skies
   Frown over the waters so free;
Then think of the lives of the poor patient wives,
   Of the men who are tossed on the sea!

At the tempest they quail, lest should danger assail
   Their dear ones, and leave them to sorrow: [sleep
As they gaze on the deep, where their men soon may
   In peace, ere the dawn of the morrow.

They anxiously wait, and resign them to fate,
The dread storm they bear, while they offer a prayer
   For the brave, who in peril must be ;
For lone are the lives of the poor fisher-wives,
   While their husbands are sailing the sea.

There is never a storm, but what many a form
   Is laid on a watery pillow :
There is never a wind, but a brother will find
   His doom on the wild cruel billow.
The hurricane loud is preparing a shroud,
And a sorrowful dirge sings the foam-laden surge.
   Every seaman in peril must be :
Oh sad are the mothers, and sisters, and wives,
   When destruction rides over the sea !

ON THE RESIGNATION OF COXSWAIN BICKERSTAFFE, OF BLACKPOOL.

TIME, the mighty king and conqueror
   Ever will a despot be ;
All things, be they art or nature,
   Yield unto its stern decree ;
Through it " the old order changeth,
   Giving place unto the new ; "
It hath ta'en the " Robert William,"
   One by one 'twill change her crew.
By its hand, the summer flower
   Giveth place to snow and rime :
Now we find the Lifeboat Coxswain
   Bowing to the monarch Time.
All the record of his daring
   Comes before the mental eye :
Gallant deeds on stormy waters,
   Oft beneath a weeping sky.
Strong of limb, with heart of valour,
   Reared beside the Irish Sea,
Breathing all its bracing breezes,
   Blackpool's pride, such men as he.

Eighteen years of faithful service,
  Done for mercy, on the wave:
Places him amongst our seamen,
  In the front ranks of the brave.
Never more his well-known figure
  In the mercy-boat will stand,
At his post, to guide her, bringing
  Those in peril to the land.
Oh! how grateful hearts have blest him,
  And his trusty, gallant train:—
Blest them for restoring loved ones
  To their home and friends again.
In the morning of his lifetime,
  Through its arid noontide heat;
He has toiled, before the evening
  Cast its shadows cool and sweet:
Now it comes, and he is weary
  With his life-work, long and hard;
For those noble deeds of succour,
  He will reap a just reward.
Look at all his decorations,
  Think of all his glorious past!
Then we know the veteran coxswain
  Well deserves his rest at last.
Healthful years be yet before him,
  Long and happy hours to spend,
By the sea, his boyhood's playmate,
  And withal his life-long friend.
Fare-thee well, true son of Neptune!
  Rest and honours fairly won:
One day thou wilt hear the Master
  Greet thee with the words "well done!"

A SEA-SIDE SUNSET.

I saw the lovely red sun set
  Into the glorious sea;
So tranquil, calm, and beautiful,
  Appeared that sight to me.

I sat and watched it slowly move,
　　Far down towards the west,
The heaving blue waves brightly gleamed,
　　With many a cream-white crest.

The shining golden sun appeared
　　To move adown the sky,
And left a crimson glow behind,
　　So charming to the eye.

And then it touched the water's edge,
　　Where sea and sky unite ;
And lit the sea across to me,
　　With soft refulgent light.

Its splendour was reflected there,
　　Till every wave was seen,
Across to the horizon far,
　　Beneath its glowing beam.

And then it dip't into the sea,
　　Till half was gone away ;
The waters looked like molten fire,
　　Beneath its dazzling ray.

And lower still it seemed to sink,
　　Into the mighty deep ;
Till but its golden edge was seen,
　　Where sky and waters meet.

A moment more, and it was gone
　　The sun was lost to sight ;
But in the western sky it left,
　　A flood of mellow light.

The bright horizon's crimson verge
　　Wore to a golden hue,
That shaded into faintest green,
　　Which melted into blue.

A sight so strangely beautiful,
　　I ne'er had seen before,
The wild waves glittered as they danced
　　And broke upon the shore.

The twilight deepened into night,
   All nature seemed at peace,—
All save the surging of the waves,
   Whose music cannot cease.

A holy presence hovered round,
   And every moment blest;
The day was done, the night had come,
   The sun had sunk to rest.

THE OCEAN'S CHARM.

A sweet and solemn feeling,
Does o'er my heart come stealing;
And my soul is filled with deep devotion,
As I list' at midnight to the ocean.
By its waters dark and dreary,
Ne'er my mental eye grows weary
Of gazing on the mighty billow,
Its vision haunts me on my pillow!
For a spell comes creeping o'er me,
As the waves roll high before me,
On the seething, surging ocean,
Thrilling me with strange emotion.
Oh, then it has a magic charm,
That soothes me like a healing balm;
Its snowy-crested foaming waves,
Rolling o'er a thousand graves!
Methinks its spirits hover o'er me
That its mermaids call before me
Noble forms, so long departed,
Weeping women, broken hearted;
The tales of shipwrecks of the past,
Men hoping, daring, to the last;
Then folded in its strong embrace,
And leaving not a single trace
Of the spot where they went down,—
By no marble pile 'tis known.
Then something says my fate 'twill be,
To slumber in the deep sad sea;—

To sink beneath the foamy crest,
Unto the grave I should love best;
A moment, and then not one faint token,
To tell for me that the waves had broken.
And they would roll, as they rolled before,
Onward, till dashed on a far-off shore.
They'd hide me there when I am dead,
Down on the sea's dark lonesome bed;
There I should lie, and heeded not,
By all my earthly friends forgot:—
With the mermaids singing all around,
With a sweetly sad and soughing sound;
In those calm depths, on a sandy bed,
With a coral reef beneath my head,
Alone to lie, mid the pearls so fair,
With the seaweed tangled in my hair.
For oh! I love the dark blue sea,
Expansive, fathomless, and free;
It is like music to my soul,
When mighty billows rush and roll.
I love it! be it calm or wild,
It lulls and rocks its clinging child.
For 'tis no inconsistent thing,
That fondest love from fear can spring
A serf may love his master so,
Regard him with the deepest awe;
Nor seek to break from bondage free,
A tyrant though that master be.
Repentant moments may disclose,
A noble nature doth repose
Deep down in that impulsive breast,
When all its passions are at rest.

. .

More solemn by far than it is at noon,
Is the beauteous sea 'neath a midnight moon
When every thing is hushed in sleep,
Save the mighty waves of the surging deep;
When moonlight falls on waters blue,
Their sheen is of the emerald hue.
And then its varied, fantastic forms,
Enhances all its wondrous charms.

The sea no man can comprehend,
Nor will it to his frail will bend;
'Tis ruled by One, the All-Supreme,
Who dwells beyond where night-orbs gleam.
Methinks the sea is nature's tie,
Connecting earth with Heaven on high;
There's something holy in the ocean—
The dark blue waves' tumultuous motion:
Oh, is it God's own spirit breathing
In mighty waves for ever heaving?
When I hear its boom in the night alone,
It has a charm that is all its own.
Oh, the solemn midnight ocean!
Oh, its waves' unceasing motion!—
It has a sweet mysterious power,
That awes me at the midnight hour.
Oh yes, the spot where I would die,
Upon its bosom would I lie,
And wait God's angel drawing nigh,—
To waft me to Eternity!

A SAIL AT SABBATH EVE.

See! the sun, in golden glory,
   Shines upon the glassy deep,
While the balmy western breezes
   Seek to lull the waves to sleep.
'Tis a peaceful Sabbath evening,—
   We are out upon the sea—
'Neath the sunlight softly sailing,
   Happy thoughts come back to me.

Tell me not the world is joyless;
   Looking on a scene like this
Wide expanse of sky and ocean,
   Seemeth near akin to bliss.
Calm, and bright, and full of beauty,
   Now the sun is sinking low,—
Lighting with its beams our faces,
   With a warm and genial glow.

Solemn, soothing thoughts come o'er me,
    At this tranquil evening hour;
Gazing on a world of waters
    Brings to mind God's wondrous power.
Sounds of Sabbath bells come stealing
    O'er the silent waters wide;
Silvery bells, so gently pealing,
    Cast a spell at eventide.

And the land seems like a picture;
    Dwarfed it is, seen from afar.
Like a city built in water,
    Where its domes reflected are.
With the radiant evening sunlight
    Playing on each house and spire;
In the windows, its reflection
    Gloweth like a mimic fire.

Look! for now 'tis fast declining,—
    Setting in the western skies;
While the sea, with mystic murmur,
    Chanteth as the monarch dies.
'Tis as if a hand from Heaven
    Sweeps across the western wave;
Touching chords of sweet, wild music,
    Such as nought on earth e'er gave.

Beautiful, and sad, and silent,
    Sinks the sun away from sight;
Kissing, ere it goes, the wavelets,
    With an amber-tinted light.
High above, the dappled cloudlets
    Peep into the water clear;
And the ocean gives each colour
    Back unto its native sphere.

'Tis as if the gates of Heaven
    For a while had stood ajar,
Showing glimpses of its splendour,
    Guarded by the evening star.
Lone and darker grows the seascape,
    Evening shades are falling round;
Still with undulating motion,
    O'er the rippling waves we bound.

Yet we all, and with one impulse,
    Let our thoughts unspoken rest;
Charmed into a holy stillness,—
    Breathing of the good and blest;
Till we, by a ray from Heaven,
    Seem to read each other's thoughts,—
Hearts draw nearer to each other,
    By the spell the hour hath wrought.

Blessëd hour of Sabbath twilight!—
    On the waves, sublimely grand,
There the soul doth hold communion
    With the far-off Spirit Land.
Often will my memory linger
    On this hour, with joy and love;
On the sea I feel the nearer,—
    To the mystic Realms Above.

THE LIFEBOAT COXSWAIN TO HIS CREW.

Come forward my men, for I heartily greet you—
    I'm happy to have you once more by my side;
Right welcome you are, for on this day to meet you
    Fills me, your old coxswain, with pleasure and pride.

You know why we meet, mates, and how I'm delighted
    To have your brave spirits beside me again;
It's sad our whole crew cannot here be united,
    Yet thankful I am that so many remain.

Well, looking to-night on your storm-beaten faces,
    Recalls to my memory how bravely with me,
You, in the old lifeboat, took promptly your places,
    And fearlessly fought with the tempest-racked sea.

You know what we went through; for, friends I've a notion
    Our courage that morning was put to the test;
Now some of our mates who were tossed on life's ocean
    Are anchored all safe in the ' Haven of Rest.''

Aye, oft, my old comrades, in dark stormy weather,
   When folks looked with fear at the sea from the land,
We all have put out in the lifeboat together,
   And none can deny she was gallantly manned.

While thankful that fortune, through dangers smiled o'er
   I now will propose, in my heartiest tones—   [me,
" Long life and good health to the fellows before me,
   Who rescued the crew of the poor " Bessie Jones ! "

"THE PALACE ON THE SEA."

(THE INDIAN PAVILION, NORTH PIER, BLACKPOOL.)

Behold ! that noble work of art,
It doth a mystic charm impart ;
Built on the mighty waters free,
O'erlooks the wide expanse of sea.
Oh, what a fine imposing sight !
Artistic, elegant, and light,
Like Oriental temple, grand—
And hark ! the music of the band,
Comes ringing sweetly on the ear,
As we the gilded structure near.
We enter, what a sight is there !
That almost seems beyond compare.
'Tis decorated all inside,
Its gorgeous hall so long and wide ;
The many windows round us seem,
To lend enchantment to the scene.
The chandeliers with glitt'ring light,
Resplendent with their pendants bright.
We seem, (all is so gay and grand,)
Transported into Fairyland ;
And thus our fancy makes us feel
'Tis too romantic to be real.
A palace on the surging deep,
Where syrens of the ocean sleep ;
The sea-fairies their wings unfold,
And tune their tiny " harps of gold."

As now the fine impressive band,
Sends forth melodious music grand;
With thrilling, deep, impassioned sound,—
That vibrates all the place around.
And then so low and sweet it falls,
The senses with its power enthrals.
The music floats upon the seas,—
Then dies away upon the breeze.
And then the vocal strains so sweet
Swell forth, to make the charm complete.
'Neath us the wild-waves weirdly roar,
Their hollow sound repeating o'er.
We rise to go, entranced! inspired!—
'Twas all the heart could have desired.
Outside, the sea looks sad and calm,
The evening air is full of balm.
The stars are twinkling in the skies,
The whisp'ring wind so softly sighs.
We leave the pier, its every light
Reflected on the waters bright;
And still in fancy every note,
Upon the zephyrs seem to float.
We quit those beauteous sounds and scenes,—
Yet they will haunt us in our dreams.

SHELLS OF THE OCEAN.

My room is decked with graceful pretty shells,
  Born in the watery world of wonders deep—
'Mong hills and valleys that man may not see,
  Where treasures 'bide that he must never reap.

They might have lived apart, in separate seas,
  Where myriads of their varied species are;
And southern skies suffuse with sunny gleam,
  Their native element to depths afar.

Or, where the dancing of the Northern Lights,
  The midnight sky illumines, o'er the wave;
And far below, they might have sported there,
  Within the precints of a rocky cave.

Oh! who shall say how many years have passed,
   Since life abounded in these little shells?
And when they yielded up their pretty homes—
   The tenants that inhabited these cells?

From pinky volute, and the cowry smooth,
   E'en to the smallest wentletraps are here;
And fathoms deep, within the far-off sea,
   They slumbered once,—I therefore hold them dear.

The ornaments that beautify the deep,
   What can surpass those lovely tints so fair?
I love them as I love earth's fairest flowers,
   No painters' colours can with them compare.

When pressed against the ear, a mystic sound,
   As of the seething surf on surges free,
These ocean gems speak of their native home,
   Through them we hold communion with the sea.

Oh! God of nature every one are Thine,
   Those beauteous things formed by Thy Holy Hand;
Thine is the wealth that lies beneath the wave—
   And all the glories of the sea and land.

A POET'S WISH.

Mine be a grave beside the Sea,
   And in some lonely spot;
Beside the waters let it be,
   Where strangers pass it not.

The booming of the breakers will
   Make music o'er my grave;
And let all other sounds be still,
   All save the sad sea wave.

My friends, there let my dust repose,
   When I shall be no more;
It is the spot where I would choose,
   Upon the lone sea shore.

When waves are bright with red sunlight,—
　With ruby glows the west;
When day and night in peace unite,
　Oh! lay me there to rest.

The waters they will come and go,
　And kiss the pebbly shore;
But I shall then be laid so low,
　In peace for evermore.

The murm'ring waves will gently leap
　Around where I would lie;
When I am in my last long sleep,
　Alone with sea and sky.

I want no flowers above me strewn,
　To deck my lonely grave;
The friendly Sea, will bring its own
　Sweet tribute on the wave:—

Green garlands spread, above my head,
　And change them every day;
Rich treasures from its deep dark bed,
　'Twill bring, and take away.

No need for granite cross to show
　My grave, when there I sleep;
For God my resting place will know,—
　His Being pervades the deep.

I want no mourners o'er my mound,
　Their idle tears to shed;
With mournful, melancholy sound,—
　The Sea weeps for the dead.

'Twill wash with briny tears my bed,
　And chant a solemn dirge;
No foot shall tread above my head,
　But roll the mighty surge!

The night-winds they will pass me by,
　And sweep along the Sea;
And give to me a passing sigh,
　Then toss the billows free.

SEA SONGS AND OCEAN ODES.

The Ocean's anthems sweet, will swell
    Upon the midnight air ;
Like funeral knell, on silv'ry bell,
    While I am slumb'ring there.

The solemn Night will fold its wing
    So soft, o'er sea and sky ;
And voices in the night will sing,
    And call me up on High.

The moon and stars will o'er me shine,
    The Sea my grave caress ;
The Sea, so bounteous and sublime —
    Will o'er my pillow press.

I fancy, yet I know not why
    Such thoughts to me are given, —
The Sea hath union with on High
    A mystic link with Heaven.

The mighty Sea, the boundless sky.
    The myriad grains of sand ;
All speak of one great Being on High,
    Proclaim their Maker's Hand.

Sure as the billows ever roll,
    His eye will mark the spot ;
And He will call away my soul, —
    He will forget me not.

Then bury me where waters lave
    The shingle day by day ;
The rippling wave sha'l kiss my grave
    On shining sands will play.

Beside the Sea I loved in life,
    Oh, lay me gently there ;
Afar from all the busy strife,
    Away from worldly care.

A lonely place, where none have trod,
    Oh! friends there let me be ; —
I seem to feel so near to God, —
    When I am by the Sea.

SOLACED.

The west wind howls, the wild sea rolls—
   They sound like solemn dirges ;
The sea-mews cry, and downward fly
   Towards the foaming surges.
The sky droops down, with threat'ning frown,
   Dark clouds roll on in masses :
The sea throws back, the heaven's black—
   Each shadow as it passes.
The shore is bare, no form is there
   To watch the Tempest's madness ;
He vents his wrath, and scowls at Mirth,
   And turns her smiles to sadness.
The fisher's home stands in the gloom,
   The wind around it wailing ;
The wife sits there, and breathes a prayer,—
   For her old man is sailing.
And all her sons, true-hearted ones,
   E'en have their father's calling,—
All fishers brave, who seek the wave,
   When evening shades are falling.
She lonely feels, yet near her steals
   Young Hope, and Faith her sister ;
They both are there, and do their share
   To tenderly assist her,
To bide at home till those shall come
   Again, who dearly love her ;
She puts her trust, as good hearts must,
   In One who reigns above her.
Hope sweetly sings, while Memory flings
   A golden chain around her ;
With precious links, as now she thinks
   That loving hearts surround her ;
Recalls the day they went away,
   And lingered to caress her ;
When to his sons, in gentle tones,
   The father said "God bless her !"
She being secure, while they endure
   The tempest on the ocean :—

A story tells — her bosom swells
    With tender, true emotion.
Now, from its nook she takes the Book
    Which heals the heart when bleeding;
The Book of Life, the old fish-wife
    Can soothe herself with reading:—
How, on the sea of Galilee,
    Christ— when on earth He 'bided—
Said "Peace, be still!" and at His will
    The mighty storm subsided!
The Word of God, of men who trod
    The earth in ages olden,
Sweet solace brings, for comfort clings
    Around those treasures golden.
And by His word she trusts our Lord,
    And prays that He will guard them;—
Shield them from harm, amid the storm,—
    And fortune will reward them.
Then Peace coms near, and dries the tear
    Which on her cheek had quivered;
Till with her wiles, the old dame smiles,
    And all her fears are shivered.
She shuts her eyes, while sweet good-byes
    Ring fresh as they were spoken;
No more she weeps—for see! she sleeps
    And Memory's chain is broken.

ON LEAVING THE SEA.

I'm leaving thee, my own dear sea,
    Expanded in thy glory;
Thy heaving breast is lulled to rest,
    The night-mists gather o'er thee;
And Solitude, in soothing mood,
    Stoops o'er thee with caresses;
Thy wrath is past, thy waves have cast
    Their crests, like silvery tresses!
Thy spirit moans in undertones
    As if t'were sadly sighing;

A message brings from far-off things,
  That in thy depths are lying.
Below the swell thy beauties dwell,
  In peace for aye unbroken;
Yet now I hear in music clear,
  Sweet words, what though unspoken.
What dost thou think can be the link,
  That binds me to thee only?
O whisp'ring sea, what can it be,
  That makes me sad and lonely—
When I depart, that in my heart
  There lurks a vacant feeling?
Unto me now, so sweet and low,
  Thou art thyself revealing;
From fathoms deep, where treasures sleep,—
  Where precious pearls lie hidden:—
From coral cells, and pink-white shells,
  Thy spirit comes unbidden;
For life is there, so wondrous fair,
  In crusted caves and bowers;
So clear and bright, yet hushed as night,
  Amongst thy tangled flowers;
Along thy tide dim shadows glide,—
  The night-clouds passing o'er thee,
Then melt away, like phantoms grey,
  In legend and in story.

Now I must cross the murky moss,
  Through corn-fields long and dreary;
The poppies bright look black to-night,
  And droop their heads aweary:
And I must pass by meadow grass
  By village dimly lighted;
By darkling dell, by ford and fell,
  When we are disunited;
By sleeping town, by forest brown,
  By farmsteads thatched and lowly;
By gurgling stream, with silvery gleam,
  That wends toward thee slowly;
By sylvan glen, by moor and fen,
  By reed, and pollared willow;
I must be sped, before my head
  Again may seek the pillow.

The wind blows cold from off the wold,
   My home lies far before me;
In sleep profound thy waves are bound.
   And night-stars shimmer o'er thee:
Toward me now thy waters flow,
   As they would fain embrace me;
Good-night, good-night, no other sight,
   From memory will efface thee!

"THE GALLANT LIFEBOAT CREW."

God bless the gallant lifeboat crews,
   Upon our Island shore;
They earn our praise, who risking self,
   Imperilled ones restore.
Their deeds of mercy, and of love,
   Are to their courage due;
These noble, self-denying men
   The gallant lifeboat crew.

Their fearless spirits render aid,
   To vessels in distress.
They promptly go, with heart and soul,
   To make the suffering less.
They leave their loved ones safe at home,
   These sailors good and true,
They dauntless, brave the rolling wave—
   The gallant lifeboat crew.

A minute's warning, and they rise
   To man their boat in haste.
They launch it out upon the sea,
   Nor precious moments waste.
With willing hands and hearts they brave
   Storms wild as ever blew,
They are true British "Hearts of Oak"
   The gallant lifeboat crew.

They dare all dangers of the main,
   However dark the night;
When fierce storms howl, and high seas roll,
   They go with all their might.

And many a shipwrecked suffering form,
   With cheeks of pallid hue,
And fainting hearts, look up and bless—
   The gallant lifeboat crew.

Then may kind Heaven protect these men,
   When out upon the wave,
Who nobly run all risk, as they
   Strive other lives to save.
And if God calls them to their rest,
   These hearts so good and true,
May He ope' Heaven's portals for—
   The gallant lifeboat crew.

And when from off the stormy seas
   These men return no more :
We'll trust that they have landed then,
   Upon the Other Shore :
And may they make their peace with God
   When Heaven is in view,
Then pass within the Harbour Bar—
   The gallant lifeboat crew.

"THAT HOUSE BY THE SEA."

The summer is gone, and rich autumn is here,
The leaves of the trees are all drooping and sere :
But yet we are happy, why should we be sad ?
With brightest reflections to make our hearts glad.
There's a spot that is dear, what though distant it be,—
Our visions fly back to that house by the sea.

I see it before me, as if I were there,
Its bright cheerful parlours, its carpeted stair :
When I listen a moment, methinks I can hear
The fond children's voices, so sweet and so clear :
I have joined in their play, and their innocent glee,—
And have felt like a child in that house by the sea.

The sweet smiling faces I now can recall,
Kind words from kind hearts, I remember them all :
In a warm flood of light, I have sat on the hearth,
And shared in the laughter, the music, and mirth :
O blest be those evenings so joyous and free,—
I have spent in my life in that house by the sea !

There oft I awoke in the hush of the night,
And heard the sea surge, with the tide at its height ;
The windows then shook with the force of the wind ;
I picture me there still at night in my mind ;
O vain the delusion ! no more I may see.—
Save in fancy, or dreamland, that house by the sea.

My Muse first appeared in that house far away,—
Made its infantile flight, on one bright summer day ;
Thus I cherish the place, 'twas the scene of the pride
That comes with success to the young and untried :
It shines like a star in the distance to me,
And I cannot forget my loved home by the sea !

THE FLEETWOOD LIFEBOAT HEROES.

Who has not heard of Coxswain Wright,
    And of his dauntless lifeboat crew ?
Who toil with all their main and might
    In fiercest storms that ever blew.
Who has not heard what noble work
    Good Fleetwood's gallant boats have done ;
Their crews will ne'er their duty shirk,
    No stauncher men beneath the sun.
"Man the lifeboat ! Man the lifeboat !"
    Hear, oh ! hear the cry ;
See Coxswain Wright old Neptune fight,
    And all his wrath defy !

Oh! oft they've passed through perils dire,
    When off the treacherous lee-shore wild;
Near Bernard's Wharf, upon the Wyre
    Their deeds brought glory to the Fylde:
For twenty-four poor Norsemen they
    Befriended in an awful gale—
Two rescues made upon one day,
    Through "Edith," and the "Child of Hale."
"Man the lifeboat! Man the lifeboat!"
    Does the cry appall?
In blinding storm each sturdy form
    At once obeys the call.

The seaman, far from home and friends,
    Tossed Lunewards from the raging main,
If signals of distress he sends,
    They never will be shown in vain;
For Coxswain Wright will see them fly,
    And promptly launch the lifeboat then:
And steer o'er billows "mountains high,"
    To save from death his fellow-men
"Man the lifeboat! Man the lifeboat!"
    Hear the thrilling call:
Good boats we boast around our coast,
    And willing crews have all.

In storms we've heard the lifeboat gun
    Boom in the night as dark as pitch,
And watched each mother's stalwart son
    The lifeboat launch, without a hitch:
Then every nerve and sinew strain
    To reach in time the hapless wreck;
And seen them then return again,
    With helpless sailors from its deck.
Help our lifeboats! Aid the shipwrecked
    Sailors in distress;
Oh! stand beside our Nation's pride,
    And God your efforts bless!

ON SEEING THE WRECKED BATTLE-SHIP "FOUDROYANT" AT BLACKPOOL.

Poor wounded ship! in her death-throes lying,
    A relic true of the glorious past;
Pathetic sight to behold her dying,
    We wait and watch, till she breathes her last!

Her grand career all the while depicting,
    When youth was hers, in the years gone by.
She dared the foe; to her end now drifting,
    The dear old warship, come here to die.

Took part in scenes that are now historic;
    Brave Nelson's flag-ship in days of old
Where he has figured in deeds heroic,
    Whose valour won us such vict'ries bold.

The great "Foudroyant" our shores defended,
    Near ten decades have her triumphs been;
Poor battered hulk! now her work is ended,
    She's drifted here for the final scene.

Staunch heart of oak! with her timbers rotten,
    Those yawning boards tell a touching tale;
Of laurels won, and of fame forgotten,
    No more the waters she'll proudly sail.

Out-lived the "Anna," and Troon's "Aurora"
    That came to ease her, but found their fate,
Among the breakers; destroyed before her,
    And left the monarch her doom to wait.

Dismantled though of her guns and splendour
    Yet veneration her form inspires;
Old Neptune makes her at last surrender,
    On Blackpool's bosom she now expires!

Farewell good ship! for thy naval glory
    Has vanished now with thy precious past;
Thy death-bed here will complete thy story,
    And "Breezy Blackpool" will view thee last.

THE FISHER BROTHERS.

There's a mist on the sea Jack, and I am aweary
    Of waiting for luck, that seems never to come ;
O life on the water is lonely and dreary,
    I'm yearning just now for a peep at my home.

They'll miss us I know when at night they assemble,
    And list' for the sound of our voices in vain ;
I know my dear Katie, who cannot dissemble,
    Will wish that her old man was with her again.

I see her just now, in the rocking chair sitting,
    A smile on her gentle face, loving and sweet:
The while her fair hands will be busily knitting,—
    The youngsters be playing their pranks at her feet.

And you lad, have ties, who will miss you already,
    Your Maggie will long for a sight of her Jack :
Your wee bonnie lassie, and warm-hearted Teddy,
    Will often be wishing their father was back.

When springtime comes round Jack, the loved ones who
    Will meet us again, if they'll patiently wait ; [miss us,
I see the sweet bairnies come running to kiss us,
    But until that time we'll resign them to fate.

I think that to-morrow I'll write them a letter,
    Of last week's good catch I am anxious to tell,
And I'll add that the pain in my head has got better—
    And end it by hoping they're happy and well.

Tis pleasant to work for the sake of the money,
    And Jack who can tell ? we may some day retire !
I've got a nice sum to take back to my honey,
    And she shall have aught that her heart may desire.

For all that my heart's feeling mournful and chilly,
    A sadness steals o'er me at close of the day ;
I think of the hours we have spent with poor Willie—
    Who now lies asleep in his grave far away.

Let us hope that his soul now is happy in Heaven,
   'Tis useless his presence to try to recall ;
I cannot but think that his sins were forgiven –
   For he was the youngest, and best of us all.

There ! let's weigh the anchor, and steer her more sea-
   She'll cheerfully go with the wind on her beam ; |ward,
The lines have all day been a-drifting to lee-ward,
   And yond is the last of the sun's lurid gleam.

He's sunk to his rest, and is weary of shining –
   Has wrapt himself up in the mist, and has gone ;
The water is still, and the daylight's declining,
   The lights in the harbour, appear one by one.

Let's anchor far out on the sea now 'tis twilight,
   And hope that to-night we may have a good catch';
Now you go below Jack, and dream until daylight,—
   While I stay on deck lad, and help to keep watch.

A DREAM OF THE SEA.

I sat in the evening twilight,
   A beautiful star shone down,
And kissed with its pale light tender,
   The leaves of a burnished brown.
I wove me a chain of fancies,
   As the night winds whispered low,
And lisped through the crimson leafage,
   So rich with the autumn glow.
For there in the vesper twilight,
   My spirit felt not alone ;
A vision there came before me,
   While heaven's bright jewels shone :—
They gleamed through the unveiled window,
   And gave to that dream-fraught hour,
A touch of the peace around them,
   The charm of a subtle power.

For there, as I sat and listened,
    The sound of the wind-tossed trees
To me were the sweet vibration
    Of waves of the distant seas:—
That broke with a measured murmur
    And seemed of my dream a part;
They beat to the rhythmic cadence,
    Of music that filled my heart.
The sound was my soul's enchanter
    And carried it far away;
I saw on the dancing water,
    The light of a summer day.
I stood in a noble life-boat,
    Nor far from the sea; behold!
It flashed in the noontide's brightness,
    All shot with the rays of gold.
A moment I wore the armour
    Reserved for my brothers brave,
Whenever the voice of Mercy
    Calls out "there are lives to save!"
Equipped in the lightsome girdle,
    They wear in the tempest wild;—
No crown, but that badge of honour,—
    I felt I was Neptune's child.
No queen in a regal galley
    Could ever have felt more pride;
But then, were the wavelets laughing
    At peace lay the sleepy tide.
A tale was to me unfolded,—
    Brave deeds of the past reviewed:
I saw the reflected glory,
    Before me 'twas then renewed.
"Oh, what if I hear a summons,"
    I thought, could I now obey,
And willingly answer "ready!"
    Or turn from the boat away?

And then came a transformation,
    I stood by a wind-churned sea;
And but for the darts of lightning,
    'Twas dark as a night could be.
And then came an echo stealing

To me from the turbid deep;
That seemed as a requiem wailing,
  For those it had rocked to sleep.
Then figures arose before me,—
  The form of a seaman true
Stood firm at his post of duty,
  In charge of the lifeboat crew:
And then at a given signal,
  He fearlessly took command;
Men fought at the lifeboat station
  For oars, till the boat was manned.
And then on the surging fury,
  In face of the awful blast,
They launched with a brave strong effort,—
  Their lives to the storm were cast.
It seemed that the mercy-angel,
  Had beckn'd o'er the billows white;
They dashed through the sea-spray misty,
  Till lost in the troubled night.
"Great Storm, through the tribulation,
  Oh spare them again," I cried,
"Nor mock at their British valour,
  At leaving each dear one's side:
For they are amongst the bravest,
  And boldest our land can boast;
Then gather them not, I ask thee,
  To lie with the sea-slain host."
I spoke to the Sea's wild spirit,
  That moaned in the deepening gloom:
"Remember they're going to succour,
  Remember the claims of home;
The scenes of thy wrecks are legion,
  The price of thy peace is great;
Be good to the brave storm-warriors,"
  I cried, for it held their fate.
Then came from its ruffled spirit,
  A sign that I could not tell;
But something that seemed responsive,
  And told me that all was well.
I watched but the vision faded,
  'Twas but an aërial thing,
And lighter than snow-flakes falling,

    Or touch of an unseen wing.
I woke, as the amber firelight,
    Its shadows fantastic cast,
And found that the gossamer fabric
    Had broken,—my dream had passed.

A SECRET OF THE SEA:—

On the mysterious loss of a tug-boat named "Secret" on her first sea trip, October, 1892.

The "Secret" sailed away one day,
    In all her virgin pride,
Upon her maiden trip to sea,
    Her powers all untried;
With men aboard buoyed up with hope,
All unprepared with storms to cope.

She never reached her destined port,
    Nor touched again the land;
The mystery of her fate remains
    In God's almighty hand.
We only know she sailed away
Upon a fair October day.

She might have struck when in a fog,—
    Been wrecked by treacherous reef,
Or by a passing craft that stayed
    Not by to give relief;
Did she her helm not answer well?
Not one is left her fate to tell!

She might have foundered in a gale,
    And left no trace behind;
Would that thy message could, oh, Sea!
    Be borne upon the wind;
By chance thou only hast betrayed
That she upon thy bed is laid.

Thou holdest in thy unknown depths,
   Whilst tossing in unrest,
Full many a 'secret' that thy waves,
   Have never once confessed;
For man can ne'er those depths explore,
Such prey is thine for evermore.

Deep in thy breast, thou tyrant Sea,
   The hidden "Secret" lies;
Thou heedest not the widows' tears,
   Nor yet the orphans' cries.
Oh! set suspense and fears to rest,
Give peace to those who loved them best.

Oh! fierce, remorseless, cruel Sea,
   To thee I would appeal:
Didst thou o'erwhelm the poor frail craft?
   The "Secret" then reveal!
There comes no answer to the shore,
Thy waves but thunder as before.

The vessel is by name and fate
   A buried "Secret" there,
Which thou, oh Sea! wilt not divulge,
   Nor tell each dying prayer;
It would at least some solace be,
The mystery rests with God and thee!

A SEA-SIDE REVERIE.

Is it a dream that I walk again
On the yielding sand, by the murmuring main?
Ah no! 'tis real, and I feel once more,
Its briny breeze on the wave-washed shore.
It smiles on me in the sunlight warm,
And holds my soul with the same sweet charm
It had of yore, when my heart was young,
When every care to the winds were flung;—
Ere sorrow came with its burden sad,—

Opprest the heart that was erstwhile glad;—
Passed o'er my life, like a dark eclipse:
I miss kind words from the dear cold lips
Of one beloved, who has walked with me,
In bygone days by the surging sea.
But sorrow sleeps; and a peace steals o'er
My spirit, sweet as in years of yore;
The ordeal passed, as our wounds can heal,
Though scars be left, that we may not feel.
Now sunshine streams on my path again,
My pulse bounds free as the restless main;
And youth comes back as I view the scene,
Of girlhood's pleasures that once have been;
A fervour glows in my soul to-night,
My heart expands, as a new delight
Thrills all my being; for I feel the sea,
A spirit holds, that communes with me.
The wild-birds warble the woods among,
Their matins sweet, and their vesper song,
But all their music is not more dear
Then those deep tones that salute my ear.
I watch the water the smooth tones lave,
A life-throb flows with its every wave:—
With every movement it takes a part
In music born in this happy heart.
Its grand old presence new themes inspire,
Responds, vibrates, as it wakes the lyre.
I watch the sun on its bosom sink,
From Memory's chalice I freely drink;—
Imbibe sweet draughts, and without alloy,
Taste once again of the old-time joy.
Ah! 'tis no dream that I muse again,
And feel the breath of the bounding main,
That bears no trace of each passing year,
But beams with beauty so fresh and fair.
Now rose-tints rest on its surface blue,
The reflex bright of the heaven's own hue;
Soon mist will fold it in night-robe white,
And I must bid it at last good-night!

THE RESCUE.

"Canst thou see that vessel drifting,
   In the offing, far away;
Canst thou see it, slowly shifting
   Leeward, through this blinding spray?

"I have not sailed on the ocean,
   Now for more than threescore years,
Not to know that yon ship's motion
   Gives us cause for gravest fears

"There behold! a signal flying,
   Showing she is in distress;
Sailors brave may soon be dying;—
   Up and save them," cries of "Yes."

"Lose no time, for if you tarry,
   They will all have watery graves;
Jim, and Tom, and Jack, and Harry,
   Muster lads, and breast the waves!

"Man the life-boat!" at the watchword,
   Men came near in numbers strong:—
Helped unasked, in manly concord,
   Got the life-boat borne along.

'Mid a shout of wild commotion,
   While the gale more fiercely blew;
It was launched upon the ocean,—
   Never went a nobler crew!

Through the surf, as shouts were ringing,
   Hard they pulled to gain the wreck;
Where the forms of men were clinging
   Firmly to the wave-washed deck.

And the veteran, looking seaward,
   Proudly watched his sons depart;
Keenly gazing, leaning forward,
   While a thrill ran through his heart.

When he saw the life-boat tossing
  On the heaving, swelling sea;
O'er its angry waters crossing,—
  Bounding fast o'er surges free.

"There!" he said, "the lads are plucky,
  They are making headway fast;
Now they gain her!—it is lucky—
  For she's lost her mizen mast.

"If I stouter was, and stronger,
  And my step was not so slow;
I'd have gone—when I was younger,
  I have oft stood at the bow.

"Now I can but watch the others,
  But the waves obstruct my view;
Yet I cry with wives and mothers—
  "May God speed the Life-boat Crew!"

Men and women stood and shivered,
  Underneath that frowning sky;
Watched, while every muscle quivered,
  As the breakers rolled up high.

Waited, with a breathless longing,
  Pressing forward in a crowd;
Then a cry of "They are coming!"
  Rose from voices clear and loud.

How the troubled sea resounded,
  How the breakers roared and splashed!
Gathered force, and then rebounded,—
  As against the cliffs they dashed.

Said the old keen-sighted sailor,
  "She is coming shoreward now;
Bravo! now with pride I hail her,
  For our Jack stands at the bow!

"Bearing true brave-hearted fellows,
  Comes the gallant little craft;
Mounting o'er the tow'ring billows
  Lightly with the wind abaft."

Near, upset, yet not defeated,
  Bravely came the life-boat near;
Gained the shore, the crew were greeted
  With a hearty, deaf'ning cheer!

"Now my lads! relate the story,
  Ye who have the tempest braved;
What success?"—with manly glory,
  Came the answer—"all are saved!"

Welcome words! behold them standing,
  While a helping hand they reach
To their shipwrecked brothers landing,
  Safely on the sandy beach.

Lord! when mighty storms assail us,
  On the leeshore, and the deep;
Help the women, guide the sailors,
  Place them safely in Thy keep!

THE BLACKPOOL LIFEBOAT CREW.

Hurrah! for the boatmen of Blackpool again;
  They've come to the fore in a praiseworthy way;
Their long-latent valour was 'roused as the main
  Broke forth in wild fury, that ne'er-forgot day.

A storm more terrific the coast never knew   [wives,
  Than that which they braved, leaving mothers and
To go on their mission, a staunch-hearted crew,
  They jeopardized freely their own precious lives.

Not once did the tempest those sailors deter,
  For twenty-one lives through their efforts were saved:
A day's splendid record, we all must aver—
  To rescue their brothers, all perils they braved.

We felt the fierce grip of the storm-fiend on land,
  And quailed at its ravages, taunting us still;
But on the Fylde foreland, thrice brave was the band,
  That fought the mad sea, with such courage and skill.

Their boat, once discarded, was put to the test,
    For men of such grit could not passive remain; [zest,
Though heavy, 'twas launched, and then manned with true
    And oh! with what triumph 'twas landed again.

In face of the gale on the waters that raved
    They coped with the wrath of the white-billowed sea;
They trusted her manfully, well she behaved—
    Won nobly their victory, all must agree.

The brave youth of Blackpool have shown us that they
    Are worthy their fathers, who brought it renown;
Upholding its glory, we bless them and say,
    The town should be proud such brave fellows to own.

A cheer for the lifeboat's bold coxswain and crew!
    For honour is due to each mother's loved son:
And may they long live to enjoy, and renew
    Their well-deserved laurels, so gallantly won!

FATHER'S BOAT.

    Over the bay, over the bay,
    The red sun throws its slanting ray;
    Kissing the bright little waves as they
    Ripple and break in silvery spray,
        Over the boulder stones.

    Over the bay 'neath the sun's last beam,
    Comes father's boat on the waves serene,
    The sunlight glinting in between
    The sails, and giving a golden gleam,
        As it comes over the bay.

    Nearer, and nearer still it glides,
    Over the water it gaily rides;
    Returning home with the flowing tide,
    Father comes to his little one's side,
        Comes from far away.

Into the bay now sinks the sun,
It has lit the way for father to come;
The boat is here, and the day is done,
The sun has sunk, and the shore is won,
    After a day of toil.

THE MARGATE LIFEBOAT DISASTER.

DECEMBER 2nd, 1897.

One morning found those Margate men, with dear ones safe at home,
With thoughts that Christmastide was near, to cheer the wintry gloom:
Those hardy, fearless fishermen, that day all strong and hale,
Turned out to watch the whitening sea, and marked the gathering gale,
That freshened as the night came on, and brought no thought of sleep,
It seemed as if a demon wild, howled on the treacherous deep!
The while the tempest shrieked, and thund'ring billows rolled up high,
An all-night watch was kept, though black became the midnight sky.
At morn, the lightships off the bar, their fitful signals bore,
A mute appeal for help, from those upon the wild leeshore.
"Go, launch the lifeboat!" at the cry, a sturdy stalwart band
Of lifeboatmen, obeyed the call, two boats were promptly manned:
"Friend to all Nations" left the strand, the boatmen's surf-boat old,
Put out 'mid blinding blast, upon the frenzied waters cold;
And one who meant to give "first aid," went with that dauntless crew.

The morn was dark, the fierce tide ebbed, a strong wind madly blew.
They from the harbour, through the surf, on Mercy's mission went,
With strength of sinew, full of hope, unto their oars they bent.
But as they crossed the Nayland Rock, a loud cry pierced the air,
Above the tempest's thund'rous voice, a wail of wild despair!
The surf-boat had capsized! too frail to those white billows ride,
The seas o'erwhelmed her, and her crew were in the swirling tide!
In sight of home, the men were tossed upon that seething sea.
The craft that went to rescue lives, their "death-boat" proved to be!
O'erturned, she drifted like a toy, the men clung to her fast,
Till nine benumbed, were forced by death to loose their grip at last.
God knows how many a voiceless prayer was breathed when in the main,
While light'ning pictures of the past, before them rose again.
But four, of all that noble crew, were saved by those on shore,—
The rest their dearest ones on earth were doomed to see no more.
Heroic, brave, unselfish men! their souls, who thus have died,
Would refuge in the Harbour find, across the Crystal Tide.
The daybreak saw some bitter tears, that coast was wrapped in gloom,
For grief-torn were the women's hearts, while orphans cried at home;—
They'd kissed their dadas sweet good-night, before they went to sleep,
And while they dreamed, their fathers dear, died on the storm-racked deep;

When those sad little ones at morn, wept by their
    mothers' side,
In vain they called their fathers back, no loving voice
    replied!
The women gathered on the shore, and strained their
    eyes in dread,
To watch the fierce despotic sea, to them " give up its
    dead."
And one poor woman, wild with grief, wept o'er each
    sea-borne form,
Her husband dear, and two loved sons, were lost in that
    great storm!
And Christmas, which they thought to greet, with joy
    like those of old,
Now finds them all 'neath sorrow's pall, their dear ones
    stiff and cold!
We may not measure half their woe, nor guage their
    deep distress;
We aid, but God alone can all those mourners soothe
    and bless;
Bereft of loved ones, who have died while doing His
    work of love,
He'll care for them, until they all unite again Above.

THE VETERAN'S RESOLVE.

How I love thee, dear old ocean!
    And shall love thee to the last;
I can ne'er without emotion,
    Think upon the treasured past,—

Spent beside thee, and upon thee,
    Playmate of my boyhood dear;
And when manhood's years stole o'er me,
    I would still to thee be near.

We have ever been good neighbours,
    Nought with thee can be compared;
Scene of all my honoured labours,
    On thy breast I've perils dared.

Comrade of my manhood early,
    Still by thee will I remain ;
Though we've fought when thou wert surly,
    Yet we soon were friends again !

In the stormy darksome midnight,
    I have tossed upon thy breast ;
And have rocked in summer sunlight,
    When thy wrath was calmed to rest.

Some may court the inland meadows,
    But I can the happiest be,
Watching heaven's lights and shadows,
    Play upon the restless sea :—

Hearing Neptune's deep tones making
    Mellow music, as of yore ;
As the ceaseless waves come breaking,
    In their gusto, on the shore.

There's one spot to me now sacred,
    By the broad expansive sea ;
Deemed by none so venerated,
    Yet 'tis all the world to me !

Once upon it, I remember,
    Stood a cottage, white and worn ;
Rich to me with memories tender,
    'Twas the house where I was born.

On the shore, where west winds bracing
    Blew upon it, stood that cot ;
Now I'll build another, facing
    Seawards, on the self-same spot !

There in freedom, at my leisure,
    Through my window I can gaze ;
Watch the sea-crafts sail with pleasure,
    And recall the bygone days.

'Mong the hearts that love me warmly,
    And are well beloved by me ;
I will spend life's evening calmly,
    Basking by the glorious sea.

Where familiar scenes surround me
 In my far-famed native town;
I will, with old mates around me,
 Dwell until my sun goes down.

Then when I have lived my portion,
 And these eyes at last grow dim;
I shall hear the grand old ocean,
 Sing to me a parting hymn!

THE HEROES OF THE FYLDE.

ALL hail the sons of Lancashire! what other land can boast
Such bold and valiant men as those that fringe our western coast;
They've shown us all what they can do, displayed their seamen's skill,
And proved to us that they are men of iron nerve and will.
The valour latent in their hearts, the mighty tempest tests,
For fear finds never once a place of refuge in their breasts.
The Fylde men on the leeshore wild, all waited firm and brave,
And watched for signals of distress gleam on the troubled wave.
St. Annes was staunch, what though she still remembers to her cost
How once in answering Duty's call her lifeboat crew were lost!
Courageous still, the "Brothers" saved a schooner's crew of four,
Who, stranded on the Salthouse Bank, were safely brought ashore.
The honour of the noblest work to Fleetwood boatmen fell;
They answered mute appeals for help—did Mercy's mission well.

They marked the aspects of the storm, and saw its
    gathering force,
No vessel fighting such a gale they knew could hold her
    course.
One noble and unselfish deed, alas! with death was
    fraught :
The smacks while making into port were in the tempest
    caught.
One, bravely battling with the storm, in direst straits
    though laid,
Descried a schooner, whose poor crew in pity sought
    their aid :
Compassion filled the fishers' hearts, though in the
    tempest's brunt,
They took the strangers off, but lo! the waves capsized
    their punt.
Two brave young smacksmen and the crew, before the
    skipper's eyes,
Went to the deep. Oh! was it not a noble sacrifice?
In thoughtful sympathetic hearts must sound the notes of
    woe,
But through the gospel let us hope that they were fit to go.

All night a sharp look-out was kept; at last a fitful light
Flashed in the dark, near Bernard's Wharf, anon 'twas
    lost to sight.
Then in the howling hurricane, there went a thunderous
    boom.
The lifeboat gun was sounded forth, ere daylight broke
    the gloom!
While wind-lashed billows rose and swirled, and broke
    with deaf'ning roll,
Like mighty demons slipped their chains, and broken
    from control:
While drenching torrents poured and helped the fury of
    the gale,
They quickly manned and launched the boat, the gallant
    "Child of Hale."
The friendly tug-boat towed her out, along the channel
    dark,
She passed the Wyre light, then she reached the hapless
    drifting barque.

Oh! none may know, but those who went, the hardships
    that they bore,
But this we know, the barque's whole crew they safely
    brought ashore!
Though they were deluged o'er and o'er between the sea
    and sky,
They thirteen "hardy Norsemen" saved, while seas
    "ran mountains high!"
Undaunted still, a second time they donned the belts that
    day,
For yet another barque was wrecked, to Luneward from
    the Bay.
Beyond the lighthouse, on the Wharf, the barque had
    found a strand,
This time the gallant Fleetwood crew the lifeboat
    "Edith" manned.
Salvation once again they took, and untold dangers
    braved.
Eleven poor Norwegians then, their daring efforts saved.
In every storm the Nation finds some heroes on our shore.
And now in glorious rescue work, 'tis Fleetwood to the
    fore!
Their arduous service of that day, with pride we now
    record.
Has twenty-four of Norway's sons to home and friends
    restored.
Where-e'er those Scandinavians be, when storms rage
    fierce and wild,
They'll breathe a prayer for Heaven to bless the Boat-
    men of the Fylde!

"BEAUTIFUL BLACKPOOL."

Beautiful Blackpool! I see thee again!
Rising before me, fair queen of the main!
Tall and majestic, thy Tower now stands,
Facing the sea, and the bright golden sands.

Beautiful Blackpool, beloved by the sea,
That sports with thee now in its boisterous glee;
Often 'tis coming to kiss thy fair face,
Clasping thee too, in its mighty embrace.

Beautiful Blackpool, for truly thou art
The theme of youth's day-dreams, the joy of my heart;
Bright scene of my pleasures, unknown to my tears,
Thou dearer hast grown with the passage of years!

Beautiful Blackpool, since childhood I own,
My fancy has woven, and o'er thee has thrown
A rosy-hued mantle, just tinged with romance,
That clings yet, and seems all thy charms to enhance.

Beautiful Blackpool, I'm coming once more,
To visit thy briny-washed, tempest-tried shore;
Oh! there is the sea! with its balmy breath sweet,
Laden with kisses its lover to greet.

Beautiful Blackpool! I look on thee now,
And feel thy soft breezes caressing my brow;
And oh! when I listen, I hear once again
Thy murmuring waves, with their ceaseless refrain.

Beautiful Blackpool, my song must now cease,
Though each time I see thee thy beauties increase;
The magical spell that endears thee to me
Is found in thy wind-ruffled, solemn-voiced sea!

Beautiful Blackpool, what sea is like thine?
Uncurbed, and expansive, the whole vision-line;
What wind is so bracing, and blows with such zest,
As that of thy health-giving, soul-cheering west?

Beautiful Blackpool, no language can tell
My love for thy sea, and which nought can dispel;
Nothing but death, oh! thou glorious sea,
Can sever the love-link that binds me to thee!

"MUSIC ON THE WATER."

Music on the water,
  As we sail along
O'er its silent surface,
  Listen to our song:

Sweet and mellow voices
   Swell upon the deep;
Fairies dance around us,
   Waken'd from their sleep.
From the depths of ocean
   To its surface bright,
They have come to hear us,
   Singing to the night.
Will you come and join us?—
   Join our little band?
We are softly sailing
   Far away from land.

Music on the water,
   As we glide away
O'er the stilly surface,
   Where there is no spray;
The sea is like a mirror,
   Smooth and glassy bright;
The crescent moon is shining
   With a silvery light.
We skim along the ocean,
   In our little boat,
With its gentle motion
   How we gaily float!
Will you come and join us?—
   We are sailing far,
O'er the moon-lit waters,
   From the harbour-bar.

Music on the water,
   Snowy sails are set,
Sleeping are the zephyrs;
   Every oar is wet
With the salt sea water:
   On we gently glide,
Happy voices blending,
   Waiting for the tide.
There is not a ripple,
   All is calm and bright,
Placid are the waters,
   'Tis a balmy night.

Will you come and join us?—
  In our little boat,
O'er the tranquil ocean,
  Sounds of music float.

Music on the water,
  What is half so sweet?
With the moon above us,
  How the moments fleet!
The limpet and the scallop,
  With their pinky shells,
Listen to our voices
  As the music swells.
The sea in lonely splendour,
  So beautiful and clear,
Music rich and tender,
  Calling fairies near.
Will you come and join us?—
  Join in our delight,—
Music on the water,
  On a moonlight night.

THE OCEAN MONARCHS.

Ye white-winged rovers through the pathless deep,
  Like living things, ye speed from land to land;
Thro' Neptune's wide dominions ye sweep,
  Beloved by Britons, dear to every strand!

Ye sailing ships, with canvas spread so fair,
  Extended freely in the fresh'ning breeze;
It gleams so white, as ye are moving there—
  Like wide-spread pinions, scudding o'er the seas.

With flags that flutter gaily in the breeze,
  As on the ocean's beating breast ye glide:
So gracefully, ye monarchs of the seas,
  A sight imposing on the waters wide.

The pride of Britain—toilers through the storms,
　The boast and glory of our sea-girt Isle;
And as we gaze upon your noble forms,
　We see man's power reflected there the while.

How beautiful ye look upon the main,
　And bearing human freights, of mirth and woe;
Their floating home, till they shall land again,
　They trust ye, though the sea prove friend or foe

The bearers of our messages are ye,—
　A bond of union over all the world;
By sail and steam, ye cleave the trackless sea,
　Blest be the ships with England's flag unfurled!

When in the docks your broad demensions seem
　So powerful and strong from stem to stern;
And masts gigantic, from the decks are seen,
　But on the sea your frailty we learn.

When tempests rage—'tis then we see ye bend,
　Seem but as floating leaves upon a stream;
Your insignificance we comprehend,
　When tested by the Mighty Power unseen.

A thrilling sight—majestical, and fine!
　Those stately ships that proudly plough the sea;
By them we trade with lands beyond the brine,
　Divided though a thousand leagues they be.

What had the commerce of the nations been,
　If 'twere not for this grand and mighty link?
Connecting lands, though oceans roll between,
　That country may with sister country drink.

By them we can unite in friendship there,
　Man shake his brother's hand across the main;
And Mother England join her children fair,
　By them uphold her dignity and name.

A ship is launched—behold it glide away,
　And spring into the world of waters free;
No longer landlocked, then it seems to say
　"Henceforth my home is on the rolling sea."

It seems to wake to life, with joyous sound,
    To *feel* the waters, as it bounds ahead :
And when a shattered, bare-ribbed hulk is found—
    Resembles some poor creature lying dead.

Oh ! give three cheers for England's gallant Fleet,
    The bold protectors of our sea-kissed shore ;
Then as we love our liberty so sweet,   [more !
    For England's Sovereign,— give three times three

LOST !

The Mackerel Boats are sailing
    In beauty side by side :
They leave the bar, and sail afar,
    All with the midnight tide ;
They're steering for the fishing ground,
    Before the break of day ;
The pale soft light of planets bright,
    Illumes their trackless way.

They glide along serenely,
    Beneath the midnight stars ;
The night is warm, no sign of storm,
    The placid beauty mars :
No gale distends their russet sails,
    No clouds obscure the sky ;
The sea's at rest, and on its breast
    No boding shadows lie.

They're anchored now in silence,
    Upon the slumb'ring sea :
No billow breaks, nor wind awakes,
    'Tis still, as still can be :
No sound is heard among the crews,—
    'Tis like a fleet asleep ;
They throw the bait, and quietly wait,
    Their fortunes on the deep.

The sun arose in splendour,
   Alike on sea and land,
It threw a ray across the bay,
   And gilded all the strand:
But when it set, it left behind
   A gold and crimson light,
Till like a flame, the sky became,
   Then waned to sable night.

The wind began to murmur,
   In whispers soft and low;
Then gathered strength, till lo! at length,
   A gale began to blow:
It wailed around the lonely quay,
   (The smacks had not come home);
No midnight hush, but roll and rush,
   Disturb'd the gathering gloom.

One long unbroken tremor,
   Swelled upward from the deep;
Its dream had broke', its vengeance spoke
   A giant roused from sleep;
For days the dreadful tempest raged,
   For days the billows tost,
The Boats no more came back to shore,
   For all the Fleet was lost!

Oh! trusting man, how soon oppressed!
The foam-flecked waters ne'er confessed:
Oh! hapless Fleet, Oh! tyrant Sea,—
Jehovah holds the mystery!

THE FAIRY BARK.

'Twas Christmas Eve, when the Land is rife
With mirth and love, and the cares of life
Are laid aside, and when fond hearts greet:
When rich and poor for a season meet
As brothers all, and our souls expand,
And join each other throughout the land.

"Peace and goodwill" for the season tends
To make us glad, as the heart unbends;
A blessèd time, for both old and young,
Since first Christ's glorious name was sung.

. . . .

A sailor stood by the bright sea shore,
A brave kind look all his features bore;—
A genial smile on his bronzed face played,
As there he stood, and the while surveyed
A little boat, that was by his side,
And his bearded face wore a look of pride,
To see the work that his hands had done,—
The ropes and sails that he one by one
Had trimmed and set; and the colours gay
He had painted there; thus in bright array,
She almost looked like a living thing!—
A graceful bird, with its out-spread wing,
And plumage bright, as if fain 't would be
Set free to rove on the rippling sea.
So fair she looked by the wave-kissed sands,
And all the work of his strong brown hands!
He'd traced a name on her side with care,
In golden letters it glittered there:
And thus completed, all spic-and-span,
He marked her beauty, and formed his plan.
His task was over, his arms at rest
Enfolded were on his massive chest;
He eyed her well, and at last said he,—
"Go find thy namesake, where e'er she be;
Without a skipper, without a crew,
I'll launch thee now, for I know thou'rt true;
And she who claims thee will love thee best,
And give thee shelter, and give thee rest.
I know not whither thy namesake dwells;
But find her out, ere the Christmas bells
Ring out to-morrow o'er all the earth.
Then seek a harbour midst love and mirth;
But none the work of my hands must claim,
Unless thou knowest she bears thy name;
I'll put thee off on the proper tack,
To seek thy fortune, and come not back!"

Thus she was charged, and was sent alone
To find unaided her future home;
And as she went from her master's sight,
His dark eyes beamed with a merry light:
For pleased he was, as he well might be,
For never a trimmer craft than she
Went on a voyage; nor looked more neat,
With fingers deft she was rigged complete:—
None gave more proof of a seaman's skill
In every detail, to sail at will
Unmanned she started, and went away,
Upon the eve of the natal day.
There lingered still on the seascape dim,
A dull red band where the sun's last rim
Had dropt from sight, on the misty verge
Where sea and sky in the distance merge;
Its good-night kiss to the land it gave,
Then sunk to rest in the western wave.

 . . . . . .

For hours and hours she was lightly tost
Hither and thither, but never was lost;
Like some poor wandering friendless child,
Seeking a home from the night-winds wild;
Seeking her namesake all the while,
Longing for rest and a welcome smile.
She sailed, and sailed, through the darksome night,
And then at last when a streak of light
Dawned in the east, and a soft wind blew,
She steered for land, though she lacked a crew;
Her bow she turned to a shore so fair,
While songs of carollers filled the air
With music sweet, as the shore she neared,
And gleaming lights of a town appeared;
When stars grew pale in the dawn-lit sky,
A wind from heaven went sweeping by,
And wafted her to a frost-bound land,
A fairy bark on a beauteous strand!
And there she paused like a timid bird,
While cheery greetings around were heard;
And hymns of praise to the skies were borne,
To hail the light of that Christmas morn.

When darkness all from the skies had fled,
The grey-hued morning blushed rosy red :
The sun arose in the glowing east.—
In splendour shone on the natal feast :—
Shot forth its rays on the wintry scene,
And touched the boat with a dazzling sheen ;
Revealed her name on her timbers bold,
Lit up in letters of shining gold.
As strangers passed on their joys intent,
A wondering look on the boat they bent ;
Then at a pause in the minstrels' song,
A maiden stept from the surging throng :
She scanned the craft, with unfeigned delight,
The name upon it had caught her sight :
A happy look on her face there came,
She read upon it her own true name !
And then her way to its side she made,
And eager hands on its timbers laid ;
Said she " some fairy with kind intent,
This tiny vessel to me has sent :
Though all alone, and without a crew,
She's fraught with wishes all good and true ;
A mystic helmsman that none can see,
Has guided her in her course to me ;
And laden thus she has found this strand,
I'll claim her now and I'll take command,
This fairy bark shall henceforth be mine."
A charm that others could not devine,
She had for her, as with joy so sweet,
She bore her off to her own retreat.
She grasped the tiller, and steered her well,
Through noisy streams, to a woodland dell ;
And far away from the busy town,
Where nature smiled in its ermine gown ;
Its jewels born of the artic night,
Were flashing there in the red sunlight,
That glancing, touched with a ruby tinge,
The trees all hung with a silvery fringe.
Its frost-gems gleamed on the crinkled leaves,
On tassels hung from the drooping eaves,
Of a harbour sacred to peace and love ;
Naught but the coo of the grey-winged dove

The silence broke; here the maiden paused,
Ere she the door of her home unclosed;
For all at once o'er the woods and fells,
There came the sound of the Christmas bells!
A joyous peal that we love to hear,
From many a belfry far and near;
They entered there at the friendly bower,
Where berries red, and a winter flower,
Bedecked the walls, and the fretted pane;
The inmates all, as in one grand strain,
Their voices lifted to give their guest,
A welcome free to her home of rest.—
A haven sweet with the maiden there,
The object bright of her pride and care,
The boat was anchored, her voyage past,
A refuge safe she had found at last;
Ere nightfall there she was laid to rest,
Like a white-winged bird in its peaceful nest.

ON THE RETURN OF DR. NANSEN'S ARCTIC EXPEDITION,

AUGUST, 1896.

We welcome back those stalwart Norsemen bold,
   Who bravely dared to sail the Arctic deep :-
To face that barren region's rigorous cold,—
   The clime where Neptune calmly lies asleep.

Asleep? nay more, embalmed in shimmering shrouds,
   'Neath gleaming ice-peaks, rests he far below
Their massive, solemn grandeur; o'er which clouds
   Discharge but freights of purest frigid snow.

Why is it there that Neptune is congealed
   The monarch Frost holds him in strenuous grip?
His throbbing being so petrified, concealed,
   That his rough bosom scarce can float a ship?

Is he enchained by bright Aurora's smile?
   (For there, the northern heavens, hold her seat);
That ice-bound, crystallized, he stands the while,
   Mute and majestic, there before her feet!

Inviolate those depths must ever be,
   Where sombre Nature rests secure and wild,
No wave uplifts on placid Polar Sea,
   Its trackless wastes lie dumb and undefiled

By human feet; for Poleward there afar,
   No man has pierced the crystal ice-bound zone;
Yet does the sailor's guiding compass-star
   Hang o'er and guard those virgin regions lone.

The while from us it yet keeps unrevealed
   The secret of that spot that knows its light:—
The untrod circle still from us concealed
   By ice blocks cold, and by its long long night.

Brave Dr. Nansen! he for three long years
   Has traversed through that ice-barred unknown realm,
Subsisting there upon its Polar bears,
   Surmounting dangers which would most o'erwhelm.

With his stout crew to man the "Fram," he went,
   As valorous as the Vikings were of old;
To reach the Pole they sailed with full intent,—
   Drift with the current 'mongst its icebergs cold.

A portion of that vast unknown they crossed,
   For miles and miles they pushed their pathless way:
Through broad expanse, in keen eternal frost
   That scarce relaxed through Arctic summer day.

Pierced they leagues further than had been explored,
   And when the faithful, gallant "Fram" was fast,
Brave Nansen, with one comrade who ignored
   The cold, like him, set out 'mid northern blast,

And penetrated that locked ocean white,—
   Taxed to the utmost all their manhood's strength,—
Braved its drear winter's hard perpetual night,
   Till huge ice-barriers stopped their course at length.

Enwrapt in furry armour, they have shared
 The Arctic's splendid solitude, and come
From those high latitudes, where hard they fared,
 With pluck undaunted, and with honours won.

Now they recount how they have perils faced,
 That did their faith and courage rightly guage;
Each other's sole companion, they have traced
 Their names upon the world's historic page.

Across the crystal desert, side by side,
 With naught to cheer the weary wanderer's eye,
But seas solidified, above the tide,
 Whose pinnacles of ice loom 'gainst the sky;—

Naught save when bear or walrus crossed their ways,
 Or sea-bird passed above the ice-blink bright;
All winter dark, but when auroral rays,
 Or moon, illumed the ice-scape with their light.

For months and months not e'en one living thing
 Once crossed their vision in that fastness drear;
On fields of bleak unyielding ice, the Spring
 But signs of constant daylight brought to cheer.

Then in returning, sounds of dog-barks broke
 The dream-like silence, falling on the ear
Like welcome music, as the echoes woke,
 For lo! they found brave Jackson's band were near.

Dear fellow-men! though there from different parts,
 They met as brothers where the waters sleep;
In other climes though strangers, there their hearts
 Warmed to each other on the frozen deep.

For there the English expedition met
 The bold Norwegians, on that coast obscure;
And brought them safe, by sea-fogs though beset,
 To native fiords, to dwell 'mong friends secure.

Thus he has come, his task accomplished now,
 We hail brave Nansen, for he knew no fear,
Back from the regions of eternal snow,
 Back to his wife and little child most dear.

Faint with o'erjoy was that young loving wife,
   For brave suspense for months her part had been;
To see him safe and full of vigorous life,
   O'erwrought her feelings at the greeting scene.

We've traced his course from this our sea-girt isle,
   And marvelled that such courage never wanes:
Why should we marvel? knowing all the while
   That Scandinavian blood runs in his veins.

All nations' interest has been centred in
   The famous "Fram," whose fate was long unknown:
Bold Nansen reached a point none dared to win,
   And Norway now is proud to claim her own!

Thrice welcome then, ye heroes, who have been
   Within the far-off mystic circle white;
Defied its rigour through lone days, and seen
   The spectral splendours of the Arctic night!

THE "BRADFORD" TO THE RESCUE!

When storms of wind, and rain and sleet,
   Convulse the ocean's mighty breast;
And mingled with the thunder's roll,
   All nature shrieks in wild unrest--
     Then hear we of our sailors,
       Full many a touching tale,
      These men that are our nation's boast,
       Must wrestle with the gale.

And when across the bleak North Sea
   The scathing blizzards wildly sweep,
A helpless vessel strikes the shoals,
   Our coastmen may not stand and weep
      'Tis "Bradford to the rescue!"
       When danger must be braved;
      The gallant boats we own with pride,
       Eight hundred lives have saved!

Wrecked on the treacherous Goodwin Sands,
  Thus many a bark her fate has met,
And crews are nobly saved by those
    Whom we to-day should not forget:
      Then give these gallant boatmen
        Support where'er you be—
      They are the sturdy coastmen brave
        That fight the fierce North Sea.

Most hearts have some they know and love
  Whom they must trust upon the deep:
Such tremble when a fearful gale
  Awakes them from a peaceful sleep:
      And when the bleak north-easter
        For long has madly blown,
      The lifeboatmen upon the shore
        May give us back our own.

The nation does a glorious work,
  Through all her boats around the coast;
Each manned by staunch, unflinching men,
  Of whom our sea-girt land can boast.
      This noble institution
        Through us must never fall;
      Uphold it, then, all you that can,
        And God will bless you all!

H.M.S. ATALANTA.

*A Training Ship, supposed to have foundered in the
    Atlantic Ocean in February, 1880.*

She sailed when the ocean was tranquil and calm,
Nor feared that the waves might be ruffled by storm
She carried the light of many a home,
Who departed in faith, and knew not their doom.
In the blossom of youth on the ocean would toil,
With the sinew and strength of the sons of our soil:
Our sailors in future, the strength did to be,
Of this beautiful land that is clasped by the sea.

In future? alas! they were destined to sleep,
Ere the fruits of their labour their country might reap.
Oh! who cannot feel for each mother's sad heart,
As it pines for the son she with pride saw depart;
While hope gaily rode on the gallant ship's prow,
And smiled, as it beamed on each young sailor's brow.
But 'twas shattered, and faded like sparks from the fire.—
On the breast of the deep it was doomed to expire:
They cherished it long, but it fled like a dream,
When the valiant crew long had basked in its beam.
They trusted the ship as she bore them away,
But where has she buried them? ah, who shall say!
Manned by young Britons in glory she sailed,—
But her fate on the main is in mystery veiled.

Did she stray from her course 'mid the vapours of night,
And strike on a reef, when there lingered no light?
She, perchance, may have answered untrue to the helm:
Did the force of a storm, in its vengeance o'erwhelm
In the wrath of a moment, and gave her a blow,
That shivered her timbers, and laid her so low?
She might have been lost when the waters rose high,
And over the billows hung darkly the sky;
While the wind with a moan, like a great living thing,
Swept over the deep, bearing death on its wing.
Then tempest would conquer, and she would be tossed,
And rocked on the ocean, and then would be lost.
God sent his winged messenger down from on high,
To carry their spirits away to the sky:
O'er the deep it descended, with pinions of white,
And bore them above to the regions of light.
And many a cry must have died on the wave,
That opened and folded the men to their grave;—
From many a voice, with the strength of despair,—
Only God, and the ocean, would hearken their prayer.
The names of their loved might have been their last
    breath,
Have blessed them while feeling the clutches of death.
Now peace be upon them, who rest there so low,
But the spot where they slumber we never may know:
Or many a vessel while ploughing the deep,
Would pay them its homage, those hundreds that sleep:

Would lower its pennon, while crossing their grave
And silently sail o'er the heads of the brave :
Would offer a tribute, some token betray,
That we honour the memory of those far away.

Then think of the orphans who mournfully weep,
The children whose fathers were lost on the deep :
Oh, God! in Thy graciousness hear them complain,
And offer Thy guidance to those that remain !
Comfort the hearts of the widows now left,
Have pity upon them, alone, and bereft !
The homestead is gloomy, the lodestar is fled,
The hands that would help and support them are dead.
We know what their anguish and heartache must be,
For those who mysteriously perished at sea :
They yearn for the tidings, that never may come,
Of a father, a brother, a husband, or son.
Not a message was sent, for no vessel was nigh,
In the midst of the waters each man had to die :
Ere he sent a remembrance to those who were dear,
To lessen their sorrow, and soothe the sad tear.
Not a sailor was spared to relate us the tale,
For their fate is enwrapt in obscurity's veil.
We cannot recall them amongst us again,
Yet honour, and glory, will cling to each name,
Then offer a prayer for the souls of the brave,
Who silently slumber beneath the cold wave.

SONG OF THE HOMEWARD BOUND.

The sunlight is streaming upon the blue ocean,
    The waves ripple lightly, with musical sound ;
Our hearts are elated, and throb with emotion,
    For home to old England our good ship is bound !

With canvas extended, like white wings, she bears us
    From far foreign strands to the " Land of the Free :
Where fond loving hearts will be ready to cheer us,
    And welcome our vessel from over the sea.

The creaking of spars, and the sound of her cleaving
    The beautiful waters, all make a glad song;
The sun warms her deck, where the soft gentle heaving
    Is felt, as she gallantly bears us along.

She carries the ensign of Britain so proudly,
    That gives her a right to preside o'er the sea;
A claim for all ships to salute her so loudly,
    Where-e'er on the breast of the ocean she be.

She bore us through storms when the billows were
    Like rolling of drums in a mighty affray;   [sounding
And over her bulwarks at intervals bounding,
    And washing her deck, in their boisterous play.

She bore us past icebergs, that looked in their splendour
    Colossal, majestic, among the sea-waves;
The sunlight behind their tall pinnicles slender,
    With opaline flames lit their crystaline caves.

We touched on the shores where the rich vines are creeping,
    And sweet-scented orange groves smile 'neath the sun:
But dearer than all is the Land we are seeking,
    And we shall rejoice when the harbour is won.

The bright rippling water the ship's side is laving,
    And white dancing foam in her wake may be found:
From top-gallantmasts the gay streamers are waving,
    That seem to proclaim that she homeward is bound.

Her sails are all filled with the soft breeze refreshing,
    As over the waves she is bounding away;
And hark! the sweet lap of the waters, caressing
    And kissing her timbers with silvery spray.

The blue vault of heaven beams tranquilly o'er us,
    The glistening sea is reflecting its hue;
All tempests are past, and our home is before us,—
    A beautiful gem in the waters so blue!

Hurrah! for that speck in the distance reposing,
    So calm and serene, and enclasped by the deep;
Ere long we shall reach it, but day will be closing,
    And peace will have fallen o'er woodland and steep.

Oh! many bright lands I have seen the World over,
  But none are so dear as fair Albion to me;
My heart gives a bound, when the white cliffs of Dover
  First break on my view, as they rise from the sea!

THE LIFEBOATMAN'S WIDOW AND ORPHAN.

"Dada's stopping! Where's he don to?
  Me's been waiting many a day;
Now me's tired, take me, Mama—
  Eddie wants no more to play.
Dada went off in a hurry
  In the wild-wind, and the rain;
Will you take me now, and tell me
  When will he come back again?

"Me can see the water yonder,
  Coming nearer up the sand;
Is it going to bring my Dada
  Is the boatie going to land?
Take your 'pandies' from your temples,
  Mama, has you dot a pain?
Will you speak and tell me truly,
  When *will* Dada come again?

"Dada kissed me in a hurry,
  When that big dun made a noise,—
Went before he'd finished mending
  Me these little broken toys.
Me can't play till he has mended
  This here little railway-train;
When will Dada come to Eddie—
  Tell me, when he'll come again?

"If my Dada's gone and left me,
  Tell me what is me to do?
Take your apron from your 'peepies'
  Mama, is 'u crying too?

Lift me up to look for Dada ;
  Me is cold, my feet is numb ;
And I want to see my Dada—
  Tell me when he's going to come ?"

    *   *   *

"My child, my child," the mother said,
  "He'll come no more to thee ;
Thy father went to sleep, my love,
  That night upon the sea.
He will return to us no more—
He landed on a happier Shore.

"That night, upon the angry sea,
  God loved thy father so,
He sent an angel from Above
  To bid his spirit go ;
It spread its hovering wings so white,
And bore his soul to Realms of Light.

"Yes, Dada and his comrades, dear,
  The storm did not appal ;
For they were doing God's work of love,
  And He hath claimed them all ;
And thou wilt one day tell with pride,
How brave and nobly Dada died.

"He'll never come again, my child,
  To mend thy broken toys ;
To love thee, and to romp with thee,
  And swell thy childish joys ;
He's waiting now for us on High,
Above yond boundless dark-blue sky.

"He'll come no more, my little one,
  To cheer this lonely cot ;
And yet I would not have his name
  By thee be once forgot ;
Remember in thy nightly prayer,
To always breathe it, darling, there.

"Come here, my child! What though with grief,
 My heart is like to break,
I'll stifle back these blinding tears,
 And live for thy dear sake;
Come, lay thy head on Mama's breast,
And I will soothe and give thee rest.

"He sees us now, but cannot come;
 Yet, if we both are good,
We'll join him, darling, if we live
 As God would have we should;
Then when we die we'll meet him, love,
Nor part again in Heaven above.

"And though thou hast no father now,
 To bring thee daily bread,
Yet if my life and health be spared
 I'll toil for thee instead;
Support from Heaven I now will ask,
For God to help me with my task."

*　　　*　　　　*

That prayer was heard, and more, for God
 Hath caused, by His command,
Into ten thousand English hearts,
 At once throughout the Land,
To rush a generous impulse free
Of sympathetic charity.

To those that were that night bereaved,
 God through His people sent
The wherewithal to get them bread,
 And hope with grief He blent;
The donors won His deep regard
Each gift would bring its own reward.

It could not bring the lost ones back,
 And yet, such prompt relief,
Would lighter make their burdened hearts,
 And thus assuage their grief;
And all who helped the poor distressed,
Would find their bounty doubly blest.

A FAREWELL TO THE SEA.

And must I leave thee, when the noontide's burning ray,
    Bathes thy broad bosom with its lovely hue?
Alas! too soon I must turn from thee away,—
    From thy rippling waters, beautifully blue.
I leave thee in the glorious splendour of the day,
    When thy surface calm and placid doth appear; [play,
But what changes will come o'er, thy wild waves as they
    Ah, many times, before the advent of another year.
Full many a storm may come and pass o'er me,
    Ere I shall look upon thee once again,—
Before I stand with pensive gaze by thee,
    And listen to thy turbulent refrain.
When I am gone thy waves will roll on as before;
    Thy ceaseless tides will ever rise and fall:
Thy restless waters still will dash upon the shore,
    And heave in might and fury 'gainst the surf-beat wall.
The sun will shine the same upon thy surface bright,
    As thy waters break upon the dull grey stone;
It will pour forth its rays, thine hidden depths to light,
    Shine upon a thousand glories, that are all thine own.
But ere I go, I turn to have another sight
    Of thy liquid volumes, that are all in all to me;
Their peerless grandeur spread beneath the radiant light:
    I love the melancholy music of thy voice, O Sea!
I see a speck of white, on the horizon's wide brink,
    Like some Argosy of old it skims the deep;
Then in thy broad expansive sheet it seems to sink,
    Down where thy peaceful waters quietly sleep.
It sails beyond the verge where human eye can reach;
    It is lost in space, and now is seen no more:
Its mirage may appear in clouds, with a foreign land
      beneath,
    Like a phantom of a ship upon another shore.
Oft have I stood to hear thy sad and mournful rush,
    Like some far-off voices chanting a low dirge;
I have watched thy waters in their vastness gush,
    And dash, and break, and surge come after surge!

Now in lone and calm solemnity art thou,
   Beneath the glorious canopy of heaven ;   now
Thy calm waves mildly chase, and o'erlap each other
   And break when they should grasp what they had
      striven !
And now I leave thy wave-beat shore, O Sea !
   To hasten back inland where I abide ;
Perhaps, who knows ?   I may never look again on thee,
   Or watch the ebb and flowing of thy tide.
For the last time now I gaze on thine open waters free,
   For I shall be so far from thee to-night ;
When I am borne away, I shall strain mine eyes O Sea
   In vain !—for thou wilt then be lost to sight !
And old Time will still pass on, and I shall be no more ;
   But it will not leave on thee a single trace ;
When I am dead thy waves will roll on as before,
   And others will stand by thee in my place.
I go :—when thou art steeped in mid-day's sunny gleam,
   As thy waters gently break upon the shore ;
Farewell ! old Sea – I know not, yet I seem
   To think I leave thee now for evermore !

ELEGIAC EFFUSIONS.

"I AM WEARY, LET ME REST."

In Loving Memory of my dear Father.

The silvery locks hung o'er his brow,
   And strength had left his weary feet;
His tottering limbs more feeble grew,
   His task was o'er, his work complete:
He'd seen o'er man's allotted span,
   And life for him had lost its zest;
His daily cry at length became
     "Oh! I am weary, let me rest—
                  Let me rest."

His blue eyes gazed before him far,
   As piercing through the shadows grey,
He seemed to see the lights of Home
   Gleam dimly on his future way;
His life's long day was nearly o'er,
   His sun was sinking in the west;
Eve's shadows fell, and thus he cried,
     "Oh! I am weary, let me rest—
                  Let me rest."

All seasons of his closing life,
   Before his vision were arrayed;
His happiest, and his mournful times,
   The spots of sunshine, and the shade:
That glorious time, the verdant Spring,
   When everything seemed gaily drest
In brightest hues; he cried not then,
     "Oh! I am weary, let me rest
                  Let me rest."

Then came the fervid Summer time,
   When bravely toiling 'midst the throng;
The sweat-drops standing on his brow,
   He sternly fought the battle strong;

FLEETING ILLUSIONS.

He nobly did his manly part,
   And freely gave the world his best
Nor cried he till the strife was o'er,
   "Oh! I am weary, let me rest
                     Let me rest."

And when the mellow Autumn sweet
   Fulfilled the Springtime's promise fair :
He reaped the fruits of early toil,
   And freed himself from labouring care :
God gave to him a fair reward
   For honest work is always blest
And heeded, when at length he cried,
   "Oh! I am weary, let me rest
                     Let me rest."

At last came Winter's withering time,
   When nature seeks for slumber sweet :
The peaceful days when hands are crossed,
   The round of life was then complete :
And as the dreamy days went by,
   Life's burdens harder on him prest :
And oft repeated were the words -
   "Oh! I am weary, let me rest—
                     Let me rest."

The chain then loosened, link by link,
   That bound him to this narrow life ;
The soul would fain its fetters break,
   And soar beyond the sordid strife :
His interest flagged in daily things,
   While pain his feeble frame opprest :
And meekly murmured were the words,
   "Oh! I am weary, let me rest—
                     Let me rest."

At last God pitied one who had
   Through nature worshipped Him so well :-
Walked in His ways from youth to age,
   Nor once at fate would he rebel :
God watched him bear afflicted age,
   And gave the wish so oft exprest :
He closed the pensive eyes in peace,
   And laid the weary form to rest
                     Perfect rest.

IN MEMORIAM:

H.R.H. Princess Alice, The Grand Duchess of Hesse.

Died December 14th, 1878.

She's gone:—amid a Nation's tears,
  And passed away beyond recall;
  Fair England's daughter, dear to all,
Her memory every one reveres.

We mourn,—but oh, alas! in vain:
  For woman's virtues all combined
  Were in that lofty soul enshrined;—
Laments will not bring life again.

The depth of that true mother's love
  Is manifest throughout all lands:
  Beside her father now she stands,
Within the Golden Gates above.

That loving, sacrificing heart,
  Endeared to all by lasting ties:
  In calm repose of death she lies,
Who played on earth a noble part.

She wished herself to gently break
  The tidings to her darling son,
  Of how his sister, fair and young,
Had gone to sleep—no more to wake

On earth, but in Eternal bliss:
  He heard, and his unbounded grief
  Gushed forth in tears without relief;
'Twas then she gave the fatal kiss

To soothe the anguish of her son,
  In that sad hour of grief and trial:
  This gentle mother's self-denial
Has touched the hearts of old and young.

She clasped the boy against her breast,
　So fervent was her loving care;
　She kissed his face so pale and fair,
For she alone could soothe him best.

But Death was in her darling's kiss,
　He came and gave the fatal blow,
　His icy fingers laid her low;
She sunk to rest in peace and bliss.

Devoted, she resigned her life
　For her young children, loved and dear,
　She went herself, and left them here,
Oh, tender mother! faithful wife!

From palace to the lowliest cot,
　In Britain and the Fatherland,
　Her pure and blameless life will stand
For ages,—they'll forget her not.

A thousand prayers have with her gone,
　A thousand blessings rest on them
　Whom she hath loved, and for whom they
She died,—and left to weep alone.

God knows how great hath been the loss,
　To our beloved and gracious Queen;
　A Nation's prayers for her have been,
"May heaven help her to bear the cross!"

ON THE DEATH OF THE DUKE OF CLARENCE,

JANUARY 14th, 1892.

L'homme propose, et Dieu dispose.

The Nation bows its head in grief,
　All England weeps beneath a pall,
To hear that God so soon has claimed
　That Royal Prince, beloved by all.

The bells are tolled throughout the Land,
  The people's hearts all throb with woe,
To find that he on whom their hopes
  Were centred, should be first to go.

Our future Monarch ; we were wont
  To think that such he might have been,
But God saw fit to take him first,
  Before our loved and gracious Queen.

Called hence was he, ere 'round his home,
  We well had marked the gathering clouds ;
He now lies cold as does the earth,
  Both slumb'ring, wrapped in snowy shrouds.

Unto his gentle mother first,
  Our loyal hearts go out in love ;
And unto those who held him dear—
  May all find solace from Above.

But more than all we think of one,
  For whom in sympathy we pray
That Heaven will pity and sustain—
  His sweet betrothed, the Princess May :—

Console the Royal maiden fair,
  Who would ere long have been his bride ;
A wounded heart, with shattered hopes !
  May fortitude with her abide.

His Royal brother was the one
  We lately watched with bated breath—
Thanks, he is spared, but now alas !
  The Duke lies in the sleep of death :—

He whom we fondly thought was safe,
  By health and hope encompassed there,
Exulting in his youth and love,
  His worldly prospect bright and fair.

But Death, impartial, cut him down
  In manhood's prime,—changed all to gloom ;
The altar-scene must be replaced
  By one slow pageant to the tomb.

That sacred chapel, where we thought
 To see his nuptials, once so near,
He yet will enter, all in state,
 But prostrate, on his funeral bier!

A wedding wreath they thought to twine,
 And deck with it the young bride's head,
Now they must weave a funeral wreath,
 For her to place upon the dead.

'Tis vain to question God's decree;
 Such sorrow comes our faith to test:
Though we lament, we can but say
 "Since 'tis His will, it must be best."

While we poor mortals vainly thought
 His happiness—earth-fleeting thing—
Had all been planned, as we prepared
 A mansion for our future King;

Nor knew that God was all the while
 Preparing one for him in Heaven—
A glorious home! where unto him,
 A *crown immortal* will be given.

IN MEMORIAM:

The late Prince Imperial of France.

Slain in the Zulu War, June 1st, 1879.

Adieu! Napoleon the brave,
 Thy widowed mother's only son;
 Thy noble, stainless life is done,—
Thy corse lies in the silent grave.

Though thou art dead, thy name still lives
 To light the page of English lore;
 Though France may look on thee no more,
A throb of pride thy memory gives.

No more for thee ambition's call
  Will bear its charm, for life has ceased:
  And every worldly aim appeased,
A veil has fallen over all.

Farewell! the last of thy great race,
  Thy patriotic life is o'er:
  Thy brave ancestors went before,
Now thou hast followed in thy place.

No mother watched thy dying breath,
  Nor soothed and kissed thee at the last:
  We cannot now recall the past,
Or wake thee from the sleep of death.

The noble gallant Prince is dead,
  Slain by the cruel foreign foe;
  The tidings fill our hearts with woe,
The star of hope of France has fled.

But what must be the grief of one,
  Who, bound to him by dearest ties,
  In anguish on his name she cries,
Or weeps in silence for her son?

We fain would soothe that mother's heart;
  We sympathise with all her grief:
  Oh! God, give Eugenié relief,—
Sustain her through her trying part.

We know she loved her noble boy:
  Her earthly idol now is broke:
  He was her every care and hope,—
In him she centred every joy.

He knelt and kissed his father's tomb,
  In silence bowed his head and prayed—
  Knew not how soon he would be laid
In death's cold sleep, 'mid tears and gloom.

His heart is still, and cold his cheek,
  And every grief is now assuaged;
  He died where fierce contention raged,
No more his kindly voice will speak.

A war-like spirit, all his own,
 Was throbbing in his every vein;
 He yearned to win a martial fame,
To raise him to a monarch's throne.

He volunteered to take our cause,—
 Defend his foster country free;
 He boldly sailed across the sea,
He fearless, faced for us the foes.

She watched her gallant son depart,
 So buoyant, from old England's shore.
 He, destined ne'er to see her more,
Yet hope was in the brave young heart.

And when afar in Zululand,
 He joined the British army there;
 Rode foremost in the ranks to dare
The dangers with that valiant band.

But oh, alas! his hopes were crushed,
 His life was briefly ended there;
 They bore his body gently here,
And placed it near his father's dust.

And like a soldier true, he died,
 Beneath a friendless foreign sky;
 None but the heathen saw him die,
No friend to linger by his side.

The Zulus played a treacherous part,
 So near a kraal, and far from camp;
 They pierced him in a donga damp,
And felled him, wounded to the heart!

Thus was his youthful life-blood spilled;
 All night there his poor body lay,
 Till by his comrades borne away,—
Such was his death that God had willed.

Our thoughts fly back to years ago;
 At Saarbruck, 'mid the deadly strife,
 The boy commenced his soldier's life,
As with his sire he faced the foe.

It wakes the mem'ry hidden deep,
   Of how he watched the bullets fly ;
   For France he feared not then to die ;
His calmness made the soldiers weep.

Our sister country's cherished ties
   Are rudely rent asunder now ;
   The light that beamed has faded low,—
The youthful Prince in slumber lies.

Let party strife then be forgot,
   Join hands in harmony to-day,
   And pray for him who died away
For France, what though she knew it not.

Fair England's dear adopted son ;
   An exile from his native land ;
   And trained beneath her friendly hand,
She grew to love the hero young.

I see the lonely Empress weep,
   While o'er his tomb she breathes a prayer :—
   Another whom she loved lies near,—
For sire and son alas ! now sleep.

From prince and peer to peasant's home,
   The mournful tidings spread so wide ;
   "Bold Bonaparte the brave has died,"
We wept to hear that he was gone.

He sought to win a regal throne
   On earth, but that has gone with life :
   Ceased, has the yearning bitter strife,
His head now wears a Heavenly Crown !

Oh ! scatter flowers upon his tomb,
   A tribute sweet to him now fled,
   Till one by one they shall be dead,
Like him shall wither in their bloom.

Then lay a wreath of *immortelles*,
   And watered by the tears that flow :
   An emblem that immortal now,
His peaceful soul in Heaven dwells.

"GONE, BUT NEVER ONCE FORGOT."

Day and night thou art before me,
   In the spirit thou art near;
Seest my passive mien at daytime,
   And at night my falling tear:
Fancy sees thee, sainted Father,
   In thy place within our cot;
Though in truth thou hast for ever
   Gone, yet thou art not forgot.

All the love we bore each other,
   Fades not as the days go by,
Twines its garland 'round the memory
   Fastened with a heart-drawn sigh:
Nought whate'er of future pleasure
   From my memory once will blot
Thy loved image; oh, my father,
   Gone, but never once forgot.

And whate'er may be my portion,
   In this world of care and woe;
May I live like thee, contented,
   Yet withal prepared to go;
Taking all things well and wisely,
   Nor repine, whate'er my lot;
Like thee mourned when past the border,
   Gone, but never once forgot.

Not forgot? oh! can thy spirit
   See thy child in sorrow here?
See the smiles I have for others,
   For thyself, affection's tear;
Where thy weary feet have wandered
   Is to me a much-loved spot;
Thou wilt never, oh, my father,
   By thy child be once forgot.

Loved and venerated dear one,
   When this pilgrim life is o'er,
May I meet thee as an angel
   On the far-off Golden Shore:
Calmly sleep ere then beside thee,
   Underneath God's hallowed plot;
From this weary world of trouble
   Gone, but by it not forgot.

Since thy soul has crossed the river,
   Mine would fain not tarry here;
Parting with thee linked me closer,
   To the glorious angel Sphere:
May I now, like thee, serenely
   Bear life's ills, and murmur not;
Seek its sunlight, shun its shadows,
   And when gone, be not forgot.

IN MEMORIAM: LORD TENNYSON.

DIED, OCTOBER 6TH, 1892.

FAREWELL! loved bard, thy life is past,
Thy soul its mortal shell has cast,
And reached the longed-for bourne at last!

That peace was thine we all shall need,
"It was a glorious death indeed,"
Said those who saw thy spirit freed.

Nor fire, nor taper, shed its light,
But through the oriel window bright,
There softly shone the orb of night:—

Its tranquil beam streamed on thy bed,
And threw a glory round thy head,
And kissed thy face, ere thou wert dead.

Thou hast but fall'n away to sleep,
A dreamless slumber, calm and deep;
At such an end why should we weep?

We could not bid thy spirit stay,
Unseen it passed in peace away,
Upon the full moon's silvery ray.

No nobler poet our Land has known,
Thy deathless spirit now has flown
To join the blest, our Father's own.

We may not see thy like again,
And now shall list' for, all in vain,
Thy pure, enobling, lofty strain.

Reared in thy dear and lonely fen,
Thou didst not court the gaze of men,
But loved alone to wield thy pen.

The world is better for thy being;
Thy life's good work, thy death serene,
Have cast an influence all unseen.

Thy teachings can we e'er forget?
We sadly mourn thy loss and yet,
We know the brightest star must set.

Watched by the ones who loved thee best,
Thy weary hands laid on thy breast,
Thou passed unto eternal rest.

God's angel was no spectre grim,
All nature hushed, kept guard for him,
Illumed the solemn chamber dim.

A light is quenched with thy release,
A minstrel's wondrous chords now cease,
Thy life has closed in perfect peace.

Thy precious dust was borne in state,
Within our hallowed temple's gate,
And placed with England's loved and great.

When thou wert with us here below,
The laurel wreath adorned thy brow,
But one more blest will crown it now!

THE MOURNING MOTHER.

My boy is an angel : he passed from this earth.
In childhood's first glory, abounding in mirth :
Oh! fondly I loved him, how could I refrain?
And aught would I give but to see him again !

'Tis hard for a mother so soon to resign
Her loved only child, to its Maker divine :
My hope and the light of my heart feels destroyed,
Instead of love's rapture, a dull aching void!

I long for the touch of his little warm hand,
For when it clasped mine, how my heart would expand !
And faster would beat with a sweet mother-joy,
To feel the caress of my own baby boy.

'Twould seem from his brief stainless life since its birth.
That he were God's angel, but lent to this earth :
And lest his white soul, that were pure as the snow,
Be soiled, it was snatched from temptations below.

And though with the parting my heart was sore-tried
'Twere better by far that my darling thus died :
While he were unscathed by life's sorrow and sin,
His soul knew no conflict ere light entered in.

Unsullied he went ; and I know that he now
Is wearing a garland upon his fair brow :
Oh ! mine were the heart-ache, but his were the joy,
Earth's anguish henceforth is unknown to my boy !

He went when this life seems most happy and fair,
All sunshine and roses, with never a care :
I fain had died for him, my grief were that wild,—
For what will a mother not do for her child !

We all have our sorrows in some way to bear,
Alone we are aided and solaced by prayer ;
When heart-strained with grieving for lost ones we plead,
Not vainly, for help in the hour of our need.

Some love may be deep and protecting, we know,
Some ardent, romantic, with passionate glow;
But clinging, confiding, transparent, and mild,
And pure is the love of a dear little child!

The sight of his playthings brought sorrow each day,
Till deluged with tears, I have placed them away;
With garments he wore, that I made with such pride,
I carefully, tenderly, laid them aside.

Oh, now that his sweet baby-voice I could hear!
That fell like glad music my lone life to cheer:
In Paradise now to a golden harp sweet,
His voice is attuned, and my spirit 'twill greet.

The while my fair child on this earth did remain,
Each day faster welded our love's rosy chain;
That bound us in spirit, my darling for aye,
For can I forget thee my child, for a day?

Thy mem'ry still haunts me, and clings to me so,
In visions I see thee wherever I go:
But thou art an angel, and near the great Throne,
In bowers of bliss, while I mourn here alone!

But why this repining? why thus should I weep?
Each day I am nearer my borderland sleep;
From which when I rise with my soul undefiled
I ever shall dwell with my sweet sainted child:

Yet I have a mission ere rest may be mine,
Before my soul's music may mingle with thine;
My life-task is set, which I needs must fulfil,
And loving my Task-Master, bow to His will.

ON THE DEATH OF A NONAGENARIAN.

Farewell thou weary one! who with
    This splendid century saw the light;
Through over nine decades has seen,
    This life's alternate day and night.

And all the changes which have swept
   O'er this fair land, that gave thee birth,
And placed it in the foremost ranks,
   Of all God's beauteous lands on earth.

And while the seasons have revolved,
   Thou too hast changed from youth to age,
Thy mission is fulfilled, and thou
   Hast passed from off this earthly stage.

'Twas meet thy soul should cast its shell,
   When withered leaves were falling 'round ;
And autumn winds were sighing low—
   It found its rest in sleep profound.

Another link that bound to-day
   Unto the past, is snapped in twain ;
The memories of the good old times,
   From thee we ne'er can hear again.

The social gathering never more
   Will see thy dear familiar face ;
The ancient form we all revered
   Will fill not its accustomed place.

Farewell! poor long-tried heart, we know
   Thy feeble hands have laboured long ;
Thine eyes, whose lids are closed for aye,
   Have shed their tears, and gleamed with song.

Oh, oft thou must have longed for rest,—
   Been ready for the reaper's hand ;
Like grain full ripe, and now the sheaf
   Is garnered safe, in God's bright Land.

We now resign thee, cold and still,
   Into the white-clad arms of Peace,
Whence thou wilt rise amongst the hosts
   That sing God's praise, and never cease.

IN MEMORY OF A PHILANTHROPIST.

(J. Crossley, Esq., Halifax.)

He's gone to his Eternal rest,
And sleepeth on the Saviour's breast,
    His earthly cares are o'er;
He filled a good and noble place,
And those who knew his kindly face,
    Will see it now no more.

The loving heart has ceased to beat,
His presence we no more shall greet;
    His gentle voice is still;
Thus ends his noble life of love,
In glory now his soul above,
    A fairer spot doth fill.

Too good to tarry longer here,
Within a higher, holier sphere,
    He rests with Jesus now;
While angels bright around him move,
And place with happiness and love,
    A crown upon his brow.

And thousands whom his love hath blest,
Have followed him to his last rest,
    And seen him laid so low;
Recalled with tears the help he gave,
And breathed a blessing o'er his grave,
    With reverential bow.

He won the poor man's kind regard,
And reapeth now the rich reward
    For every generous deed;
He riches gave — himself denied,
A noble man he lived and died,
    In truest christian creed.

The widows, and the frail and old,
Weep o'er that form now dead and cold,
    And breathe a silent prayer;

The orphan children bless his name,
So pure and spotless, not a stain
    Has ever rested there.

His mission now on earth is done,
And we behold his "Orphan's Home,"
    With dome that points to Heaven :—
A monument henceforth 'twill be,
For future ages yet to see—
    A gift so nobly given.

'Twas thus he laid him down to rest,
He felt aweary and oppressed,
    And yearned for his last home :—
He gently bade his friends " good-night,"
God's angel came before his sight,
Then 'midst a flood of holy light,
    The Saviour's voice said, " Come!"

LINES ON THE DEATH OF MADAME PATEY.

Her voice is hushed, and never more
    Will fall upon our ears again :
Its wondrous tones no more will charm,—
    We listen for that voice in vain.

For it is still, and ne'er again
    Can we recall her thrilling song :
Her sweet impressive strains though hushed
    Will linger on the memory long.

Oft have we listened, all entranced,
    And cheered her when there came a pause :
Now that melodious voice is still,
    Her ears are deaf to all applause.

Her kindly heart could but respond,
    She sought to please the clamorous throng :
The glorious songstress whom we loved,
    When dying, sung her farewell song.

But as they sat enraptured, lo!
   The singer's spirit all but fled;
For even while she warbled there,
   The angel hovered o'er her head.

Her closing sympathetic notes,
   Will, with remorse, remembered be
Her death-song's last prophetic words
   Fell sadly, "There a corpse lay she."

Her song has ceased for ever here,
   Fled with her soul so far away;
That mournful ballad's sad refrain,
   Will haunt the heart for many a day.

Her lips are sealed for evermore,
   So silent now beneath the turf;
Farewell! we grieve that we shall hear,
   That tuneful voice no more on earth.

It now has joined the angel band,
   In happy, joyous songs of love;
'Tis singing sweetly in God's Land,—
   The peerless Regions far Above.

IN MEMORY OF AN OLD SHRIMPER.

It is well that God in mercy,
   All the future from us hides;
Veils our fate that we may humbly
   Trust in Him, what-e'er betides.

Quickly He hath ta'en poor Rimmer,
   Veteran toiler of the sea;
Ne'er a warning that the summons
   Was to come, that morn had he.

Stricken by the hand of Heaven,
   While at work beside the wave;
Truly he hath died in harness,
   Full of years, and staunch and brave.

Hardy son of Father Neptune,
　Fallen in his bosom there:
Would the waves could bring a message—
　Tell to us his dying prayer!

In the dark, cold winter morning,
　To the lone and silent shore,
Wandered forth the poor old shrimper,
　And, alas! returned no more.

Not a loving hand was with him,
　While he drew his dying breath:
Not a loving voice to soothe him,
　In the cold embrace of death.

All alone with sky and water,
　But the beating of the surge,
Might at last have lulled his spirit,
　With a low and solemn dirge.

Grieve not, kindred! God's good angel,
　Unperceived would be at hand,
Hovering o'er his head that softly,
　Pillowed on the yielding sand.

But the widow's heart is aching,
　She will miss him from his place:—
Look in vain within the cottage,
　For his old familiar face.

Father, wilt Thou give her comfort,
　Bless and soothe the agèd heart:
Cheer her, till they are united
　Once again, and ne'er to part.

SACRED MEMORIES.

How we cherish sacred memories!
　Keep them close within the heart:
Some so sad, that to recall them
　E'en, will make the tear-drops start.

Memories shared not by the stranger,
   Safely locked within the breast;
By the golden key of silence,
   Truths for ever unconfessed.
Each heart holds its precious memories,
   To itself supremely dear;
Guarded in its treasured storehouse,
   Summoned thence, dull days to cheer
Vanished scenes, and past emotions,
   Each retentive mind recalls;
All preserved and venerated,
   Safe behind the strength'ning walls.
Bygone trials and tribulations,—
   Sorrows that were hard to bear;
Robbed by time of half their sadness,
   Clothed in robes now sweet and fair.
Clouds that once have passed above us,
   Thrown their shadow o'er the light;
Rise before us, hallowed memories,
   Silvered now, and gleaming white.
Sacred griefs, subdued and mellowed,
   By the soft'ning hand of Time;
See we now in brighter raiment
   Crusted, as with wintry rime.
Fondest memories of the absent,
   Faithful souls for ever flown;
And the changeful years invest them,
   With a glory all their own :—
Memories of our loved and lost ones,
   Treading now the Heavenly Aisles;
Left behind a blest remembrance,
   Treasured words, and vanished smiles
Sweet sad memories! ne'er unbosomed,
   In the heart's recesses sleep;
Buried there, nor break the stronghold,
   Where they rest secure and deep;
Only called forth to be nourished,
   In the drear and lonely hour;
Solitude can wake their slumbers,
   Bid them rise, and wield their power.
Such can never pine nor perish,
   Years but make them dearer grow;

Folds them in a fadeless glory,
   At life's close they brightest glow.
They are wrapt in robes of silence,
   When we meet the young and gay;—
While with happy friends surrounded,
   Thoughts revered are placed away.
Things remembered since our childhood,
   Woven deep into the heart,
Are the tender ties of memory,
   Till of us they form a part:
Mingled with our every fibre,
   Grown with us from out the past,
Memories that will never leave us,
   Till we've breathed on earth our last!

IN MEMORY OF A POET.

Farewell! belovèd bard, whose lays
   Oft-times have charmed this heart of mine:
   For He who gave the gift divine,
Hath claimed him in his early days.

Farewell! for God's ways are not ours:
   Too soon, we think, He snatched the prize:
   A veil is yet before our eyes,
Each troubled heart its grief still pours.

The widow's and the orphans' cry
   Of anguish, yet to Heaven ascends:
   'Twill not be long before He bends
Upon them all His pitying eye.

We miss the voice, the face, the smile,
   He's gone, yet he hath left behind
   The reflex of a master mind,
A noble "monumental pile":-

His memory to perpetuate·
   And to the world still keep it green:
   We are the richer for his being,
But those he loved are desolate.

His form was sought from boyhood's years-
    The nucleus of a happy throng;
    Beloved his fellow-men among,
Where he has walked, we find their tears.

He might have erred; oh! who has not?
    Yet Mercy found him at the last—
    Obliterated all the past,
And bore him to the brightest spot.

We never more shall hear again
    The fresh outpourings of his soul,
    That would the throbbing heart console;
Such was the power of every strain.

Nor will again that magic pen—
    The hand-maid of poetic thoughts—
    Obey their dictates; it hath wrought
Him honour, mongst a host of men.

And now that fertile pen must rust,
    For poesy it no more may yield;—
    The hand is cold that pen could wield,—
We drop a tear above his dust

Ambition beckoned him to fame,
    He reached it, but alas! too soon
    His sky grew dark, before 'twas noon,—
Yet laurel-wreaths adorn his name.

He bore his cross, and now is crowned:
    He sleeps alone, where sweet flowers shed
    Their fragrance o'er the hallowed dead,
'Neath fairest patch of English ground.

His highest flights of fancy here
    His purest, idealistic dreams
    Of what should be; were trancient gleams
Of what he now has realised there.

Freed from the mean confines of earth,
    The soul untrammelled soared up higher,
    To swell the sweet angelic choir,
In Paradise it had new birth.

Against its bars it fretted long,
   Aspiring to a perfect state ;
   God gave it grace to pass the gate
That leads unto the sainted throng.

And now in bright ethereal bowers,
   Where nought the fair Elysium mars,
   He dwells in peace, beyond the stars—
A white-robed angel, crowned with flowers.

And when my songs have ceased below,
   Perchance I then shall meet him there ;
   He'll greet me on the " golden stair,"
And place a chaplet on my brow.

TO A YOUNG FRIEND,

On the Death of her Mother.

Thy Mother is dead,—I must tell thee my child,
The earth-star has vanished that on thee has smiled :
But gently—the tidings are sad to thee now,
For grief has its furrows upon thy young brow :
The tenderest chords of thy heart are awake,—
And touch them too roughly, perchance they may break.

Thy Mother is dead,—she will never again
Give comfort unto thee in anguish or pain ;—
She'll never come near thee again on this earth,
To soothe thee in sorrow, or join in thy mirth :—
No never steal near thee, and noiselessly tread,
To kiss thee, and tuck thee at night in thy bed.

Thy Mother is dead,—and she will not be here,
To offer thee counsel, or wipe the sad tear ;
Oh, never again will she walk by thy side,
Nor through the dark ways of the world be thy guide :
She'll never caress thee or speak to thee more,
The bright golden dream of thy childhood is o'er.

Thy Mother is dead,—didst thou grieve her poor heart?
Oh, then with contrition thy bosom will smart;
Thy faults would come thick at the sight of her corse,—
Thy conscience be pierced with a pang of remorse;
Thou canst not redeem them, nor bring her again,
Then hush, for the bitterest tears are in vain.

Thy Mother is dead,—she is sleeping so low,
The truest best friend that thou ever canst know;
She now lies at rest in the cold sodden ground,
Go ask for support then, and kneel on that mound;
And pray for this cloud to be lifted away—
For hope to illumine thy pathway to-day.

Thy Mother is dead, she has gone to her rest,
Her spirit abides with the loved and the blest;
Be good, my dear child, to the end of thy days,
And pray to be kept from temptation's dark ways:—
And then at the last the blest Home thou shalt share,
Thy Mother will meet thee and welcome thee there.

Thy Mother is dead, she is happy at Home,
Thou mayst not go to her till Jesus says "come";
Remember my child there's a mission for thee
To do here below, ere thy earth-bonds are free;
Then cheerfully go with thy heart and thy might,
To win thee a place in the Regions of Light.

Thy Mother is dead,—and her soul is afar,
Among the glad angels, beyond that bright star;
And she will come back to her darling no more;
She waits for thee now on the far-away Shore;
Then follow the path that thy Mother has trod,
If thou wouldst inherit the Kingdom of God.

IN MEMORIAM:
The Crews of the St. Annes and Southport Lifeboats,

*Drowned while on a mission of rescue,
December 10th, 1886.*

I CALL the Muse, but lo! to-day,
  It falters when I bid it come—
Unequal to its mournful task,
  It feeble is, and all but dumb.—
So weak, it scarce can frame the thoughts
  That rise in wild chaotic gloom.
Oh, cruel Storm! Oh, mighty Sea!
  Great is thy spoil, wide is thy tomb!
Man feels his strength while on the land,
  But have we not to-day been taught
That when 'tis tested by the sea
  His boasted power is set at naught?
Such tempests prove his utmost skill
  Is naught beneath their awful sway;
His craft becomes a broken toy,
  With which the billows madly play.
Who can depict that midnight scene—
  The struggle on the wrathful main?
'Tis not for us to ask of God
  " Why did they not return again?"
Scared not by danger went they forth
  To bravely battle with the blast;
In blinding storm, on raging sea,
  "Twas Duty first, and Self the last.
Talk not of war, till you have seen
  A deed like this, then, if you can,
Compare:—is he who slays, or he
  Who strives to save his brother man,
The nobler? Let your conscience speak,
  And what it whispers must be right:
The Father knows, the angels know,
  All deeds are done within their sight.

Lord! surely men who die like these,
  Thou wilt receive, and call them Thine?—
Who perish thus upon the deep,
  Have they not won Thy love divine?
We trust they have,—nay, know they have,
  For going at Mercy's own behest,
Would she not intercede; for Thee
  To place them with the good and blest?
If they had walked on life's broad way,
  Oh, did they not at last redeem
The past, by that heroic deed,
  And see in death the glory gleam?
And may not England well be proud
  Of sailor sons like unto these?
Her prayers and blessings go with them,
  When Mercy bids them dare the seas.
Since sympathetic human love,
  Must now be strong in every heart:
May not a monument be reared,—
  When heroes such as these depart?
But for that noble act humane,
  They might have all been with us still:—
The women spared those pangs of grief,
  That come with desolation's chill.
Remorseful tears they now may shed
  Death unforeseen oft wounds us so;
Oh! pity them, and pray with me,
  For One to aid them in their woe.

"THY WILL BE DONE."

Grieve not, poor wounded hearts, bereft
  Of one most dear to you on earth:
  For all who knew your loved one's worth,
Will feel for you, whom she hath left,

To sadly mourn; through day and night—
  When darkness veils each tear-stained face;
  But strive amidst your grief to trace
The path from darkness unto light.

And strive to calm the throbbing brow,
  And still the anguish in the breast;
  Your lost one sweetly sleeps at rest,
" With Christ, which is far better," now.

'Twas well you all were near to say
  " Good-bye," and kiss her ere she died;
  With heart-strained watchers by her side,
Her spirit softly passed away.

How vain to boast of life, when we
  Have seen how soon it can be ta'en;
  The " silver cord " has broke in twain,
We know not where Death next may be.

Weep not; she walked in peaceful ways
  On earth, and made her presence dear;
  With all her kindred's love to cheer,
And cast a blessing o'er her days.

Throughout her brief and blameless life,
  She won kind friends afar and wide;
  Now she has crossed the mystic tide,
And left this weary world of strife.

Her soul its mortal husk has shed,
  And passed the mystic border-gloom,
  That intervenes between the tomb
And Heaven, whither it hath fled.

Her life was pure, God in His love
  Saw good to take her far from here;—
  Unto a bright and happier Sphere,—
To join the angel host Above.

Oh! then, bereaved ones, strive to cease
  To grieve for her now called away;
  " *Thy will be done,*" is hard to say,—
And yet those words will give you peace.

"HE IS NOT DEAD, HE ONLY SLEEPS."

We laid our loved one gently down,
   And placed the daisies on his breast;
The tired hands had ceased their toil,
   In peace he passed away to rest;
But when the soul from bondage leaps,
It is not dead, it only sleeps.

Yes, still it lives; what though apart,
   It has but left its mortal shell;
And while we watched it softly go;
   All fear of death it did dispel:
We know, though yet each mourner weeps,
He is not dead,—he only sleeps.

Sleeps, sweetly sleeps, oblivious now
   Of all the cares that once opprest;
Beneath a loving Father's eye,
   He softly passed unto his rest:
Faith says, through darkness while it peeps,
"He is not dead, he only sleeps."

Nor pains, nor sorrows, pierce him now,
   His yoke for ever he has cast:
God's handmaid, Mercy, smoothed his way,
   His mortal suffering soon was past;
He now lies 'mongst his native steeps,
He is not dead, he only sleeps.

To wake again to sacred joys,
   Within a holier Land than this;
Around the mighty Throne of Grace,
   To swell the throng in endless bliss;
All will be his the good soul reaps,
He is not dead, he only sleeps.

When light and darkness joined their hands,
   And vigils of the night were o'er;

As it resigned to rosy dawn,
   He slept, to wake on earth no more :
God o'er him now a watch still keeps.
He is not dead, he only sleeps.

We watched him through this world's dark night,
   Until the weary eyelids closed,
At dawn, when Heaven's new light broke in
   Upon his soul, then he reposed ;
To wake when he has crossed the deeps,
He is not dead, he only sleeps,—

Sleeps calmly with the pure and blest,
   A life well-lived was his while here :
"His end was peace," and now his grave
   Is watered by the fervent tear ;
His fav'rite flower above him creeps,
Till he is called, he rests and sleeps.

IN MEMORY OF A LANCASHIRE BARD.

Once more the veil has lifted been,
   A soul has passed into the light
That glorifies the great Unseen,
   And knows no more of mortal night.

A brother bard's dear memory claims
   A loving tribute to his worth—
The love which kindred nature frames,
   Enwraps the soul now called from earth.

Though each the other knew not, yet,
   If we were strangers in the throng ;
In spirit oft methinks we met,
   Within the mystic realms of song.

He wore his unsought laurels here,
    But richer wreaths will deck his brow;
Within that holier, brighter Sphere,
    Whose gates for him have opened now.

Though he adorned a lowly place,
    He humbly strove to serve his God;
Departed now, we love to trace
    His waymarks in the path he trod.

His aims were good, his home-songs are
    In Truth's blest keynote, hence his fame;
And his were what is better far,
    A duteous life, an honoured name.

A wild bird's warblings by the way,
    That helped to make the woodlands ring;
Is missed when it has hushed for aye
    By those who loved to hear it sing.

He trilled the people's heart-songs sweet
    Through him their woes they could express;
The poor his buoyant notes would greet,
    For he could cheer them in distress.

The minstrel whom we held so dear
    Who touched the chords of truth and love,
Has only been rehearsing here,
    Before he joined God's choir Above.

From honest labour he hath found
    Too soon for us, eternal rest;
His christian virtues will be crowned
    In glory, 'mongst the pure and blest.

Farewell to all his heartfelt lays,
    His earthly burden now is cast;
No more he treads life's thorny ways,
    He sleeps in perfect peace at last.

When my rehearsal shall be o'er,
    And I have laid aside my lyre;
He'll meet me on the crystal Shore,
    To join him in the angel choir!

"OUR JANEY."

You ask me why I weep to-day,
The tears will all unbidden flow;—
Because a dear one's passed away,—
     Our Janey.

You knew her not, oh! had you known
Her spotless life, her depth of soul,
You would have loved her as your own,—
     Our Janey:—

And wept with me, that One Above
Should take our darling home so soon;
For all who knew her could but love,
     Our Janey.

We might have known that one so fair,
So good, so pure in mind, would go;—
That God would soon take to His care,
     Our Janey.

She was not fit for here; her mind
Soared far above the things of earth;
God's Word ennobled and refined,
     Our Janey.

She loved us, but her thoughts would reach
Full oft to One whom she revered;—
Christ's life its lessons sweet could teach,
     Our Janey.

In innocence a child was she,—
A trustful, sympathetic child;
And yet a woman true could be,
     Our Janey.

She lingered on the border-line
Which seems to separate the twain;
The traits of both could she combine;—
     Our Janey.

I think I see her even now,
Before me as when warm with life,—
Her earnest eyes, her thoughtful brow;
                    Our Janey.—

Her movements full of quiet grace,
Her simple, meek, and guileless ways;—
Her slender form, her pensive face;—
                    Our Janey.

We little thought she would be called
At last so quickly from our side;
Death came, but never once appalled,
                    Our Janey.

For, "Blest are they that hear the Word
Of God, and keep it;" were her last
Dear words, and then no more we heard.
                    Our Janey.—

The soft sweet voice was hushed for aye;
So beautiful in death was she,—
An angel in her white array,—
                    Our Janey.

We keep her little treasures yet,
And fondly prize them for her sake;
Without them could we once forget,
                    Our Janey?

The bloom of summer time has fled,
The autumn rain falls thick and fast;
The sodden grass droops o'er the dead,—
                    Our Janey.

The quiv'ring leaves begin to fade,
The storm-cloud dims the azure sky;
The night-winds wail where she is laid,—
                    Our Janey.

Where-e'er we look for her around,
Or call her name, 'twill be in vain;—
On earth can never more be found,
                    Our Janey.

If you had met her in a crowd,
Naught would have marked our darling there:
The one of whom we were so proud,—
      Our Janey.

No feature, save perchance the eyes,
Could once arrest the strangers' gaze:
They had not known our treasured prize,—
      Our Janey.

'Twas through those orbs her spirit shone,
And made her radiant at the last;
In sweetness then she stood alone,—
      Our Janey.

And by the angel-smile she wore,
She must have caught a glimpse of Heaven:—
Its crystal courts appeared before.
      Our Janey.—

A vision of celestial things,
To mortal senses all unknown;
Or heard a seraph's rustling wings;—
      Our Janey.

Come back! come back, oh! could she come
If but a moment back again:
And speak to us once more at home,—
      Our Janey.

They were not for a world like this,
Her gentle tones, her beaming smile:
But oh, to-night I long to kiss,
      Our Janey.

That cannot be, but yet it seems
Remorse a sudden grief will tinge;
She can but come to us in dreams,—
      Our Janey.

It seems so hard that hopeful youth,
So full of promise should be ta'en:—
In whom there shone such love and truth,
      Our Janey.

Yet we had wished it thus could be,
If time had spoiled our fragile flower;—
In youth's first bloom we e'er shall see,
                    Our Janey.

We mourn, but what can that avail?
The angel child has perfect peace;
Nor pain, nor sorrow, can assail,
                    Our Janey.

If mortal love be such as this,
What must be God's? Oh! boundless bliss!
Why fall ye tears? He knows 'tis best,
That gentle Janey's gone to rest.

HIS BEST REWARD.

A NOBLE soul, and as brave as true,
    Was lately summoned to cross the bar;
Whose many virtues but known to few,
    'Tis meet that such were extolled afar.

There beat a loving and genial heart,
    Beneath the jersey of navy blue;
He played a brave and heroic part,
    As volunteer for a lifeboat's crew.

He knew in life what it was to face
    The boiling wrath of a storm-lashed main;
The lifeboat's course when 'twas hard to trace,
    All feared she ne'er would return again.

He knew what it was to snatch from death,
    His fellow-men o'er a surging grave;
When those on the shore have held their breath,
    Or murmured prayers for the boatmen brave.

He knew what it was to land and hear
    The praise and cheers of the anxious crowd;
His loved ones' welcome he held most dear,
    Of well-won honours he was but proud.

Though prized the medal he owned and wore
    For lifeboat work on the stormy deep ;
He'd one reward that he valued more,
    And ne'er forgot till he went to sleep.

'Twas one received from a little girl,
    Long ere his spirit was called to Heaven ;
Of that reward he was wont to tell,
    With tears of joy 'twas received and given.

The clasp and kiss of a grateful child,
    Upon the shore, by the rushing wave :
Her thanks broke forth in a rapture wild,
    For noble service he freely gave.

That child's young sister he'd rescued there—
    Had brought her forth from the surging sea ;
Thus earned her blessing and childish prayer,
    No prouder moment in life had he.

She felt that something to him she owed,
    A sweet child's impulse ne'er fails to charm :
The grateful heart of the girl o'erflowed,
    In fervent kisses, so true and warm.

A father he, and each clinging kiss,
    Touched tender chords in his kindly breast :
No thought of honours or fame was his,—
    For love and duty he'd done his best.

That soft caress on his sun-burnt cheek,
    His deed of gallantry well repaid ;
The noblest natures befriend the weak,
    Brave hearts are proved at a cry for aid.

He's drifted now to the Silent Land,
    For him the storms of this life are o'er ;
His bark is moored on a Brighter Strand,
    In God's safe Harbour for evermore.

One last reward, and by far the best,
    And one which none can receive on earth,
Will yet be his, with the good and blest,
    For God is just, and rewards true worth.

A TRIBUTE TO THE MEMORY OF THE RT. HON. W. E. GLADSTONE.

Who found his rest May 19th, 1898.

That star of finest magnitude has set,
Whose light illumined many Lands, that yet
Will feel his influence; we can ne'er forget
    His grand career!

For years the bark of State he wisely steered
Through troublous waters,—trusted was, and cheered,
A helmsman grasped the tiller who revered
    And feared his God.

His fine physique, colossal mental powers,
He used aright, spent well his God-sent hours;
And gave his best to this fair Land of ours,—
    Served well his Queen.

His life's an inspiration,—how complete!
It graced this wondrous century, so replete
With progress; and through it we trace his feet
    In lines of gold!

We know his name will live, whom nations mourn,
Its reflex glow for ages yet unborn;
Nor decked with star nor title, he has worn
    True virtue's crown.

'A grand old man!' nay more than that, for we
Know that he was as God would have us be;
In purity of heart, and life, was he
    A *good* old man!

His inner sanctuary,—his home-life pure,
Apart from State, held lessons to endure;
Bore scrutiny, for to a faith secure,
    His soul was moored.

In dignified nobility he moved,
With sway magnetic, loved us, and was loved;
We miss his benign presence, now removed
    To Realms of Peace.

We could but look and marvel, while we bowed
Before his genius; his vast life-work showed,
The Statesman, Scholar, Author, was endowed
    With gifts from Heaven.

While on Fame's pinnacle in strength he stood,
He did the world a great and glorious good;
A central figure, kingly, whom we could
    But venerate!

He strove with highest aims, whose soul has fled;
Beloved, he sleeps with England's mighty dead;
A thousand lips have blest that honoured head,
    Now laid at rest.

Oh! may his life, its grand work nobly done,
Be emulated by each mother's son;
In Heaven he'll have his guerdon, richly won,—
    His Master's praise.

His name rings like one grand melodious chime;
His life illustrious, and his death sublime;
'Mid prayers he passed the bounds of space and time,
    In peace profound.

He chafed not at the bars, but passed away,
In solemn, sweet serenity, for aye;
Upon the morning of *Ascension* Day,
    God claimed His own!

PASSING HENCE.

    Day by day the veil of Heaven,
        Lifts, to let a soul pass in;
    One by one do spirits enter,
        Cleansed, and purified from sin:
    First some loved one must ascend,
    Then a true and trusted friend.

Those are glorified who leave us,
　　Crowned with honour, bent with years:
Ripe and ready for the sickle,
　　Such demand no idle tears:
Work is finished,—life complete,
Unto such then, rest is sweet.

They have no desire to tarry,
　　Through each stage of life have passed:
Stand they waiting to be garnered,
　　Welcome being the call at last:
Weary souls are ever blest,
Passing thus, in peace to rest.

But howe'er they may be ready,
　　Leave they many an aching heart;
Those whom we have truly cherished,
　　Cause a pang when they depart:—
Leave a void where they have been,
Yet we keep their memory green.

CONSOLATION.

When a dear one has departed,
　　And our fond hearts are bereft;
To the lone and stricken-hearted,
　　There is this sweet comfort left:—

That though it was hard to sever,
　　Costing us such bitter pain;
Yet they are not lost for ever,—
　　We shall meet them once again:—

Hear then how for us they've waited,
　　With a welcome and a smile;
Joy! to think we're separated
　　"Only for a little while."

Now we think they were the dearest,
　　When we find that they have fled;
And the heart-ties were the nearest,
　　Such are memories of the dead!

Still we've other hearts to cherish,
   'Mid the sacredness of grief;
Prize them now, before they perish,—
   Let the effort bring relief.

Something yet to strive for, seeming
   In the cloud a silver band;
Through the darkness Hope is gleaming,—
   Let it take us by the hand.

All our love will be requited;
   Here true consolation lies,—
We shall soon be reunited,
   In one Home beyond the skies.

Christmas Chimes.

CHRISTMAS.

Christmas is coming, in garlands of snow,
    Out of the vista of Time;
The white wreaths are shining like gems on his brow,
    And his beard is bespangled with rime.

Out of the realms of the mystic Unknown,
    He comes to the Present in smiles;
As cheery and pleasant as those that have flown,
    And full of his legends and wiles.

His voice is the wind as it sweeps o'er the land,
    And sings over mountain and vale;
Then give him a welcome, and clasp of the hand—
    For see! he is hearty and hale.

His hair is bedecked with the silvery snow,
    His breath is the wintery chill,
That stifles the pond, and the rivulet's flow,
    And arrests the sweet voice of the rill.

He bears the good things that he only can bring,
    To garnish the festal array;
While Plenty and Peace sit aloft on his wing,
    He bids us be happy and gay.

Then give him a welcome to every hearth,
    To preside over laughter and glee;
For he is the bearer of pleasure and mirth—
    And who is so merry as he?

CHRISTMAS EVE.

Over the snow, the crispening snow,
The people are hurrying to and fro.
    On the Eve of the Natal Morn;
Crunching the crystals beneath their feet.
Some gaily trip through the gaslit street,
    Some are weary, and sad, and worn.

Over the snow, the drifted snow,
They greet each other as on they go,
    For 'tis now when all hearts expand:
From over the border, and far away,
They meet on the Eve of the joyful day
    From the distant parts of the Land.

Over the snow, the shimmering snow,
Under the stars, as they peep below,
    Far into the cold white world.
From loving friends who must dwell apart,
Kind offerings passing from heart to heart,
    Are over the Land being whirled.

We see the spirit of Mirth abroad,
In the market town, and the country road,
    For it floats in the frosty air:
And Plenty smiles on the festive scene,
For linked together they oft are seen,
    In the homes of the wealthy there.

And here is Poverty, gaunt and grim,
It hangs about in the starlight dim,
    And its haunts are the narrow ways:
But what is better than all the rest,
The spirit of Charity, always blest,
    For it brightens the wintry days:

In noiseless gossamer robes of white,
It sheds a lustre into the night,
    As it flitteth from door to door—
A beautiful, pure, and heaven-born thing,
The bearer of happiness under its wing,
    As it hies to the homes of the poor.

CHRISTMAS MORN.

Unlocked are the gates of morn,
And Christmas enters, as the silence deep
Is broken; while the sound of merry bells
   On the chilly air is borne.

And long ere the dawn has shed
Its dim grey light, and covered all the stars,
Glad music, swelling from a thousand throats,
   Over all the land is spread.

On the frost-encrusted earth
A host of Christians stand: with one accord,
They burst in songs of praise, to bless the day
   Of the great Messiah's birth.

There, with uplifted eyes,
They sing, and wake the echoes of the hills;
The glorious chorus in sweet silvery strains
   Floats upward to the skies.

While the hallow'd morning breaks,
And rosy color streaks the eastern skies,—
They're chanting still: beneath the fading stars,
   Till every sleeper wakes.

The heavens look cold and sad,
And snow-charged clouds hang o'er the frostbound streams:
Yet people in the fulness of their hearts,
   Have made each other glad.

A CHRISTMAS GREETING.

Take my hearty Christmas greeting,
   On the joyful natal morn;
May all good things sent from Heaven,
   Unto you and yours be borne.

Hark! a thousand joy-bells pealing,
    All proclaim throughout the land,
It is Christmas! all men brothers,
    Shake each other by the hand!

Emulating Christ our Saviour,
    Heart to heart in love be bound;
And the poor ones with our blessing,
    At the plenteous board be found.

May your Christmas-tide be happy,
    Rich with boons that make life fair;
Merry hearts with mirth o'erflowing,
    All untouched by grief or care.

Angel fingers drop from Heaven
    Crystal snow-flakes, pure and bright
Clothing Nature while she's sleeping,
    In her wintry night-robe white.

Berries bright adorn the hedge-rows,
    With the frost-gems all among;
Where the hardy robin cheers us,
    With his welcome winter song.

When the wintry blast is coldest,
    Warmest then our hearts should be;
By the cosy coal-fire glowing,
    Friends unite in festive glee.

Blest ourselves, while blessing others,
    Love and peace will be our share;
Then with hearts in thanks uplifted,
    Welcome in the glad New Year!

HOW TO SPEND CHRISTMAS.

The season should be fraught with joy, then do the best you can
To spend it well, to make it bright, and this should be the plan:—

Go first of all on Christmas morn, and kneel in praise
　　and prayer,
Then lift your voice in hymns of joy, to greet the Saviour
　　there.

In happy homes, old friends and kin should meet from
　　far away.
In "Peace on earth, goodwill to men," should pass the
　　natal day;
To happy be, let heart and hand that day be open wide;
Make others blest, if you would spend a merry Christmas-
　　tide :

Find joy in making others glad, with cheerful heart and
　　voice,
And in the midst of all forget not *why* we all rejoice :
But keep in mind the One whose birth has blest our
　　winter day ;
Let not your hymns be empty sounds—be earnest when
　　you pray.

Nor yet forget the aged, the poor, the sick with weary
　　heart ;
By loving words, and timely gifts, some joy to such
　　impart ;
And look at those in lowly life, if you would be content ;
Then render daily thanks to God, for all the mercies sent.

And if affliction be not nigh, let every one be glad :
At Christmas-time, of all the year, we never should be sad.
But be at peace with all the world, and have a conscience
　　clear ;
In no man's debt, and you will end with joy the good
　　Old Year.

With lightsome heart, you then will join the festive
　　throng with glee,
And be a welcome guest around the laden Christmas-
　　tree—
Be found among the cheery hearts who love the sprightly
　　jest,
And join the music and the dance, and merry games
　　with zest.

At yule-tide while we love the most the warm and cosy hearth,
Let out-door recreation, too, enhance the season's mirth;
To walk, to skate, to ride or drive, and hardy pastimes seek
For youth, if they would have the bloom of health upon their cheek.

Amid your pleasures, be not deaf to what the wise can preach;
Find time for calm reflection, too, on all the good they teach;
Be wise and merry, and each day, fling round on every side
What good you can, and God above, will bless your Christmas-tide.

THE DYING YEAR.

The year has grown old, it is withered and cold,
   'Tis going, with its joy and its sorrow;
And soon we shall greet, the untried, and the sweet,
   Fair infantile year of to-morrow.

Now Time does enrol, on his full-lettered scroll,
   Another account to his keeping:
And soon he'll unfurl, as his wheels swiftly whirl,
   Another blank sheet while we're sleeping.

Then Fate wields her pen, and the fortunes of men
   Sets down, and engraves them for ever;
We cannot erase whatsoe'er she may trace,—
   For she works for the bountiful Giver.

God grant by her side may sweet Mercy preside,
   And what though it cannot unbend her;
Whate'er she decree, that our destinies be,—
   'Twill veil in its wisdom so tender!

But break not the spell of a solemn farewell,
   While gloweth the blazing log-fire;
With God be at peace, ere its pulses shall cease,
   In prayer let the Old Year expire.

The while that we kneel, let our conscience reveal
   The errors, that daily betide us;
Then offer a prayer, that the coming new year
   Bring light from our Father to guide us.

Full many a home may be folded in gloom,
   And many a heart-tie be riven;
And many a face may be missed from its place,
   But think of the loved ones in Heaven!

For the past give a sigh, now the year will soon die,
   Give thanks for the blessings that reach us;
To some it were stern, yet from grief we may learn,
   The beautiful lessons it teaches.

Its visions arise in the black midnight skies,
   And ghosts of its memories olden;
On the walls of the past, its dark shadows are cast,
   And yet it had gleams that were golden!

Yon snow-laden cloud, is its funeral shroud,
   The past like a dream comes before us;
Oh! lead us aright, gracious God, in Thy might,—
   And keep Thou a loving watch o'er us.

TO THE NEW YEAR.

Sweet little cherub, what dost thou bring,
Hidden beneath thy bright little wing?
Sunshine and shadow thou bearest I know,
For such is the fate of all mortals below.

And yet thou art coming light-hearted and gay,
And strewing good wishes around thee to-day;
But thou wilt grow older, thy cares will increase,
Thou canst not be always so young and at peace.

Whate'er be our portion we welcome thee still,
Tho' with every valley thou bringest a hill:
Burdens and crosses, to drop at thy call,—
Thou has plenty of pleasure to balance them all!

Then come little stranger—Recorder of Fate,
Preside at thy post, for we anxiously wait:
Whatever thou bringest, dispense it with care,—
Distribute thine happiness everywhere.

A NEW-YEAR GREETING.

My friends, I wish you one and all,
   A happy, glad, New Year:—
That sorrow may not on you fall,
   But all be bright and fair.

I wish the frail, infirm, and old,
   A happy, peaceful, year:
Protection from the winter's cold,
   Of comforts have their share.

And may the honest toiling poor
   Have strength for Labour's call:
Prosperity, with bounteous store,
   To recompence them all.

To all the little children fair,
   Around the cheerful hearth:
I wish a happy, bright new year,
   To teem with joy and mirth.

Their voices give my heart a thrill,
   God bless each little face!
And may each one be spared to fill
   A noble, useful, place.

In spirit we may meet again,
   To greet another year:
And until then, may you remain
   Beneath our Father's care.

We know not what the coming year
   Is bringing on its wing ;
But let us strive to meekly bear
   The crosses it may bring.

The Young Year's coming new to all,
   With fresh unopened hours ;
Hush! let the Old Year's curtain fall,
   Be silent while it lowers.

RESOLUTIONS FOR THE NEW YEAR.

May these resolutions be kept this New Year;
First, let us be constant in praise and in prayer;
Each night, and each morning, through life as we plod,
Forget not devoutly to kneel to our God.

Next, be well employed, daily duties fulfil,
Whatever our task, do it well, with a will ;
Nor waste precious time, for too swiftly it flies
Go early to bed, that we early may rise.

In all things be temperate, never abuse,
The things that were meant for our rational use ;
Be patient, vile tempers and passions repress,
'Tis selfishness only that leads to excess.

Resolve next, to utter no harsh unkind word,
Invectives too strong, nor let slander be heard ;
Speak only of good, nor infer there is guile,
Far better be silent than others revile.

A good rule is this, for the forthcoming year,
To pay all our debts, and to keep straight and clear;
And if we should find that our income is small,
Then just in proportion our wants should all fall.

All those who are able, and easy can live,
According to means to the poor ones should give ;
The wealthy their riches remember to share,
Thus help all to have a bright happy New Year!

NELLIE'S CHRISTMAS.

She woke in the morning twilight dim,
As the welcome strains of the grand old hymn
Went floating up on the frosty air,
And 'roused the child in her chamber there.
She quickly rose from her little bed,
Then bent her knee, while her prayers she said:
She sought her stocking, which was replete
With Christmas presents, both good and sweet.
Then drest in haste, ere she raised the blind,
While happiest day-dreams filled her mind.
The window curtain she held aside,
And viewed the landscape, so white and wide:
She gazed above at the cold grey skies,
And marked the glow where the sun would rise.
The child in her faith looked up afar,
And sought for the holy mystic star,—
The guiding light that had smiled on earth,
And shown the place of the Saviour's birth.
And then she looked on the lawn below,
Where stood the carollers out in the snow,
Who sung to Nellie how Christ was found,
And gladdened her heart with the joyful sound.
And then she jauntily tript the stair,
And found the room where her parents were;
She lovingly went to each dear one's side
And wished them a merry Christmas-tide.
Then neatly drest in her crimson frock,
She went and answered the postman's knock;
He brought her greetings from many a friend—
The brightest missives the heart can send.
Then breakfast came, and the birds were fed,
By Nellie's hand, with the crumbs of bread.
Then wrapt in furs, and with feet well shod,
She next set out for the House of God;
The church bells rang with a merry sound,
The while she trudged o'er the snow-clad ground:
Beside her mother she entered there,
The temple sacred to praise and prayer;

Where evergreens bright with the berries red,
Were twined 'round pillars, and hung o'erhead.
She heard the pastor's sweet preaching then,
Of "Peace on earth, and good-will toward men."
She joined the hymns, and the anthems grand,
That told of Christ and the "Better Land."
Then forth she went from that sacred dome,
With eager steps to her own loved home :
With a merry heart and a smiling face,
At the well-spread table she took her place :
Of all good things they could well afford,
She there partook, at the Christmas board.
Then forth she went in the snow again,
To where poor people lay low with pain ;
To children sick in the various wards,
She gave her toys, and her books, and cards.
Less favoured they, than our Nellie sweet,
Who came beside them with noiseless feet,
Those poor pale children, that suffering lay,
She happier made on that blessèd day.
And then she hied to her home once more,
Her duteous deeds for the day were o'er.
When tea was over, they sat at night
'Neath lamplight glow, by the fireside bright :
With joyous heart, and with childish glee,
Our Nellie played 'neath the Christmas tree.
And with her young companions gay,
The evening hours were whiled away,
And rest-time found them with hearts content.
A happy day had our Nellie spent.

   *   *   *   *

'Tis New Year's Eve, and the guests are gone,
And in her chamber there kneels alone
Our blue-eyed Nellie, in night-robe white,
Beside her bed, in the calm moonlight :
With head bowed down on the coverlet fair,
She says this prayer for the dying year:

    "Father in love and might,
     Hearken my prayer to-night,
     Here in the dim moonlight,
      And all alone.

I bow on my bended knee,
Lifting my soul to Thee,
Father look down on me,
    From Thy great throne.

Answer my simple prayer,
Teach me this coming year,
Patiently how to bear,
    With every ill.
Keep me from sin away,
Show me each passing day
How I can best obey
    Thy holy will.

Pity this child of Thine,
Suffer Thy light to shine
Into this heart of mine,
    And make me good;
Teach me to serve Thee, Lord,
Grant that Thy gospel word,
Into my mind be stored,
    And understood.

Jesus was once so weak,
Teach me to be as meek,
See that the truth I seek,
    Nor am defiled;
Make me, oh Father, now,
Pure as the falling snow,
And as I older grow,
    A better child.

Well be my future spent,
Teach me to live content;
Thanks for the blessings sent,
    Forgive the past;
Grant that the angels' home,
Far from all earthly gloom,
Over yon starlit dome,
    Be mine at last."

These simple words from her heart she said,
Then rest she sought on her little bed;
At peace with God, and with all the world,
She watched for the New Year being unfurled.
But sleep stole over her senses soon,
While gazing up at the solemn moon:
The heavy lids o'er the blue eyes closed,
She sweetly smiled as she there reposed.

The moonlight fell on her features fair,
And kissed the curls of her golden hair,
Its dusky beams o'er her pillow shed,
A sacred halo around her head.
When midnight bells rang the Old Year's knell,
They rang too late for our little Nell!
Their music welcomed a New Year in,
Unmarked by sorrow, unstained by sin;
And when its light through the window crept,
Our sainted Nellie in peace still slept:
Her soul had fled with the dying year,
Beyond the reach of all earthly care.
Before the dawn of that New Year's day,
The child's bright spirit had passed away:
An angel came on the moonbeam bright,
And bore it up to the Realms of Light!

A CHRISTMAS GIFT.

She daintily tript down the long busy street,
  On a loving mission of bounty bent;
She braved the pitiless wind and the sleet,
  At her Father's bidding she freely went:
Her merciful errand but quickened her feet,
  For she felt that day was being nobly spent.

Her form was in warmest of garments arrayed,
  Not a fear had she for the winter storm;
The happiest smile on her countenance played,
  For the heart within her was young and warm:
The bright touch of health on her cheeks was displayed,
  And in ev'ry line of her lithe young form.

She passed by the poor, and the affluent child,
  As December's daylight began to wane:
She passed by the houses that cheerily smiled,
  And the gay shop windows with lights aflame,
Where the withering breath of old Boreas wild,
  Had congealed the vapour upon the pane.

At last she arrived at a neat, humble cot,
  Where she paused, and knocked at the lowly door;
And when it was opened it showed her a spot,
  With Poverty's seal from its roof to floor;
But oh! from that moment she never forgot,
  The cleanly aspect that cottage wore.

Two worthy old dames, who had better days seen,
  Had resided there since their fortunes fell;
Their poverty fain from the world they would screen,
  They never a tithe of their woes would tell;
And never once pondered on what "might have been,"
  But they trusted God, and felt all was well.

Resigned, and unmurm'ring, in peace they dwelt there,
  And they envied not what the rich can hoard;
Each morsel they had they would lovingly share,
  Contentment smiled on their scanty board;
They cherished each other with sisterly care,
  For love is a lux'ry the poor can afford.

One came to the stranger who stood there so white
  (For the snowflakes lay on her cloak and gown);
She seemed like a ministering angel of light,
  As her Father's bounty she there laid down;
With kind loving words and a smiling face bright,
  It was softly placed in the old hand brown.

Frugality there was allowed not to sleep,
  For the most was made of the smallest crumb;
That sweet Christmas gift made the old woman weep,
  But her thanks for a moment refused to come;
For words will not flow when the feelings lie deep,
  Yet "the eyes will speak when the lips are dumb."

By the hand's warm pressure her joy was exprest,
  And the smile that broke o'er the care-worn face;
Few words did she say, but enough to attest,
  That the maid with sunshine had filled the place;
Thus she went from that cottage rejoicing and blest,
  For she nearer was to the Throne of Grace!

NEW YEAR'S EVE.

Another year has winged its flight,
    Since last we met each other here;
And now we meet again to-night,
    With joyous hearts and words of cheer.

How fast the year has passed away,
    Since last we joined in converse sweet!
Its each alternate night and day
    Has run its course,—'tis now complete.

I see your faces 'round me ranged,
    So happy and so radiant now;
They are the same, though some have changed—
    For Time has touched us on the brow;

But some with such a gentle hand,
    That he has scarcely left a trace:
Where Grief he brought, they left their brand
    Imprinted deeply on the face.

As back we look upon the past,
    Now Memory sees the spots of light:
And where a shadow has been cast,
    It makes the rest appear more bright.

We know not what our fates may be,
    For Mercy deftly holds a screen,
That man the future may not see,
    He is but certain what has been.

All my good wishes go with you
    Into the future, dim and far;
I would that Hope to you were true,
    That Faith may be your guiding star.

Then may we each and all be spared
    To meet again another year,
And all relate how we have fared,
    Without the semblance of a tear.

The year is like a mighty book,
    Which we have made complete to-night;
Each page is full, one backward look
    We've ta'en, before 'tis lost to sight:—

For it will soon be placed away,
    Henceforth 'twill be beyond our grasp;
But ere it leaves us, *let us pray*,—
    Thus close it with a golden clasp!

THE MEETING OF THE YEARS.

Out of the Land of the great Henceforth,
    There came a young beautiful child:
A sweet fair thing, with a snow-tipt wing,
    And it gaily nodded and smiled.

It wore a flowing garment of white,—
    Nearly concealing its form;—
That Mercy had thrown, in a way of her own,
    As a shield from many a storm.

The child was timid, and fresh, and pure,
    And paused on the threshold of Time;
Then it glided in, with a dimpling chin,—
    At the sound of the midnight chime.

It met a veteran, bent and grey,
    Coming out of Time's Temple so slow,
With a mournful look, and he carried a book,
    Which he gave to the child, with a bow.—

The child stept up to the vacant Throne,
    Where the sire had reigned in state:
Then it took his place, with a pleasing grace,
    And opened the Volume of Fate.

HOPE WITH NEW YEAR'S DAWN.

The young year glided in unseen,
   And took its place when all was dark :
From realms of space and time serene,
   Sent here for us to live and mark :
Oh! may we nobly fill its days,
And golden way-posts strive to raise.

Hope, born anew, arose from out
   The first faint dawn-tints in the sky,
On New Year's morn; and gazed about,
   Ere downward it began to fly :
This earth to heaven, with golden thread,
Connecting, as it swiftly sped.

To cheer its lovers waiting here ;
   For they are legion who can feel,
That it doth dry the grief-drawn tear,
   And next to Faith, has power to heal
The broken spirit, bring a balm,
Diffuse a sweet and holy calm :

And buoyant make the drooping heart ;
   'Tis thus we watch with upstrained eyes
Its advent; for it doth impart
   A radiant glow, like that which dyes
The morning's gorgeous mantle bright,
That gives the dawn-clouds rosy light.

Like a white dove thus Hope descends,
   With New Year's dawn 'tis welcomed here
And angel-like, its presence lends,
   To us a foretaste of the Sphere
Unknown to pain ; thus peace it brings,
And sweet contentment 'round us flings.

Delusive 'tis to him who clings
   Too closely to the things of earth :
Forgetting that from heaven it springs
   That from the skies it has its birth ;
Though yester-year it seemed to wane,
It, phœnix-like, can rise again.

To life and toil Hope gives a zest,—
   Makes us hold on, when dark despair
Had near' o'ermastered; 'tis our best
   Attendant through the coming year:
It tinctures all our joys below,
And makes life's current brisker flow.

NEW YEAR REFLECTIONS.

We are passing along through this life below,
And our gracious Father has given us now,
From our futurity's endless store,
A new year, stainless as those before.
Unlived, unmarked, in His hand it lies,
A mystery, pure as the far-off skies;
Its months and days are of virgin white,
And may we fill them, and make them bright
With noble actions, and deeds of love,
So win a blessing from Him above.
Oh! that no record of wrong or sin
Would mar the year we have ushered in!
But may it stand in the ranks of Time
A bright example, unstained by crime;
Whilst grace and goodness its name adorn,
Be honoured by thousands yet unborn!

We are passing along, and the fleeting years
Bring waves upon us of smiles and tears,—
Of joy and gladness, of grief and woe,
In lights and shadows they come and go.
As Time glides by on his pinions fast,
The old year sinks in the silent past:
'Tis but a memory, never again
Will come its pleasures, nor care, nor pain.
How wise is God's considerate plan,
That He permitteth the mind of man,
To recall past joys; with a vivid power
We live again through each long-past hour
Of dear delights; and they o'er and o'er
So real and forceful can flash before

The mental vision. While mortal pain
Once felt in passing, comes ne'er again
At man's own will; and it must we know
Be done in mercy to us below.
But Memory keeps through the lapse of years
Our bygone sorrows embalmed in tears;
Subdued and softened, she holds them still
And brings them forth at her own sad will;
But smoothed by Time, like the pebbles grey
Upon the rivulet's well-worn way.

We are passing along, and we may not stay.
'Tis birth and growth, then slow decay;
Time works his changes, as one by one,
The seasons come, and the days speed on.
Now looking back on the vanished year,
The gleams of light through its mists appear;
Though rich it were in some memories sweet,
In works of goodness 'twas incomplete.
And though the past we can ne'er erase,
May we illumine this year of grace;
And so improve on the one now dead,
Make this revered when its days are fled.

Farewell old year! We have watched it die
In the arms of Winter, 'neath grey-hued sky;
Its young successor we gladly greet.
Unknown, untrodden, it is but meet,
To bid it welcome; and may it bring
To you, dear friends, on its glowing wing
Bright gifts from Heaven; and through it fall
God's sweetest blessings upon you all!
May no misfortunes its annals dim,
Impressed in memories sad and grim;
May no dark shadows upon you frown,
But God's approval good efforts crown;
His holy light through the new year shine,
His peace be with you, and love divine!

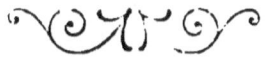

A PRAYER FOR THE NEW YEAR.

Father of righteousness, Father of light,
Oh! in Thy graciousness hear us to-night,—
Bend in Thy mercy to list to our prayer,—
Give us new hearts with the coming New Year!

Father, forgive all our sins of the past,
Grant that all guilt from our souls may be cast;
Look down in pity on us from Thy Throne,
Hear us! nor leave us to wander alone!

Father of goodness, upon Thee we call,
Ne'er to forsake us whatever befall:
Deign to look down from Thy glory on High,
Hearken Thy people in penitence cry!

Hallowèd Father, may this be Thy will,—
Guide us, and bless us, and keep us from ill:
In Thy beneficence, Father Above,
Lead us aright, in Thy goodness and love!

Guardian Father, oh! this would we ask,
Give us but strength for our labour and task:
Strength to be kept from the dark sinful way,—
Strength to resist all temptation, we pray!

Merciful Father, upon Thee we lean,
Give us Thy guidance, Thou mighty Unseen!
Help and support us, and teach us oh Lord,
How to obey, and to follow Thy Word.

Father Omnipotent! Thee we implore,
Soothe the afflicted, and care for the poor!
Fear we Thy Hand when in vengeance it lowers,
Thanks for the blessings, oh God! that are ours.

Help us to keep good resolves that we make,—
Shrink from all baseness, and live for Thy sake:—
Love one another, and lift through Thy Hand,
Some of the shadows that darken the land.

Worshipful Father! Whose name we revere,
Soften the road for Thy people while here;
Make us, good Keeper, more pure, that a place
Each may deserve, in Thy Kingdom of Grace.

Dark is the past with man's evil and wrongs,
Pure is the future, to Thee it belongs;
Now Thou art sending another New Year,
White and unlived in, unblemished and fair!

Father, we pray that this opening New Year,
When it shall close, on its annals may bear
Records sublimer than those that have gone,
Bright with the traces of noble deeds done.

Father of glory! oh! let us pursue,
Nought but the good, and be steadfast and true;
When this New Year shall drop into the past,
Let it shine forth with a light that will last:—

May it stand out, when 'tis past, from the rest,
Clothed with a halo so sacred and blest;
Better than aught we have passed through before,
Spent in the service of One we adore.

Lord in Thy wisdom, oh! show us the way,
How we may best Thy commandments obey;
Show us our duty, nor let us depart,
Put into each of us now a new heart.

Bountiful Father, we ask at this hour,—
Naught is too much for Thy infinite power,
Make us anew, we beseech Thee to-night,
Shed on the heads of Thy pilgrims Thy light.

Great is Thy love for Thy children we know,
Deeper, far deeper, than that we bestow
On one another; oh! Spirit of Love,
May we all merit Thy favour Above.

Father we crave Thou to us wilt reveal,
Knowing Thou knowest how worthless we feel,—
Daily Thy presence; dear Master Divine,
Lift up the erring and call us all Thine!

Earnestly, hopefully, Father we plead,
Wilt Thou befriend us ?—protection we need ;
Suffer us all to inherit that peace,
Born of a conscience, when virtues increase.

Out of the future the young year we see,
Comes full of mysteries known but to Thee ;—
Rich with fresh hopes its first moments appear,
Be it a blest and a happy New Year!

Father in heaven, we kneel to Thee now,
Hear our petition! as humbly we bow ;—
Make us all worthy a home with Thee there,
Kneeling, we trust Thee, and greet the New Year!

RANDOM RHYMES.

PAST AND PRESENT.

A conversation between Laura and her Grandma.

Laura. "I'm going to be married dear Grandmama soon;
   Our wedding is going to take place in next June:"
Gran. "You! going to be married? you silly young thing!
   Such foolish ideas from your mind you must fling;
   But nowadays girls are so forward and pert,
   For most of them seem so determined to flirt
   When *I* was a girl, sixty years ago now,
   I had not your pleasures, you'd say I was "slow;"
   I never played tennis, nor skated, nor danced."—
Laura. "O tell me dear Granny, how then has it chanced
   Those white satin slippers you came to possess,
   And yon fine brocaded low-bodiced white dress?
   You showed them me once, I remember it well,
   You said that you'd worn them when you were a girl.
Gran. "Yes Laura, I did, now the act I recall,
   Yet certain I am I ne'er danced at a ball;
   I bought them to wear at a party at home,
   When just a few *girls* to my birthday would come
   I never was one who was fond of display,
   And thus the fine things were soon treasured away.
   A dance is not now what it used to be *then*,
   'Tis made up of parties of maidens and men;
   And those who indulge in an innocent dance,
   Sometimes are led into a maze of romance;
   Most truly this is an "electrical age,"
   Doing things with despatch is becoming the rage;
   And *love* even now soon ignites to be sure,
   But love soon aflame is not bound to endure.
   In *my* younger days, then a maid was a maid,
   I minded my work, and was modest and staid
   I never once flirted, nor cared for the men;"

Laura. "Yet Grandpapa courted and married you then?
Gran. " Yes dearie he did, but 'twas all his own doing,
   I kept at my spinning, while *he* did the wooing;
   He followed me long, but I kept him at bay,"—
Laura. "But Granny, you let him at last have his way?"
Gran. "I did my dear child, when I found that his love
   Was pure as the dew that descends from above:
   I tested him long, ere I gave him my heart,
   And sad was the day he was called to depart.
   But *you* are too young to be married child yet,
   The words of your lover now try to forget;
   And drive from your head his nonsensical talk.
   It seems but last week that I learned you to walk!
   You stay a few years in your unfettered state,
   And don't be afraid you will then be too late;
   For marriage brings bushels of care in its train,
   In fact all my days I would single remain,
   If I were as young and as pretty as you;"
Laura. "You *once* were, then Granny why did not you do?"
Gran. "O Laura! 'tis rude to ask questions, I thought
   That you better manners long since had been taught:
   I was not encircled like you my dear child, [
   The love of my parents upon me ne'er smiled:
   They went to their rest in my infantile days,
   And left me alone in the world's thorny ways:
   A brother's and sister's sweet love I knew not,
   A life among strangers was then my sad lot:
   And when to woman's estate I had grown,
   I wanted to have a nice home of my own."
Laura. "And *I* want one Granny now just same as you,
   For I am now twenty, and he twenty-two."
Gran. "But *you're* no excuse to be married my dear,
   You've got a good home, and kind relatives here:
   And marriage for you is a really bad plan,
   To leave your mamma for the sake of a man!"
Laura. "But Granny look here, though Pa does not com-
   He has plenty to do with us all to maintain; [plain,
   And when I leave home I relieve poor Papa,
   And Clara and Harry will see to Mamma:
   Then Edgar has said he is dying for me,
   And thus 'tis a charity, do you not see?—

	I save a dear life, and I save Papa's purse,
	So things will be better, instead of being worse :
	I make Edgar happy, and spare Papa's store,
	That you and the others may all have the more!"
Gran.	"O *that* is your logic, you clever young miss,
	But don't think that wedlock is nothing but bliss :
	It is my dear child a most serious thing,
	'Tis not all so fair as the flowers in spring :
	Then look well around, ere you venture to leap,
	For under the surface stern duty lies deep ;
	Consider things well, for there's time enough yet,
	Or when 'tis too late you may some day regret.
	I hope that young Edgar is true and sincere,
	Look well at his heart ere he takes you my dear :
	Learn all his past life, and reject him my child,
	If *once* he has walked in the ways of the wild ;
	And if his young life has been all that it should,
	He'll bear to be tested, if honest and good :
	But if he recoils at the questions you ask,
	Be certain that something lies under the mask :
	Mind too that the lad has a blessing in you,
	Let wisdom and prudence your conduct pursue ;
	Whatever the portion that falls to your share,
	Remember you always must *bear* and *forbear*."
Laura.	"I'll promise dear Granny to be a good wife,
	My love for my Edgar will cease but with life :
	But how you mistrust him, dear Grandmama, when
	I know he's a jewel, a prince among men !
	He vows that when once he my husband is made,
	He'll love and protect me through sunshine and [shade]."
Gran.	"'Tis all very well for a lover to vow,
	I've known them to break them too often ere now ;
	Though now you think Grandma is doting and old,
	You'll value my words when I'm lifeless and cold.
	I think Laura dear, I have now had my "say,"
	You've got my advice, but may go your own way :
	I only have warned you dear child to beware,
	And not to go blindfold right into a snare :
	For life is too earnest, no shadow or dream,
	And men are deceitful, and not what they seem.
	Then marriage they say is a lottery, child,
	And when to the altar we once are beguiled,

          We all take our chance, be it better or worse;
          To some 'tis a blessing, to others a curse:
          But here is a truth which we cannot disguise,
          That fifty draw blanks where there's one draws a prize!"
Laura. "But *you've* tried it Grandma, and don't seem to rue?"
Gran. "Because child my partner was noble and true:
          A man in a hundred was Grandpapa, dear,
          And go the land o'er you'll not find his compeer."
Laura. "I've found him in Edgar dear Granny, you mind
          I draw a first prize when I wed him, you'll find;
          He's good and sincere, and you *know* that he is,
          And talk as you like, I am going to be his!"
Gran. "Well child, I suppose you must do as you please,
          But love was worth more in the old days than these!"

YORKSHIRE FACTORY GIRLS.

They rise at morn, with cheerful hearts,
    While factory bells are ringing;
And make towards the lofty mills,—
    Their shawls around them clinging.

With dresses neat, and clattering clogs
    Though wet and wild the weather,—
They trudge contentedly to work,
    In joyous groups together.

In winter-time, at early morn
    So dark, and chill, and dreary.
Respond they to the mill-bell's call,
    With faces bright and cheery.

They pride themselves in well-done work,
    And in their prompt attendance;
And draw their weekly recompense
    With native independence.

On Sundays see them in their pride,
    With neat and shining tresses;
Fine things they wear; and in the style
    Are all their well-earned dresses!

They love a happy song or jest,
    By way of recreation;
And they enjoy a hearty laugh,
    And social conversation.

Go where you will, throughout the land,
    Amongst all creeds and classes,
None will excel in face and form
    These bonny Yorkshire lasses!

AN OLD MAID.

When I was a girl, I remember it well,
    For I had not the head of a sage;
I wanted to grow, and look older you know
    By far, than I did, for my age;
I wanted to be a grown woman you see,
    And did all I possibly could,
To try to appear as if older, 'tis queer
    When youthful, we most of us should.
My age I then told just as free and as bold,
    As girls will all do for a while;
I boasted of mine till I reached twenty-nine,
    But there I stood still!— you may smile.
And ever since then, I've concealed from the men
    The date, and the year of my birth;
I never shall own, it will only be known,
    When I have departed from earth!
I fain would conceal the slight traces that steal,
    On what was my once " marble brow";
For to tell you the truth, I am " past my first youth,
    I really must own to that now.
I never have met with my ideal as yet,
    Though I so long single have stayed;

I've done with romance, you may see at a glance
  I am what people call "an old maid!"
Of suitors 'tis true I have had just a few,
  But none that I'd link with my fate;
Some asked me to wed, but I loftily said,
  "Not yet,"—for I wanted to wait.
Some praised my fair face, but I kept them in place,
  Whenever they made an advance;
With one I'd have had, it was equally bad,
  For he did'nt once give me the chance!
My real lover died, and it can't be denied
  That his death filled my heart with regret:
I grieved for a time, for he went in his prime,
  And I cherish his memory yet.
And thus for a while, with a satisfied smile—
  Though scorning attentions men paid—
I haughtily said, with a toss of my head,
  "I never will be an old maid!—
To sit at my tea, with a cat on my knee,
  And tell all the gossip I'd heard:—
And never be seen but in spectacles green,
  The prospect seems really absurd!—
And then they're so prim, with some old-fashioned whim,
  And always so awfully "slow";
Ah! had I then known I should be one, I own
  I should'nt have railed at them so.
When I could not find just the man to my mind,
  I began to be rather afraid—
As years kept going by, and no offers had I—
  That I *might* have to be an old maid.
But that is all past, and I *am* one at last,
  Ah yes, and a merry one too;
I've a plentyful purse, so I might be much worse,
  And I always find plenty to do.
I've a nice tabby cat, you be certain of that,
  I never feel lonely and cold;
I can sit at my ease, and do just as I please,
  For I have not a husband to scold.
With nephews and nieces my pleasure increases,
  They love to come see me, and still
When aught goes amiss, then the best of it is
  I can send them away at my will!

When assistance they want, it is "go and fetch Aunt,'
   They know I will give them my aid;
I'm ready to call, and make out for them all.
   So you should'nt despise an old maid.
Then never despair all you maidens so fair,
   For I am content, and am blest;
I'm happier far, than some married folks are,
   I laugh and I sing with the best.
There's much we can do in this world it is true,
   Though wedlock may be not our lot;
Some old maids have wrought, both in deeds and in
   Much good, that will ne'er be forgot.   [thought,
I try to fulfil with a hearty goodwill.
   The duties that on me are laid;
And let you all see that there really can be
   A useful and happy old maid!

"THAT NAUGHTY DEMON DRINK!"

(CHILD'S TEMPERANCE RECITATION.)

One thing I now will shun I vow,
   Though I am but a child;
Strong drink, I mean, which long has been,
   A demon fierce and wild;
To shame and sin it draws one in,
   And who so low would sink?
Oh! I for one will always shun,
   That naughty demon "Drink!"

When I grow tall, I'll show you all,
   The good I'll do some day;
I'll do my best, to "down" the pest,
   And chase it right away;
There's power in me, could you but see
   Though this you little think;
I'll bring it out, that it may rout,
   That naughty demon, "Drink!"

If they should try to tempt me, why
  I'll always turn aside ;
And say them nay, for who shall say
  What evil, drink may hide ?
And then at last, when youth is past,
  I'll have more gold to clink ;
Then those who waste their coins to taste,
  That naughty demon "Drink!"

And all you here, companions dear,
  Come join me in the right ;
Though we are small, yet if we all,
  But try with all our might,
To lend a hand to those who stand
  So near to ruin's brink ;
We yet may save, all those who crave,—
  That naughty demon "Drink!"

Say what you will, it does some ill,
  It is our greatest foe ;
Then you and I, from now must try
  To fight, and lay it low ;
Such works of love, to God Above
  Will form a closer link ;
Then let us pray, that we may slay—
  That naughty demon "Drink!"

"SPEAK OF A MAN AS YOU FIND HIM."

When meet you a man whom you think is no sham,
  And if a staunch friend you should prove him ;—
If straight are his ways, then give him your praise,
  Win others to know, and to love him ;
The mischevious tongue would fain do him wrong,
  Heed not his detractors behind him ;
Say what you think true, and you never will rue,
  But speak of a man as you find him.

The mind that is base is revealed in the face,
    And so is the one that is narrow;
Some men may be good, but their " plebian " blood,
    Is scorned by the mean and the shallow :
We all have a fault, so as well 'tis to halt,
    Before we condemn one another;
Think well of a man, then, as long as you can,
    Until some grave fault you discover.

But prove it well then, ere the man you condemn,
    Be sure that your censure he merits :
And probe well the case, look the facts in the face,
    False rumour stern justice discredits.
And lend him your ear, that himself he may clear,
    'Tis always the fairest and surest :
For vile tongues we know have often ere now,
    Reviled e'en the best and the purest.

The heart that is pure can no slander endure,
    Suspicion the guileless ne'er reaches :
Their trust's oft betrayed, they're in base coin repaid,
    Experience stern lessons such teaches :
The ignorant mind, of the type unrefined,
    Too oft is the harbour for slander :
'Twould have us believe that all hearts will deceive,
    All people from virtue now wander.

From Envy is bred, and by Malice is spread,
    Untruths that are really appalling;
We all need to mind, or in some way we find,
    We under their influence are falling :
Speak well if you can, 'tis a capital plan,
    To raise some poor sister or brother :
Be silent for aye if you only can say
    Disparaging words of another.

If proved 'tis to you, that 'tis only too true,
    What gossips had whispered about him ;
Then tell him I say, in a straightforward way,
    The reason you slight him, or doubt him :
And if you should deem he deserves no esteem,
    And merits your friendship no longer,
Then shun him say I ! and your pity defy,
    For duty must ever be stronger!

But never be friends till his ways he amends.
    And seek not again to approach him ;
Unless with a view, his bad traits to subdue,
    As teacher to firmly reproach him.
If you win him back to the straight narrow track,
    And make him of friendship deserving ;
If rescued is he, then your efforts will be
    Approved by the Father we're serving.

THE COUNTRY COUSIN.

"GOOD-NIGHT, my dear cousin, I really must go,
You press me to stay, but I still answer 'no' :—
For if so much longer with you I remain,—
I shall just be too late for the nine o'clock train.

" And you know what a long lonely road I've to go ;
When I step from the train, I must plod thro' the snow ;
But I'm glad it is moonlight, for that is a boon,—
I thought I would come while there shone the new moon.

" But you in the town do not give it a thought,
You *here*, set our country contrivance at nought ;
Your streets are well paved, and with gas all alight,
So you don't know the value of *moonshine* so bright.

"And you my dear cousin, must come to see me ;
Now when will you come ?—to-day,—let—me—see ;
It is Thursday to-day, will you come next week soon ?
You then will enjoy the full light of this moon."

" You really can't come quite so early, you say ;
Well then, my dear cousin, you set your own day ;
I shall gladly receive you some fine afternoon,—
But be sure to come when there's light from the moon !

" And now I *must* leave you, 'tis time I should go ;
Remember me kindly to Auntie you know ;
I shall have a nice walk, for the moon is so bright,
So now my dear cousin, I wish you good-night !"

"WHAT MUST I WEAR?"

"Oh, what must I do, and what must I wear?
I *must* be in fashion, or people will stare;
I noticed Miss Lighthead has got a new hat,
She looked so bewitching, *I'll* have one like that;
Except the red feather, I'll have one pale blue,
'Twill look more becoming, *I* think so, don't *you*?

" Oh, where must I go, and what shall I wear?
I'm bored with being here for my outings are rare,
It's such a nice day, I will put on, I think,
My hat and fur jacket, and go to the rink ;
They'll show to advantage a day such as this,
I'll outshine the others, oh, won't that be bliss !

"Oh, how do I look? and what must I wear?
This dress is old-fashioned, I had it last year;
I don't think it suits my complexion and height.
I always look best in a dress rather light;
I'll wear it no more ;—but now stay, when I think,
I will, when it's altered, and re-trimmed with pink :

"Oh, how did she look? and what did she wear?
I'm longing for details, describe them with care;
Then say if she's slender, a blonde, or brunette?
If pretty, no doubt she's an awful coquette ;
What shape was her bonnet? and how was her hair,
They say she's in style, but I don't think she's fair !"

She wore a nice dress, that was simple and neat;
Her face beamed with smiles that were kindly and
She dressed like a prudent and sensible girl, [sweet;
Befitting her means and her station so well ;
Her manners were all that a maiden's should be,
So modest, and yet unaffected and free.

Now some of you maidens who take such delight
In talking of dresses from morning till night,
Come listen a moment, and take my advice;
Let not your sole object be " how to look nice ;"
Be more intellectual, then you will find
You nobler will be, with a well-cultured mind.

Oh, maidens, dear maidens, I wish you'd think less,
Of outward appearance,—the style of your dress;
Don't *let* fashion be your ambition and aim,
Or you will be proud, and conceited, and vain:
But make it your object the mind to adorn,
'Twill shine when your trinkets and dresses are worn.

To make then your lives be the better enjoyed,
Be ever with good useful work well employed:
But frivolous finery, cast it away!
Let thought be engaged in a nobler way:
For some of you girls, if you'll only confess,
Are given to thinking *too much* of your dress.

A LADY'S LEAP-YEAR PROPOSAL.

My very dear Sir, now to you I aver,
   I've liked and admired you for long:
My presence you've sought, till I've actually thought
   Our love has been mutually strong.
You've said for a while, how you've lived on my smile,—
   Been happy to know I was nigh:
Your low tender tone, when we've wandered alone,
   The glance of your fine speaking eye,
All tell me a tale: but I cannot prevail,
   Upon you to say the one word:
Sometimes you're inclined, but you don't speak your mind,
   Such diffidence seems most absurd!
Though you've not confessed, I've your sentiments guessed
   By signs has your love been disclosed:
Oftimes and again, I have tried you in vain,
   And yet you have never proposed!
I fear you are shy, so I really must try,
   And show what a woman can do;
This year I've the chance, so I'll make the advance,
   And pop the great question to you!
Then will you be mine? would you like to resign
   The life of a bachelor free,—
Its pleasures and pains, and its losses and gains,
   And live and be happy with me?

Don't open your eyes, as if feigning surprise,
   As often we fair maidens do ;
And say with concern, when my meaning you learn,
   "Oh ! this is so sudden of you !"
Just say " yes " or " no," that my fate I may know,
   Be truthful, whatever you do ;
Be candid I pray, in which-ever you say,
   For have I not been so with you ?
Then say what you think, nor too modestly shrink,
   For fear that your words may offend ;
If me you reject, I shall always respect
   Your pluck, and shall still be your friend ;
But if you will take this bold offer I make,
   I'll give both my hand and my heart ;
If you're not averse, now " for better for worse,"
   To claim me " till death us do part."
I promise you this, if my fortune it is
   To thus be your help-meet for life ;
For Love's own sweet sake, I'm determined I'd make
   A loving, and dutiful wife !

POMP AND VANITY.

    "O wad some Pow'r the giftie gi'e us
    To see oursel's as others see us !"—*Burns.*

In a northern county's proud old town,
That now to a thriving port has grown,
There stands a beautiful house of prayer,—
The church of God, in its glory there ;
Wherein the worship of Him should be,
In prayer devout on the bended knee ;
Should be, alas ! for the soul of man,
He has gone astray since the world began ;
To most it is but a meeting place,
With scarce a thought for the Throne of Grace.

High on the roof of this church one day,
In coloured plumage, so bright and gay ;
Was seen a peacock, with outspread tail,
Like a stately ship, with expanded sail !

It seemed to think that it cast a charm,
As it stood erect in the sunshine warm:
Then strutted on in the fair sunlight,
That showed its gorgeous feathers bright.
It looked imperious, flaunting there,
With its head held high with the proudest air:
And the bird looked down with an actual frown,
On the murky roofs of the good old town;—
Surveyed the whole with disdainful eye,
As it perched on the topmost ridge so high;
Then walked about and its charms displayed.
The bird was having a church parade!
The folks looked up, and they all averred
It was the proudest, gaudiest bird!
To choose that spot before those below,
God's house of prayer! for its pompous show :
" Vain bird!" said they, " 'tis a great disgrace,
To flaunt thyself on that sacred place!"

* * * * *

The scene is changed :—it is Sabbath morn,
And on the breezes is softly borne.
The sound of bells, from that old church tower,
To tell to all it is service hour.
Towards it now in their best array,
The goodly citizens wend their way;
Behold! there comes with a measured tread,
A host of men, in their coats of red,
Adorned with white;—they are soldiers fine,
And form a long and imposing line:
Each wears his sword, and his high cockade.
The *men* are having a church parade!
They move along, with their forms erect,
While all the ladies so grandly decked,
In costly, beautiful, new attire,
Those martial uniforms all admire.
They pass the portals, and enter there,
With solemn aspect, the house of prayer:
When all are seated, in long straight rows,
Each one to God for a moment bows;
Then casts sly glances around them each,
And when the parson begins to preach,

They *try* to listen, for they so prim,
Seem all attention, good folk to him;
But all the time are their thoughts astray,
And wander far from his words away!
The ladies glance at the soldiers there,
While the soldiers stare at the ladies fair;
As each one sits like a stately queen;
They go to *see*, and in turn *be seen*;
While each is conscious of how she looks,
They scan each other behind their books;
They join in singing, and *seem* to pray,
All parrot-like, in a formal way;
Some pray in earnest, but *most*, I fear
Are hypocritical, insincere!
If truth be told of that brilliant host,
'Twas of each other they thought the most;
And of themselves, and their garments fine,
'Twas *not* of God, and of things divine.
The service ends, and they all file out,
But heaven has opened its waterspout;
They dash along, but their clothes are drenched,
Their pomp and ardour is quickly quenched;
Their lace hangs limp, and their feathers drop,
Their drabbled dresses the pavements mop;
With smiles all gone, and with faces wry,
They gaze aloft at the weeping sky;
The rain has ended their flaunting show,
Which all was vanity, now they know!

*　　　*

Oh! which sinned deepest now, man, or bird?
He censured it, as you all have heard;
But which was vainest? I answer "man!"
Refute it now if your conscience can?
And if you're needing a further proof,
The bird when perched on the old church roof,
And choosing it to the church-yard sod,
Not once pretended to worship God.
And though its feathers it there displayed,
They were its *own*, and by nature made;
Man's clothes were made from the lower herds,
While wings and feathers of poor slain birds

Adorned the ladies' new bonnets fine,
That ne'er were made by the Hand divine.
Man scorned the bird, but he needs to halt,
For he committed the greatest fault;
Such mock religion *I* think profane,
'Tis only taking God's name in vain!

A CYNIC'S OPINION OF THE "NEW WOMAN."

Behold! the "new woman" is coming apace!
Athletic in figure, with resolute face;
In rational dress, is she coming to stay?
With firmness of purpose she's pushing her way.

Behold she has mounted her "bike" for a ride,
She's wearing her bloomers, and sitting astride!
Her limbs are unhampered with feminine skirts,
She loves her cravats, her coats, collars, and shirts.

If she and a male-friend are out for a round,
The one with the other we nearly confound!
The "new woman's" dress now has reached such a pitch,
'Tis difficult often, to tell which is which!

She leaves her home circle and feels no remorse,
She'd rather be riding her fast iron horse!
To spin on her cycle for miles is her plan.
The "new woman" beats from the field the "old man."

This up-to-date woman, with masculine airs,
Braves coarsest of jeers, and the rudest of stares;
'Tis not her strong point to be ultra-refined,
The "new woman's" pride is the strength of her mind.

She stoops o'er her cycle though shoulders grow round,
Though oft she falls from it, and sprawls on the ground;
She works at it hard, all her strength to display,
Her feminine attributes losing each day.

For modesty now is a virtue most rare,
Too forward and fast is this amazon fair;
Machines do the work that was woman's of yore,
Invention has brought this new being to the fore.

She manages just to keep out of the inns,
But visits her club when she goes on her spins;
She smokes cigarettes, and talks slang when she can,—
In manners and speech tries to be like a man.

She has several methods of showing her charms,
She sculls her own boat till she hardens her palms;
She rides with her brothers, the first in the chase,
She drives her own ponies, but this with more grace.

Gymnastics, and shooting, and cricket, she tries.
Hard work, if called play, she but seldom denies;
In gaiters and "knickers," and breast-shield arrayed,
Defying decorum, at football she's played!

If you would arouse her with words that will vex,
Just tell her she's one of the "weak softer sex;"
Then, if you're a man, ere the words are well said,
She'll retort that *you're* softer than *she* - in the *head*!

Look out! wise young man of the old-fashioned school,
Beware! or she'll certainly make you a fool;
The new woman's coming! nor will she turn back,
She'll over you ride, if you stand in her track!

THE SAME ON THE "NEW MAN."

The up-to-date "male" the "new man" shall be dubbed,
By woman he likes to be petted and snubbed;
He thinks it a favour to sit at her feet,
Make him but her slave, and his joy is complete.

She knows well the powers to her sex that belong,
The key to his heart is the tip of her tongue;
She knows by that weapon what game she can kill,
He soon falls a victim, and oft 'gainst his will.

Man grows more effeminate each passing hour,
As woman is wielding her wonderful power:
The first and the foremost she's striving to be,
He'll fall, when she gets to the top of the tree!

He's vain and conceited, and selfish as well,
The money he squanders, no mortal can tell:
He's fond of excitement, whatever its cost,—
Must have some amusement, if not, he is lost!

He thinks the " new woman " his rival, for sure,
Her clever progression he yet must endure;
She makes him more feeble and finicking grow,
He fears to her absolute rule he must bow.

But when he's in love, he's an object indeed,
He always will let his beloved take the lead;
Delighted he is when she's holding the sway,
In great things and small, then she gets her own way.

She sees through him right to the core of his heart,
Her glance thrills with joy, or with pain makes it smart;
In varying moods with his love she can play,
Her every caprice he will gladly obey.

She just knows the value of all her sweet smiles,
She reckons him up, with her womanly wiles;
He's woman's inferior, feels he too oft,
He's proud to be called by her " silly," and " soft!"

The budding " new man," ever grateful is he,
If she will permit him her escort to be;
To render her homage whenever he can,
To pose as her servant, delights the " new man!"

Though he all the while is the butt of her wit,
He deems he is honoured if him she will skit!
He even seems pleased when she laughs him to scorn,
For love makes him simple, if so he's not born!

But when he is married we pity him most,
When he of his freedom no longer can boast:
Meek, humble, and patient, he sits in the nook,
While minding the baby, and trying to cook!

His wife, the " new woman," she usurps the " lords,
By mounting the rostrum, and sitting on " Boards,"
At meetings and lectures, and concerts and balls,
Or "biking" and "shopping," or paying her calls.

If he should revolt, would from serfdom be freed,
Most dearly he pays for his grievous misdeed;
He's henpecked, belittled, far more than before,
And made such mean conduct to deeply deplore.

Poor hapless " new man," how I pity his state!
He longs to assert himself now, when too late;
He needs to stand firm, nor his courage let cool,
Or else we must call him a faint-hearted fool!

THE QUEEN'S JUBILEE AT NORWOOD GREEN.

One glorious week in lovely June
   Was festive on the village green;
For young and old turned out to keep
   The Jubilee of our good Queen.
Said one old dame who forward came,
   In Sunday garments drest:—
" Mun Norrad Green, to honour t' Queen
   Is dooing it little best."

She spoke the truth, for all around
   Hung flags and coloured streamers bright;
And music lent its cheering charm,
   To every one's intense delight;
The young were gay, in fine array,
   And danced with pride and zest;
True, Norwood Green for England's Queen,
   Was doing its little best.

The village Queen drove past in state,
   Beneath a sunshade large and gay;
Then pent-up loyal feeling burst,—
   For cheered she was upon the way

Sweet maids were there, both young and fair,
  Who many charms possest;
All Norwood Green for England's Queen,
  Was doing its little best.

The women all had " fragrant " tea,
  'Twas " finely flavoured too," they said;
And out upon the village green,
  The tables were with good things spread:
Blue skies above smiled down in love,
  Upon each joyous guest;—
For Norwood Green for England's Queen,
  Was doing its little best.

And moving in the rustic crowd,
  Some local " leading lights " there were:
To whom were due the thanks of all—
  The main-spring of the whole affair:—
Each dame and maid they happy made,
  And by their bounty blest;
So Norwood Green for England's Queen,
  Was doing its little best.

With sports the time was passed away,
  The children played their games in glee;
And all unbound with one accord,
  To celebrate the Jubilee:
" We'st niver see t' Queen's Jubilee
  Agean," they all confess'd;
So Norwood Green for our good Queen,
  Has done its very best!

" THREE THINGS."

These sayings you perchance have heard
  Repeated many a time:
Yet some may not, so here they are,—
  I've put them into rhyme.

"Three things a woman should be like,
  And yet *unlike* should be;"
If you are curious now to know,
  I'll mention all the three.

She should be like the townhall clock,
  Keep punctual time, 'tis clear;
And yet *unlike* that clock, for all
  The town her voice to hear.

And then she should be like a snail,
  Within her house should stay;
Yet *not* like it, to carry all
  Upon her back, we say.

Then she should like an echo be,
  Speak but when spoken to;
Yet *not* like it, to *always* have,
  The final word, 'tis true.

These sayings were in Grandma's days,
  And things were different then;
Before the modern women came,
  To stand beside the men.

BLACKPOOL'S ATTRACTIONS.

Go look at its palaces, lofty and splendid,
  Whose domes glitter bright 'neath the clear sunny sky
The Muses find haunts in those beautiful temples,
  And lend them a charm that you cannot deny.
Then turn your eyes westward — what is there before you?
  A sight that will charm in the highest degree;
It fades not, it fails not, and wants no renewing
  A whole wealth of glory — the wide open sea!

Go watch its broad billows come swirling and breaking,
  And bearing the ozone so bracing and sweet;
They playfully flow up the steep to approach you,
  And creamy-white foam-flakes they fling at your feet.

And when it is ebbing, behold to its margin
    The wide stretch of sand is a playground so free;
The fine open beach has a host of attractions,
    While yet in the distance there gleams the bright sea!

Go visit the drama in all its perfection,
    Each artiste excels in a well-chosen role;
Go hearken the music in scenes operatic,
    Which ravish the senses, and enters the soul;
So many resorts there are open around you,
    And each worth a visit, you all will agree:
Go see them, and yet you'll be bound to acknowledge
    The greatest attraction of all is the sea!

Go walk on the cliffs in the cool of the morning,
    Inhale the fresh breeze as you tread the green turf:
Descend if you like, to the shingle below you,
    Among the grey boulders all kissed by the surf:
You've heard the sweet music of art so enchanting,
    But here you have Nature's wild melodies free:
Oh! sweeter, and sadder, and deeper the spirit,
    Of music that breathes in the waves of the sea!

Once look at the sea when the sun is declining,
    One glance, and behold you're transfixed to the spot:
When seen in the height of its heavenly splendour,
    A sunset at Blackpool is never forgot.
At night there bursts forth all the blue lights electric,
    Enhancing the beauty of all things you'll see:
A guide to the homeward-bound steamboats, and making
    Look lonely and grander the dark solemn sea.

Then there is the newest of power impelling,
    With magical forces, the beautiful cars;
And truly it seems, so the world is progressing,
    The highroad of science is now without bars:
Here all the new methods of swift locomotion,
    And latest sensations well tested can be;
But what is most healthful and far more delightful,
    And grandest of all is a sail on the sea.

Go look at the two noble piers and extensions,
    The elements bravely they seem to defy
Like Ajax of old; and confront they as boldly
    The Storm King, whene'er he descends from the sky;
Go tread the pier decks, if you love not the motion
    Of sailing, and yet o'er the ocean would be;
The essence of life and of health is around you,
    So fresh and untainted, the breath of the sea!

Go see the tall Tow'r, whence the view is delightful,
    The Big Wheel, the Gardens, where Pleasure is Queen;
Though these may have rivals in places more inland,
    'Tis rarely we know that their equals are seen;
But not in the cities, not even for riches,
    Is seen the one sight that fills thousands with glee:
The acme of splendour, there ever unrivalled—
    The glorious view of the limitless sea!

"AUNTIE."

    Auntie, Mamma's maiden sister,
        Always ready to attend
    On Mamma, and to assist her,—
        Always is the children's friend.

    Auntie has a form so slender,
        And has such a youthful face.
    You would think Mamma the elder;—
        Such in truth is not the case.

    Loving, kind, and ever willing,
        Helping Mamma how to plan;
    Into youthful hearts instilling
        All the goodness that she can.

    Was she ever sought in marriage?—
        Ever asked to be a wife?
    Yes, and might have kept her carriage
        But prefers a single life.

    Note, and you will soon discover
        What a favourite Auntie is;
    How the children dearly love her—
        Give to her a good-night kiss.

In the morn when each one rises,
  How she loves to give them joy!
Have for them some glad surprises,
  In some pretty longed-for toy.

Good, devoted Auntie, ever
  Pleases with some new device;
At her needlework so clever,
  Always making something nice.

Daily are the children crying—
  "Auntie" this, and "Auntie" that;
Is she weary of replying?
  No, she loves to join their chat.

What if someone yet should claim her?
  Useful Auntie, alway near:
Should she marry, could we blame her?
  If we knew he held her dear.

Think how Auntie, good and cheerful,
  Would be prized if going away;
We should see the children tearful,—
  Hear them crying, "Auntie, stay!"

THE CUNNING MOUSE.

A Song for Children.

When all in the house are in bed and asleep,
A little grey mouse from a corner does creep:
It slily peeps 'round with its little black eyes,
Until a few crumbs on the floor it espies;
It cautiously, noiselessly, glides from its nook,
Then round the whole parlour it takes a good look:
It greedily clears up the crumbs of white bread,
Excepting two morsels with poison bespread!
          It nibbles and scatters,
          It fritters and shatters,
          Contriving and clever,
          Yet caught it is never,
This little grey mouse is the pest of the house!

It runs in and out 'mong the tables and chairs,
And then makes its way to the foot of the stairs;
Then does what next day will make everyone cross.
It gnaws the stairs carpet, and piles up the floss;
And oft it stands up on its little hind feet,
And works with a will ere it deigns to retreat:
For what do you think does this cunning mouse do,
But fritters the carpet completely in two!
   It nibbles and scatters, &c.

For many a night does this mousie go there,
And patiently gnaws at the step that is bare:
It crumbles the wood with its little sharp teeth,
As if it would see what there is underneath:
When weary of wood, then some paper it finds,
To hastily tear it to fragments it minds;
And carries the pieces to where it likes best,
Of them and the floss then it makes a warm nest!
   It nibbles and scatters, &c.

In vain they set traps which have baits of nice cheese,
These from the *outside* mousie eats at its ease:
A vessel of water is placed for it soon,
Upon whose flat edge is a meal-spread old spoon,
Which, being nicely balanced, they wisely intend
The mouse shall tilt over on reaching the end;
It gravely sits up, gives the spoon a good stare,
Then shaking its head, thinks " I must not tread there!"
   It nibbles and scatters, &c.

Each one in the house, from the master to Bess,
Were beaten by mousie, they had to confess;
Though 'ticing its baits, it was "wise in its day,"
Not once to temptation did mousie give way.
Now see ye the moral? compare if you will,
A man to a mouse, and a truth you distil;
Man falls into traps ere he well is aware,
Thus weaker he is than a mouse, I declare!
   It nibbles and scatters, &c.

Now just one more word, for I'm not going to preach,
But surely this mousie a lesson might teach;
Of prudence and caution, to each of us here,
To heed not the tempters, whatever their sphere;—

Resist every snare that is placed as a test
To prove which of us is the wisest and best:
Be not beaten twice, by a mouse, or you'll rue;
Then keep from the traps that are waiting for you.
    In every-day matters,
     The tempter oft scatters,
     Traps cunning and clever,
     Yet caught be not ever.
Do more than a *mouse*, be the pride of your house!

A GRANDFATHER'S ADVICE.

JUDGE not from folks' appearances,
 It does not always do;
A man may look so poor, and yet
 Be just as good as you.

What matters if his clothes are patch'd,
 And shabby is his hat?—
His manners too, be rough and plain,
 He's none the worse for that.

These's many an honest noble heart
 Beneath a shabby vest:
And men who look so prim and smart,
 Not always are the best.

For there have been the worst of men,
 Clad in the finest suits;
And those who seem so kind, sometimes,
 Have minds as low as brutes.

And there are awkward, bashful men,
 Who have not good address,
Whose minds have noble thoughts, but lack
 The power to express.

While some who have a fluent speech,
 May have but meagre brains:
Or use their tongues but to deceive,
 For selfishness, or gains.

Some men may be but poorly clad,
  And yet have bags of gold;
Some carry all upon their backs,
  For others to behold.

Birth, wealth, and education, place
  Some men in high command;
But *moral goodness* ought to take
  The lead, o'er all the Land.

High intellect, and genius too,
  Should raise a man's estate;
But moral goodness there should be
  Ere he is truly great.

And in whatever class 'tis found,
  It lights the soul with grace;
To it should others pay respect,
  Whate'er their social place.

Combined with greatness, then we find
  The highest beings on earth;
The sphere of life has naught to do
  With true intrinsic worth.

Let men be rich, or poor, or dress'd
  In rags, or golden lace;
If honest, generous, good and true,
  And free from aught that's base,—

They are the men whom you may trust,
  Whate'er their rank may be;
Where wealth and goodness are combined,
  True gentlemen we see.

The one is like a polished gem,
  Refined, and set with skill;
The other in its natural state,
  Yet both are diamonds, still.

Then test a man to prove his worth,
　　Watch every word and look,
And read the index of his heart,
　　As you would read a book.

But judge not from appearances,
　　It does not always do;
A man may look so poor and yet
　　Be just as good as you!

Promiscuous Pieces.

THE QUEEN'S JUBILEE, 1887.

O glorious year! Wherein one golden day
   Stands out in blushing June among the rest:
The people rise one impulse to obey,
   That our good Sovereign's Jubilee be blest.
        With works of love:
For five decades of honoured life have sped,—
   Their lights and shadows crossed the changeful scene
Since first the Crown was placed upon her head,
   Began her rule, a fair young maiden Queen.
        And from Above,

A hallowed light has fallen on the Throne,
   Through all the years of good Victoria's reign:
Its halo widened 'round her as it shone,
   And blessings brought her, and the courtier train.
        In childhood sweet,
She those prophetic words spoke from her heart:
   " I will be good!" And she has since fulfilled
That promise well; nor stooped to once depart
   From virtuous ways, with which her life she willed,
        Should be replete.

Paths pure and chaste are those she ever trod,
   Here we the secret of her greatness see.
Exalted, yet she humbly bows to God,
   Thus kneels before—though she a monarch be
        A higher Throne.
As maid, as wife, as mother, she has knelt:
   As widow, Empress, and a Queen the while:
And she beloved, has made her influence felt
   By all her subjects on this beauteous Isle:
        Nor here alone:

Revered she is by those across the sea ;
    Her Empire's dusky people own her worth ;
Ten thousand thousand join this Jubilee,
    And as they love the Land that gave them birth,
        Her name they hail.
A nobler head the Crown has never graced ;
    And when we pray, that name is on our lips,
Whose lustre gilds the dreary ocean waste,
    And sheds a glory on her gallant ships,
        Where-e'er they sail.

Progression stamps this grand Victorian age,—
    The Land has been prolific of great men :—
The Statesman, the Philosopher, the Sage,
    Divine, Inventor, Knights of sword and pen,—
        Each left his mark.
The labour-fruits of many a useful life,
    We all enjoy to-day ; on every hand,
Conception and Construction have been rife,
    Inventive genius dropped upon the Land,
        Its mystic spark.

What other fifty years such wonders wrought,
    In art and science, thro' the hand and brain ?
What fifty years so many changes brought ?—
    O prosp'rous, glorious, and eventful reign !
        And England's Queen,
A bright exemplar stands before the world ;
    Hath power for good through her dominions wide ;
And wheresoe'er her flag may be unfurled,
    Our hearts exult with loyalty and pride :—
        When-e'er 'tis seen.

They crowned her youth in flowery June, 'twas meet
    They should, in that sweet month of promise true ;
When Nature dons its crown, and thus we greet
    The time to pay to her a tribute due
        From every place.
The Nation lifts its voice in grateful praise,
    This glorious reign 'twould fain perpetuate ;
For those hereafter, monuments we raise,
    To bear her name, and thus commemorate
        This year of grace.

The regal splendours of her life we find,
   Chase not away serenity and peace;
Her Court reflects her own sweet tranquil mind,
   And thus each passing year doth but increase
           Her sovereign sway.
Beside the cares and pomp of Throne and State,
   The sympathies of a true woman move:
Which make the royal lady more than great,
   And claim for her deep universal love,
           Without decay.

The good Prince Consort of her early years
   Has gone, who would with us have blest her now;
With son and daughter sleeps beyond all tears,
   The glory-circle 'round each angel brow,
           In yon bright Spot.
But hush the lyre, if once a mournful strain
   Recalls those sorrows in that noble breast,
So meekly borne, they sacred must remain,
   For Time has kindly lulled those griefs to rest,
           Then wake them not.

May God beneath His shield let her repose,—
   In peace permit her to adorn and light
These earthly realms, till called away to Those,
   Where loved ones wait for her in raiment white
           As glist'ning snow.
Her royal children's love around her clings,
   And while she sits enthroned, endeared to all,
Support unto that widowed heart it brings:
   And soothes her as life's evening shadows fall,
           Upon her now.

Long may our good illustrous Queen be here!
   May guardian angels watch her palace door;
Bring blessings rich and sweet her life to cheer;
   Long may her hand the sceptre hold before
           She lays it down.
God make her happy, till He bringeth on
   Her second coronation; when be sure,
The crown she wears will be replaced by one
   More beautiful, of crystal gems so pure,
           A Heavenly crown!

But Father yet our gracious Ruler spare:
   Thanks be to Thee, for through Thy wisdom 'tis
That one so good is o'er us; we declare
   The World a greater Jubilee than this
      Has never seen.
She rules by love: and ever by her side
   Stands white-robed Honour; thus all hearts rejoice
With one accord: for hark! afar and wide
   Her people sing with loud exultant voice,—
      "God Save the Queen!"

YOUTH.

Live as you will, or where you will, or howe'er long you may:
What though your life be strife or calm, or with the grave or gay;
The first score years the longest seem, and they are oft the best:
So varied are their incidents, far more than all the rest.
And oft old age the impress feels they left upon the mind,
The dearest loves, the fondest hopes, to them are oft confined.
Whate'er those early years may bring, though full of woe or weal,
They set their seal on after years, their influence then we feel.
They see the transit from the babe into the lisping child,
Who views the world from narrow bounds, and deems it undefiled,
As are the pure and spotless snows upon the virgin steeps;
And grief comes not, but "home" and "play" are all the joys it seeks:
Its heart is light, no "cares of bread" disturb the free young mind:
Free as the bird upon the wing, light as the wandering wind.

Blest is that happy trustful time, so full of guileless joy,
When all its pleasure centres in a little new-bought toy.
In those first twenty years of life where childhood is
    embraced,
Impressions which we then receive, are never once
    effaced.
The careless girl, the heedless boy, their free and artless
    ways :
Those recollections linger long, and brighten after days.
And oft the doings of early youth, the very place, and
    scene,
Comes to the mind as age creeps on, though most is lost
    between.
And next it sees the youth and maid, that sweet romantic
    time,
When all seems bright, and every sound rings like a
    merry chime.
'Tis then the time that "love's young dream" makes
    life begin to glow :—
The first, the sweetest, purest love, the heart can ever
    know!
When fancy paints in roseate shades, they deem it but
    their due ;
Nor think the lovely tints will die, and leave a steel-grey
    hue.
Oh! buoyant youth, full soon in life the glowing colours
    fade ;
'Tis meet that years mature must wear a sombre sterner
    shade :
And like our English northern skies, the neutral tints
    prevail :—
And when a brilliant red is seen, it but portends a gale.
But what must be the youth of those who reared in sin
    and shame,
Lack innocence, and childhood sweet, is but a mocking
    name ?
To whom the dear words "home" and "love" are but an
    idle sound :
Oh! would that fewer wretched ones like unto these
    were found !
For such as these, we pray to God that in the coming
    years,

They rescued be from that black net, which now their
    youth ensnares.
Sad too for those who in their youth feel stern Mis-
    fortune's frown ;—
When grief the tender blossoms blight, and bows the
    spirit down :
For such as these we can but hope their fortunes be
    reversed ;—
That ere they reach the noontide's prime, the mists be
    all dispersed :—
The sun break through the chastening gloom, and shed
    a genial ray :
Which, tempered by a soothing wind, may chase the
    clouds away.
For oft the wild and stormy days will set in bright repose;
As those that have a sunrise clear, sometimes in gloom
    will close.
Oh! if this precious time be yours, enjoy it while you
    may ;
But let Discretion hold the reins, and Reason lead the
    way :—
They'll guide you into paths of joy, apart from those of
    sin,
To which one false step from the right, a draught may
    draw you in.
And though a thousand luring lights around your path
    may flare ;
Be not like moths, and headlong fly into the deadly
    glare.
Where'er those twenty years are passed, in mansion or
    in cot ;
Whate'er our grade, 'tis all the same, they cannot be
    forgot.
What in those golden days we sow, in after years we
    reap ;
Youth ! wake the good, condemn the bad into a lasting
    sleep !
Howe'er this early time is spent, 'tis one recurring theme,
On which is based in after years, full oft some vivid
    dream.
Reflections on those twenty years, though well or badly
    spent ;

Will in proportion bring us peace, or pain and discontent.
Whate'er those twenty years have been, though happy or
    opprest;
God grant that naught enacted then, may mar age
    twilight's rest!
Be happy in your youth and health, return Mirth's play
    ful nod;
Yet in the midst of blessings sweet, be mindful of your
    God.

BIRTHDAY LINES, TO AN ABSENT FRIEND.

On this thy birthday would that I could greet
    Thine ear with what my heart desires for thee:
I have no gifts to lay before thy feet,
    Such would be thine wert thou but near to me.

These lines at least will unto thee convey
    My wishes for thy welfare, oh, my friend;
More bright and blest return each natal day,
    Peace, Love, and Hope, be with thee to the end.

I see thee now as if thou still wert near,
    Thy voice is hither borne upon the wind;
And in its whisp'rings faint I seem to hear
    The sweet responses of a thoughtful mind.

Long days be thine, and where-so-e'er we be,
    I will not thee from memory's tablet blot;
Oh, would that thou shouldst think good friend of me
    On this thy birthday, though I meet thee not.

How soon 'tis here again! years will revolve,
    Each passing date for some one bears a mark;
Each opening year we make some new resolve,
    To help to guide us through its shadows dark

But when these milestones on our way are passed,
    Which 'mind us all how we are marching on;
Our noblest plans alas! dissolve too fast,—
    The days go by, the good is left undone.

Fair rosy visions we but see in youth,
    The while we mount the hill aglow with hope;
The summit gained, we see the wholesome truth,
    Youth's fancies fade when we descend the slope.

Unsatisfied, do we not sometimes crave
    A higher, fuller, nobler life while here?
In narrow limits fettered, and the grave
    But frees the soul to seek a better Sphere.

Look but at daily life, what trivial things
    Warp our existence; it consists of nought
But shreds and patches, yet on noiseless wings
    The soul soars high with every purer thought.

And does not life, when all is done and said,
    Resemble patchwork? shades of dark and light?
Drawn close together with a silken thread,—
    Form one grand whole, if they are placed aright.

A lovely piece of work some are when done,
    Some intermingle every varied hue;
Some far too dark, of sombre brown or dun,
    Some well designed, in colours chaste and true.

Blest is the mortal with aspiring soul,
    Who yet to smallest duties bends the heart
Contentedly: they both exert control,
    Till they enlarge this life,—each doing its part.

Contented, should we go our daily round,
    To know the joy that faithful duty reaps;
True happiness, it ever will be found,
    Upon the bosom of Contentment sleeps.

Then these attend thee, through each passing hour,
    Till life enriches, as the time speeds by:—
Attains the sweetness of the God-made flower,
    While it fulfils a purpose pure and high.

I leave in the care, whate'er betide,—
    As through the maze of life thy footsteps roam,—
Of One who is the weary pilgrim's guide,
    And who at last will lead thee safely Home.

"MY MOTHER."

Who watched me from my earliest year,
Oh, with such loving, tender care,
And would my little troubles share?—
                      My Mother.

Who was it that so oft caressed
Hushed me to sleep upon her breast,
Whose voice hath lulled me oft to rest,—
                      My Mother.

Who taught my infant lips to speak,
And kissed my little rosy cheek,
And spoke in patient words so meek?—
                      My Mother.

Who would my every sorrow soothe ;
Who guided all my early youth,
And led me in the path of truth?—
                      My Mother.

Who taught me then to say my prayers,
The comfort of these after years ;
Who gently dried away my tears?—
                      My Mother.

Who when I was a little girl,
Cast o'er my life a loving spell,
Its influence now I feel so well,
                      My Mother.

What tho' since then long years have fled
Who tucks me in my little bed,
And breathes a blessing o'er my head?—
                      My Mother.

Who gives me still a "good-night kiss,"
And then I go to sleep in bliss,
I feel so happy after this,—
                      My Mother.

What tho' I am a maiden now,
Who gently soothes my aching brow,
And gives me counsel, sweet and low—
              My Mother.

Who comforts yet my youthful days,
In countless little winning ways,
And ever for my welfare prays—
              My Mother.

Since first I lay upon thy knee,
Oh, what do I not owe to thee,
For all that thou hast done for me,
              My Mother.

I fear I never can repay
Thy loving kindness day by day;
But I will honour and obey,
              My Mother.

Yes, I will try, and do my best,
To do the duties that are prest,
On me, till thou art called to rest,
              My Mother.

Oh, mayst thou long with me abide,
Through many a year, o'er every tide;
Long mayst thou linger by my side,
              My Mother.

In Heaven there waits a rich reward
For all thy years of toiling hard;
God o'er thy life is keeping guard,
              My Mother.

OBSCURE HEROISM.

England is proud of her soldiers and sailors,
   Heroes alike on the land and the wave;
Yet there are lives that must go unrecorded,
   Women and men who are dauntless and brave.

Heroes and heroines in the home circle,
　Nursing the sick ones, and helping the poor;
Sisters of Mercy, with hearts true and tender,
　Coming like angels of love to the door.

Heroes and heroines, wearing no badges,
　Pass by us daily when out in the street:
Living through ordeals, privations, or anguish,
　Passed by unheeded as dust at our feet.

Not to the world do they trumpet their virtues,
　Getting no laurels, nor seeking renown;
Prized but by those who are nearest and dearest,
　Happy indeed if such heart-ties they own.

Gems of humanity, bearing no tokens
　Giving no signs of the valour within:
Living uncared for, then dying unhonoured,
　Bearing their crosses that crowns they may win.

Martyrs to sickness on couches are lying,
　Patiently bearing some torturing pain:
Waiting unmurmuring, till the good Father,
　Calls them away, or restores them again.

Living in hope of a blessèd Hereafter,
　Biding their time, and yet yearning to go:
Often the truth of the Scripture recalling
　"Those whom He loveth, He chasteneth" so.

How many hearts that are noble surround us,
　Here in the Land of the true and the bold:
Courage and fortitude wait for ignition,
　Down in the hearts that seem dormant and cold.

Ready to die for the sake of a stranger,
　Waiting the summons of peril or pain:
Uniform lives may not bring them to action,
　Energies latent, unnoticed remain.

Sombre-clad ministers work for the Master
　Carry the Scriptures to places obscure:
Into dark alleys, 'mong vice and corruption,
　Only such know what they have to endure!—

Going to the sorrowful homes of the dying,—
    Holding a light to dark souls in their woe,—
Going to the homes of the poor and dejected,—
    Lifting the shadows where-ever they go.—

Preaching the Gospel to brothers and sisters,
    Giving them comfort whenever they can;—
Risking their lives for the soul of another,
    Nearest the angels in form of a man!

Beautiful lives grace the high and the lowly,
    Many are gone ere we know their true worth;
Oh! but we know there is One will reward them,
    What unto *His* are the glories of earth?

THE ELLIS MEMORIAL CLOCK TOWER.

A landmark fair salutes our eyes,
Uprising 'gainst cerulean skies;
What is this stately ornate pile
That o'er the landscape seems to smile?
A grand Clock Tower! not built in vain,
To celebrate the "Record Reign:"
And to the memory of a man
Who lived upon the wisest plan;
A village pedagogue, who taught
Within this school, and strengthened thought
By knowledge, which he did impart;
Thus gave the boys a better start
For life's stern battle;—trained them then
To all make wiser, better men.
This meet memorial now is seen
Of one who honoured Norwood Green
As being his birthplace; all now take
This gift with thanks for his dear sake.
He showed us all what can be wrought
By temp'rance, thrift, and careful thought.
A truly self-made man was he
Who rose from lowly birth to be,

An affluent one, as we have seen,
Yet gentle, and of modest mien.
He set forth many a golden rule,
In youth, within this dear old school,
Whose tower his honoured name now bears,
To keep it green through future years.
Then give three cheers for those who raised
This useful clock! let them be praised
For their good gift. By it we see
That time is money; punctual be
Then to each duty, and this clock
Will not our good endeavours mock;
For it will teach us all alike,
To value time when it doth strike;
To us each passing hour 'twill tell
To keep good time, and spend it well.
All honour to the family be
Who thus have marked the Jubilee;
For all who are of wealth possest,
Ennobled are by doing their best
To those less favoured; for we mind
That wealth must all be left behind
When we go hence; 'tis understood
'Tis only blest in doing good
To others; gold can ne'er be given
To pass the rich ones into Heaven!
They live and die the most content
Who of their surplus wealth have spent
To aid the poor; nor sought to hoard,
Who give thus, "lend unto the Lord;"
All such with open generous hand
Will earn a place in His fair Land.
Then here's good health to England's Queen!
And those who gave to Norwood Green
This handsome tower! may all be blest,
With years of joy, ere called to rest.

"PART IN PEACE."

Oh! part in peace with those you love,
    You may not meet again;
In after years, when they are gone,
    'Twill cost you bitter pain;—

If you have dropped a careless word,
    The time when last you met;
'Twill fill your heart with keen remorse,
    And foster vain regret.

For what avails our self-reproach?
    We cannot then recall,—
Repentance brings not back the words,
    We let in anger fall.

Then part in love, with kindly words,
    From those so near your heart,
For sweet will be the after-thought,
    If thus in peace you part.

A gentle word will linger long,
    And 'tis the soonest said,
And in the avenues of time,
    'Twill dwell when they are fled.

Oh, "let not then the sun go down
    Upon your wrath" at night;
Their spirit may be called away,
    Before the morning's light.

And when too late we would recall
    The heedless words that fell,
Unguarded from our lips, they haunt
    Us like a funeral knell.

We cannot ask forgiveness, when
    The loving heart is still;
We cannot give them life again,
    It is the Maker's will.

And part in peace at early morn,
　　When only for the day;
Perchance ere night-fall may grim Death
　　Snatch those you love away.

A friendly pressure of the hand,
　　A tender parting word,—
And fling a kind wish after them,
　　Heartfelt, what tho' not heard!

If those we love should first transgress,—
　　Against our hearts rebel,
Oh, let us not retaliate,
　　But hasty words repel.

In grief the richest gems are dark,
　　Tears dim their lustre bright:
When troubled waters wage within,
　　The day has lost its light.

For when the soul with grief is pent,
　　Then beauty has no charm,
Until the ruffled waters cease,
　　And wax subdued and calm.

Then let us part in peace at morn,
　　In peace at eventide;
With those we love, they never more
　　May linger by our side.

'Twill save us many pangs of grief,
　　Their love for us increase,—
'Twill spread a halo round the soul,
　　To part in love and peace.

TO MY FATHER ON HIS SEVENTIETH BIRTHDAY.

Now "three-score years and ten" have passed, above thy
　　honoured head;
Alas! God's promised life on earth to man for thee is
　　fled.

If I could hold the hand of Time, or once arrest decay,
I would for thee, but father mine, I cannot bid them stay.
'Tis not for me to lengthen years, or smooth one time-wrought line:
That mystic power lies within a higher Hand than mine.
The wish, the fervent wish, is there, but human strength is frail;
It makes me sad, as day by day, I watch thee slowly fail;
The feebler step, the dimmer eye, the locks as white as snow;—
All plainly show life's tranquil eve is stealing o'er thee now.
Yet still the mind's sweet afterglow beams from those kindly eyes,
Awhile we revel in its light, before the splendour dies;
And twilight shadows gather 'round, for that approaching night,
When thou wilt sleep, and wake at dawn in everlasting light!
How soon a lifetime runs its course, a few short years at most;
Or more, or less, of life on earth, can now be thine to boast.
A backward glance with mental eye upon thy past career,
Enwreathes with smiles thy saxon face, thy thoughts must bring thee cheer.
And yet I see a glist'ning tear come trembling from thine eye;
Who can review the past with smiles, unmingled with a sigh?
For who has reached thy honoured age, and tasted naught but joy?
Our portion ne'er is happiness while here without alloy;
The rainy days will come among, and they are sent 'twould seem,
To make the sunny ones to us, by contrast brighter gleam.
And as the years glide swiftly by, we prize them more and more;
The solace 'tis of age to draw from Memory's treasured store.

The past is sure, the future vague, known not to seer or
    sage;
The interest in this life grows less, with fast advancing
    age.
When not reverting to the past, the mind is fixed afar,
Upon that fuller life in store for us across the bar.
Thy face to-night reflects thy life, with all its past
    decades;
I see it rippling in thy eye, with all its lights and shades.
My first remembered happy hours were spent I know
    with thee;
I marvel how thy mind unbent to join my baby glee;
And how unselfish was thy toil, in those long-vanished
    years,
When I a careless prattling child, knew not thy daily
    cares.
And now when I at last have grown to fully know thy
    worth,
Behold! I find thy term expired, thou'rt ripe to leave
    this earth.
The fruit while lingering in the husk each day will riper
    grow;
The grain assumes a deeper gold, before we lay it low.
Each day thy spirit mellows in the sunshine of our love
Before it joins the good, the blest, the beautiful, Above.
Thy few remaining years of life, are left for me, thy child,
To recompense thee for that love which on my youth has
    smiled.
And after now, the years to come, which may to thee be
    given,
Thou wilt be living "over time," by kind indulgent
    Heaven.
Ere long the "pearly gates" on High will be unclosed
    for thee;
Then all the glory there beyond revealed to thee will be.
The Maker knows when thou shalt go, the very time and
    spot;
Yet it has wisely been ordained, that we shall know it
    not:—
By One who holds the universe within His hallowed Hand,
The centuries would cease to roll, if He but gave
    command!

'Tis well, and yet I pray that long to us He thee will
spare ;
I tremble as I picture home when thou wilt not be here,—
Our little circle incomplete, a link lost from the chain :
Yet this is selfish, for I know, our loss will be thy gain.
May blessings fall upon thy head, while yet above the
sod ;
And light divine, upon thee shine, until thou meetest God.

A RUSTIC BEAUTY.

I've seen a bonny maid to-day,
   As strangers we have met ;
Yet that expressive face of hers,
   I never can forget.

She seemed so like a sweet wild flower
   That out of place was born,
And growing by the dusty path,
   Neglected and forlorn.

Unvalued it was rudely passed,
   And trampled 'neath the feet ;
Uncared for, still it reared its head
   To waste its fragrance sweet.

A rustic beauty, unrefined,
   But sweet and fresh to see :
A maid unconscious of her charms,
   As simple flower could be.

That fascinating face of hers,
   I seem to see it still ;
I try to cast it from my mind—
   It comes against my will.

I read her eyes—those sweet dark orbs
   To me betrayed her mind ;
And traits incongruous were there,
   Which nature had combined.

And from those tell-tale, bright brown eyes,
    Beyond her own control,
Which spoke of sadness, then of mirth—
    There shone a spotless soul!

A PLEA FOR THE MINERS.

You pray for those who sail the sea,
    And all its perils dare:
But there are those you mention not,
    Yet need your daily prayer:—
As well deserving fervent words,
    To reach the Throne divine;
You ask me whom? I answer those,
    In peril in the mine.

You see them not, you mind them not,
    Nor know their life below;
But think of them, when basking in
    The firelight's ruddy glow;
For manly, brave, undaunted hearts,
    Toil in those dark confines;
Yes, when you pray, remember those
    In peril in the mines.

The blessings of a warm coal-fire,
    Have cost some precious lives,—
Have rent some hundred loving hearts
    Of mothers, and of wives!
The collier works in Danger's grasp,
    From morn, till day's decline;
For daily bread, he bravely dares
    The peril of the mine.

We English, love the firelight's glance,
    As 't were a living thing;
For 'round this "Golden Milestone" oft
    The fondest memories cling;
Then when upon the cheerful hearth,
    With loved ones you recline,
Forget not those who toil beneath,
    In peril in the mine.

Down where no daylight penetrates,
   The deepest, darkest bore;
In subterranean windings damp,
   They there unearth the ore;
No wreaths of glory, or romance,
   With work like their's entwine;
Yet honour to those honest men,
   In peril in the mine.

For fathoms deep below the sod,
   In weird oppressive gloom;
Has been for miners all too oft,
   A mighty living tomb!
Though Death in ghastly form be there,
   They dread not his designs;
Oh! may God guard, and save all those,
   In peril in the mines!

HOPE.

There is a little cherub near,
   That hovers round thy brow;
Whose voice can banish many a tear,
   With whispers sweet and low.

Oh! may that angel ne'er depart,
   But long with thee abide;
It comfort gives to many a heart,
   When worn, and sad, and tried.

Its name is "Hope," and it is young,
   It singeth oft to me;
It lingers near with prattling tongue,
   And fills my heart with glee.

Then prize it, while it tarries yet,
   To cheer thee on thy way;
For guidance sweet we all may get,
   While basking 'neath its ray.

When racked with sorrow, bowed with grief,
    And Hope we thought had fled;
Oh! what a joyful glad relief,
    To see it still ahead.—

And beck'ning with a radiant smile,
    Like some bright glorious star;
For us to follow it the while,
    On paths of light afar.

THE MOTHER'S PRAYER.

Behold a poor, but cleanly cot,
    Whose windows face the woodland glen
One casts a light the whole night long,—
    A beacon star to way-lost men:
Around it autumn winds blow cold,
And rack the trees by field and fold.

Within a lowly chamber dim,
    A gentle, pretty, fair-haired child,
Was ill and prostrate on her bed:
    Her little heart all undefiled,
Clung to her mother, day and night,
Nor long would trust her from her sight.

The mother sat beside the bed,
    And watched her child with loving care:
None knew the anguish in her heart,
    To see her darling lying there:
The young life hanging by a thread,
As fever tost the restless head.

That little wasted tender form,
    Was more to her than worlds of gold;
For oh! that mother's heart was tried,
    With other sorrows, all untold:
Her child was her one comfort sweet,
Without it, life were incomplete.

She watched with concentrated mind,
   That ever comes with mother-love:
Strong to endure, she bided there,
   With strength direct from One Above:
Restrained her tears, she dared not weep,
And scarce would close her eyes in sleep;—

With yearning soul strained every nerve,
   To nurse her dear one back to life;
A twofold weight of grief she bore,
   As mother, and as anxious wife;
Her heart-wrung tears were dropt aside,
All signs of woe she fain would hide.

Oft in her midnight vigils lone,
   While gazing on her sleeping child,
O'erflowed that purest thing on earth,
   Maternal love, in visions wild;—
'Tis all absorbing, and intense,
And seeks no earthly recompense.

She mused, desponding, in the gloom,
   "Sweet child I miss thee at thy play,
No little footfall greets my ear,
   Thy shoes and frocks are laid away;
I centre all my joys in thee,
More than my life thou art to me!—

"But oft I would too harshly chide
   My little sufferer lying there:
And oh! I fear, my fragile child,
   I have not tended thee with care;
If God will only thee restore,
In future I will prize thee more."

'Tis ever thus with human hearts;
   When those we love seem passing hence,
Remorse invades the troubled breast,
   And loudest speaks in our suspense:—
The grief-fraught mind when backward cast,
Will censure self in scenes long past.

Upheld by faith, with cheerful mien,
   In accents low she soothed her child;
And when its violet eyes sought hers,
   Into their wistful depths she smiled:
And oft she knelt and blessed her there,
And breathed to Heaven a heartfelt prayer.

She murmured meekly " Oh! my God,
   Be pleased to hear me when I pray;
Bring back my precious child to health!
   Oh! call her not from earth away!
Thou canst relieve all mortal pain,
Oh! make my darling well again.

" Kind friends are mine, sent through Thy love,
   But what avails all mortal skill?
By sympathetic hearts sustained,
   I wait with them, Thy holy will;
Thy gracious aid I now implore,
Please God my little one restore.—

"Thou canst do aught, then deign to hear,
   And answer this my pleading prayer;
Oh, spare to me my only child!
   So pure of soul, so frail and fair;
I love her more than tongue can tell,
Oh! bless my child, and make her well!"

And even as she rose there came,
   Two God-sent angels from Above;
They poised unseen, but not unfelt,
   For one was "Hope," and one was "Love!"
Their radiance filled her quivering heart,
And gave her strength to bear her part.

Look up, thou sore-tried mother then,
   Thine is a sacred mission here;
God will defend the soul opprest,
   He notes a woman's heart-drawn tear;
Through tortuous paths His hand we trace,
"Through suffering thou wilt see His face."

"Give me my dolly, mamma please;"
  Broke forth in child-tones, sweet and low:
That voice, been hushed for many a day,
  Then set the mother's heart aglow;
Responding with impassioned kiss,
She murmured, "Thank Thee Lord for this:
The crisis past, she then and there,
Poured forth her soul in grateful prayer.

TROUBLED HEARTS.

How many hearts in sorrow,
  Go through the walks of life,
Taking their burdens with them.
  Into the scenes of strife.—

Doing their daily duties,
  Going to their dreary task;
Giving their smiles to others,
  Wearing a cheerful mask.

Deep in their hearts at daytime,
  Hiding their grief from sight,
Locking it up at morning,
  Setting it free at night.

Seeming the while to strangers,
  Callous, and cold, and calm;
Longing in truth for solace,—
  Yearning for rest and balm.

Woe to the heart in sorrow,
  Bearing it all alone;
Never a friend to enter
  In through its case of stone.

Woe to the soul beclouded,
  Having no faith or creed;
Never a prayer to offer,
  When in the hour of need.

Blest is the heart though troubled,
　　Finding a glad relief;
Into a kind friend's bosom,
　　Pouring its weight of grief.

Blest is the true believer,
　　Whatever he has to bear;
Seeking and finding comfort
　　Of God, through a heartfelt prayer.

"GOODNESS BRINGS ITS OWN REWARD."

As with weary feet we traverse
　　Through life's steep and thorny ways,
With few earthly joys to greet us
　　And illume the sunless days;
Though temptations may beset us,
　　Though the road be rough and hard;
Let us ever this remember—
　　Goodness brings its own reward.

Wending through the narrow pathway,
　　Keeping always to the right;—
Looking forward to the distance,
　　Where there gleams the guiding light;—
Ever let these words be with us,
　　Never truer sung a bard,
In whatever field of duty—
　　Goodness brings its own reward.

Striving after good will bring us
　　Blessings, whatsoe'er betide;
And through every sad misfortune
　　One will be our stay and guide;
If we only love and trust Him,
　　And all evil things discard;
Knowing He has ordered wisely,—
　　Goodness brings its own reward.

Though we may have our oppressors,
   Darkening all our duteous days,
And for patience and forbearance,
   Never get one meed of praise:
Yet will conscience deep within us,
   Quickly tell us when 'tis marred;
So it comforts when 'tis clearest—
   Goodness brings its own reward.

Know we this, that right must conquer,
   Sin but leads to shame and pain;
If from rectitude diverging
   Halt at once, and try again:
Ask for strength, that light may enter
   And our wandering steps retard;
Be assured we shall be answered—
   Goodness brings its own reward.

May we watch our words and actions,
   Careless ones too oft are rued;
And the world, so prone to evil,
   Trifling faults has misconstrued:—
Magnified them, and condemned us,
   May we then our conduct guard;
Holding as a true conviction—
   Goodness brings its own reward.

Though our lives be dull and joyless,
   In a narrow humble sphere,
Lonely, with frail hopes to cherish,
   And few loving hearts to cheer;
Yet if we but do our duty,
   And our Father's laws regard,
He will surely recompense us -
   Goodness brings its own reward.

It will not be long in coming,
   Know you that in each good deed,
Full reward lies in the *doing*,
   Steps are they which Heavenward lead.
Then when we have ceased life's labour,
   And are laid beneath the sward,
Then our souls in Heaven will realize,
   Goodness brings its own reward.

"I HEARD THEE SING."

I heard thee sing; thy voice fell on my ear
Sweet as the syren's, ocean's caves forsaken;
Till mem'ries, which had slumbered, soon were waken,
    Loved forms came near.

Those 'witching strains on themes I love, for me
Had all the sweetness that to earth is given;
Oh! music so enchanting, must of Heaven
    A foretaste be!

I listened, still enthralled, and felt thy power,
Thy mellow voice was full of force and feeling;
And with its pathos came a sadness stealing,
    That charm-fraught hour.

The strangest sadness, which is born we know
Of deepest rapture; and withal so soothing;
The soul beneath its thraldom seemed removing
    From things below.

My swelling heart to one sweet touching song
Was all responsive; spell-bound as I listened,
One form supernal rose in robes that glistened,
    From out a throng.

For hallowed memories, which till then had slept,
Before my vision passed in quick succession;
O'er-strained the heart, and ere I found expression,
    Behold I wept!

I saw an old man, with a time-touched brow,
A gloriole o'er his white hair was shining;
The dear arm-chair where he was last reclining,
    All vacant now!

The mental mirage made by music sweet,
To me appeared, but for a moment only;
The fireless grate, the hearthstone cold and lonely,
    No voice to greet.

My father's spirit, seemed embodied there,
Through every tone of that sweet song was speaking,
Then face to face with him mine had been seeking.
    I breathed a prayer.

I blest thee then, what though my tears rained fast;
Thy theme then changed, and lo! the vision faded;
Thy thrilling song, thy beauteous voice, had aided,
    To wake the past.

Oh! music, source of most intense delight,
And deep emotion; while the soul uplifting,
It lulls us, till we seem the nearer drifting,
    To Realms of Light!

TO A LADY:

On her Silver Wedding, and on her Leaving the neighbourhood of the Authoress.

Oh! gentle lady, I have known thee long,
And marked thy goodness through my youthful days,
Permit me then, to give to thee a song,—
A tribute, ere we go our separate ways.
What though of different rank, and thou hast dwelt
In ancient hall, and I in lowly cot;
Yet thou hast made thy kindly presence felt:
Thy woman's heart has brighter made the spot,
'Round thy abode; and though but rarely seen,
Yet have the poor oft felt thy offered hand:
Thy christian virtues through thy life serene,
Have been a guide unto the promised Land.
We fain would have thee near us, but since thou
Art going, amid the deep regret of all;—
We pray that One, may on thy head bestow
The choicest blessings that to mortals fall.
For five-and-twenty years of wedded life,
Have now been thine, in sweet retirement spent:
The mother's joy, the bliss of honoured wife,
Have with the summer of thy life been blent.

Yes, children blest thee, first the noble boy,
Was gladly welcomed with a mother's pride;
And then a daughter came to crown thy joy,
Came when the May-flowers decked the country side.
And now has come the silver day at last,
A gleaming milepost on thy life's highway;
Whence thou canst now review the happy past,
And backward look upon thy bridal day.
All nature seems attuned in concert sweet,—
In whispers tells that gladsome thou shouldst be;
Thy bright home circle be to-day complete,
And loving tokens find their way to thee.
To-day in all things seems a silver vein;—
The silvery clouds so lightly sail along;—
In autumn woods, the robin's silvery strain,
Is mingled with the silvery streamlet's song.
The quaint old hall, thy home for many years,
Must be so dear as some familiar face;—
The scene of all thy youthful joys and cares,
Thy cherished memories cluster round the place.
Yet Sorrow came, and spread its sable wing,
And dropped its burden deep into thy breast;
Awhile the birds have ceased for thee to sing,
Thy spirit mourned for loved ones gone to rest.
But God sustained thee through each bitter grief,
For thou hast known the solace of a prayer;
When thou hast sought, He gave to thee relief,
And lighter made the yoke for thee to bear.
If I had but the power to make thee glad,
Beyond a simple offering such as this;
O lady thou shouldst never once be sad,
But all thy future life be full of bliss.
And what is ever more than rank or wealth,
And when possest can ne'er be prized too well;
The precious boons of happiness and health,
May these be thine, where-ever thou mayst dwell
Fresh joys await thee in thy future home,
A lovely vista opens to thy view;
The smiles of friends will chase away the gloom;
And hope will lift thy heart to all things new.

Farewell dear lady, may good fortune shine,
On thee, and on thy faithful partner true;
And may ye through our Father's grace divine,
Be spared to see your Golden Wedding too!

SABBATH DAY.

Sweet Day of rest, we welcome thee,
    The most of all the seven ;
When we can cast aside our cares,
    And turn our thoughts to Heaven :
How sweet to breathe a thankful prayer,
And worship One we know is there.

Sweet Day, to those who labour hard
    Throughout the weary week ;
And when they all have done their work,
    At last their leisure seek :
And find when all the six are done,
That they can rest upon this One.

Oh! Father teach Thy children all
    To love this blessèd Day ;
And hold it holy for Thy sake,
    In all we do and say:
For Thou hast ordained for the best,
That we should have a day for rest.

Teach us to keep Thy laws divine,
    And bring the wanderers back,
From sin, and let them Homeward walk
    Upon the righteous track :—
And Father, teach them how to pray,
And how to spend the Sabbath Day.

"WAITING."

Waiting, with the golden sunlight
    Falling on his silvery hair ;
While he peacefully reclineth
    In his oaken, high-backed chair.

Waiting, while his locks are glist'ning
  In the rays that Heaven has sent;
In his features, now reposing,
  Hope and fortitude are blent.

Work is over, he is weary;
  Long he's laboured in the field:
He has sown, and reaped his harvest,—
  Garner'd all that life can yield.

Waiting there with resignation,
  Sweet to see in one so old;
Spending hours in looking backward,
  Basking in the beams of gold.

True it is that memory fails him—
  Fails in daily trivial things,
Yet 'tis, in recalling bygones,
  Faithful still, and comfort brings.

Age is full of retrospection,
  Memories cheer it to the last—
Early scenes that rise before it,
  Gild the present with the past.

It has time for calm reflection,
  Sweet delight in something done;
While 'tis near the hallowed Gateway,
  Leading to the Life to come.

Yet the soul will have its yearnings,
  To be free and soar away;—
Long to hear the welcome summons—
  "Leave those prison walls of clay!"

Still it bides within its temple,
  Though the walls are crumbling down,
List'ning for the angel's whisper—
  Waiting for a crystal crown.

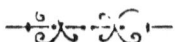

A MOTHER'S LOVE.

What love is like a mother's love?
  What care is like to hers?
When we are bowed with grief, or pain,
  Her heart with pity stirs:
A tender, deep, unselfish love,
  We cannot prize too well,
That twines itself around the heart.
  And nothing can dispel.

Who can bestow such soothing care
  As she alone can do,
And touch with such a gentle hand?
  None but a Mother true!
And from our childhood's early days
  Her love and care we feel;
Her influence, on our years mature,
  Has left a lasting seal.

Oh! children dear, you little know
  Her fond devoted care:
Her hidden depth of love for you,
  Attends you everywhere:
When you were little helpless babes,
  She nursed you day by day:
The debt of gratitude since then,
  You never can repay.

Oh, think of what you owe to her,
  Reward her kindly heart,
For all that she has done for you,
  Ere she and you must part.
Confide in her, and she will soothe
  Your every passing grief;
She'll softly kiss away your tears,
  And make your sorrow brief.

Those blest with a good mother's love,
  Possess a wealthy store;
And ever as the years steal on,
  Revere her more and more.

A time will come, perchance ere long,
  When she must pass away;
Her sweet familiar voice be hushed;—
  Then love her, while you may.

A Mother's love! the words convey
  A volume in their sound;
A treasure deep of untold worth,
  By sacred feelings bound.
It clings to us in adverse years,
  Through sunshine, shade, and strife:
Her faithful, pure, and holy love,—
  Forsakes us but with life.

LINES ON THE DEATH OF A FAVOURITE DOG.

How I loved thee, faithful Rover,
  Who could help but hold thee dear?
For thy every look and action,
  Proved to me thou wert sincere.
Far more so, in real affection,
  Than some shallow human hearts;
Thus thy bright and brief existence,
  Lessons deep to such imparts.
Noble, grateful, true, and loving,
  Such wert thou, while life was thine;
Honest worth, with no dissembling,
  Marked this canine friend of mine.
Master, mistress, all, have missed thee;
  Full of promise thou hast fled;
Boy and maid, thy daily playmates,
  Wept to find their fav'rite dead.
Thou hast revelled in thy youth-time
  Felt "how good it is to live;"—
Made the most of canine pleasures,
  And thy love didst freely give.
Thou wert, as by intuition,
  Quick to know who liked thee best;

Fondly gave for it with interest,
　　Love that bore the truest test.
With thy natural keen perception,
　　Thou couldst always comprehend,
Marked by outward demonstration,
　　Who at heart was thy true friend.
Never more thy form will greet me,
　　How I miss thee at the door!
Eyes that beamed, and spoke thy feelings,
　　Now are closed for evermore.
Fare-thee-well, devoted creature,
　　Mortal could not bid thee stay;
Oft 'tis thus, that things we cherish,
　　Are the first to pass away!

"SUMMER TIME WILL COME AGAIN."

Forward look, nor be downhearted,
　　Lift the shadows from your brow;
There are blue skies far above you,
　　Though the storm-clouds veil them now.
Know ye that the brightest sunshine
　　Ever follows after rain?
Cheer up then, and trust the future,—
　　Summer time will come again.

Dreary hours the white-robed Winter,
　　Brought ye in his withered hand,
Ere his icy ermine mantle,—
　　Disappeared from o'er the land.
Dull despair must never conquer,
　　Sad repinings are in vain;
All distress will quickly vanish—
　　When the summer comes again.

Though the sea-birds now are flying
　　Low upon the white-ridged sea,
Soon with sunlight all its waters,
　　Will one wealth of glory be;

And the bitter cold north-easter,
   Long with us will not remain ;
Softer winds will soon caress us,—
   Summer days will come again.

Look ahead, for in the distance,
   Are the silver shafts of light
In the darkness now appearing,
   Wait, and all will soon be bright.
Hark! what music is awaking,
   Breathing hope in every strain ;
All good fortune will attend you,—
   When the summer comes again.

THE AGED.

Respect and love the old and frail,
   And honour their grey hair ;
For all, throughout their toiling lives,
   Have had enough to bear.

Then children, kindly treat the old,
   Let them be loved by you ;
And guide their feeble trembling steps,
   Have patience with them too.

For some day you will be the same,
   If God your lives should spare ;
Your forms will stoop, your faces wear
   The trace of grief and care.

Oh, do not laugh and jeer at them,
   Because they are infirm ;
But listen to their counsel wise,
   And from their wisdom learn.

Then try and make them happy here,
   Turn not their words to scorn ;
They've known this world long years before
   The time when you were born.

Oh, wound not then their careworn hearts,
　　But honour and revere.
The old, the feeble, and infirm,
　　They will not long be here.

And gently lead them by the hand,
　　Speak kindly to them now;
And let your arms protect their forms,—
　　Support their steps so slow.

What though their brows be furrow'd now,
　　With lines of age and care:
Those wrinkles on their hollow cheeks
　　Have been not always there.

Remember that they once were young,
　　Though dim now is their sight:
Their brows were once so white and smooth,
　　Their eyes were once so bright.

At most, they have not long to stay,
　　For life is short at best;
Then cheer them on their lonely way,
　　Till they find peace and rest.

For who can look upon the aged,
　　Descending Life's rough hill;
And feel not reverence and respect,
　　Through every fibre thrill?

May God look down and bless the old
　　In mercy and in love;
Till He shall call them to Himself,
　　To dwell in Heaven above.

THE PARTING.

Oh, Marion dearest, fare-thee-well,
　　Sweet idol of my heart;
For now the dreaded hour has come,
　　When thou and I must part.

The tears are streaming from thine eyes.
   They bathe thy cheeks so white;
But I must go, amid thy sighs,
   Good-night beloved,—good-night.

Behold! yon full orb mount the sky,
   So beautiful and clear;
But ere it sinks again to rest,
   I must away from here.
It grieves my heart, oh, gentle maid,
   Our happiness to blight;
But one day we may be repaid,
   Good-night, beloved, good-night.

My calling takes me far away
   To win a golden name;
To life's stern duties I must go,
   To bring thee wealth and fame.
Though darkness falls around us now,
   There yet will dawn a light;
I will be true to thee I vow,
   Good-night, beloved, good-night.

Whate'er in future may betide,
   Where e'er my lot is cast:
Through weal, or woe, my love for thee
   Will linger to the last.
I turn to leave thee, full of hope,
   Life's battles I must fight,
With many hardships I must cope
   Good-night beloved,—good-night.

Whatever be my future fate,
   Where e'er my footsteps roam;
How sweet will be the thought, that one
   Will wait my coming home.
Now I must leave my heart's fond pride,
   From thee I take my flight;
I must not linger by thy side,
   Good-night beloved, good-night.

Once more I kiss thy cheek so fair,
   I can no longer stay;

Once more I press thine hand in mine,
  Before I turn away:
Oh! send a kind wish after me,
  When I am from thy sight;
And I will long remember thee,—
  Good-night beloved,—good-night!

GUARDIAN ANGELS.

Have you in the solemn midnight,
  In the darkness, bent your ear;
And have seemed to *hear* the silence
  Felt it as a presence near?

'Tis methinks the wings of angels,
  Rustling near us in the room;
Visions bright in space around us,
  Guard us, in the midnight gloom.

Unperceived, they hover o'er us,
  Faithful watchers through the night:
Till they at our Father's calling,
  Vanish ere the dawn of light.

LINES ON THE OPENING OF THE FORTH BRIDGE,

—— MARCH 4TH, 1890. ——

Hurrah, true Britons! ye have made complete
To-day, a grand memorial of our age:
And by this mighty structure ye have raised
Have shown to all the world that art at last
O'er Nature triumphs: Caledonia's sons
Have o'er her now a splendid victory gained;
Nor was it won alas! without the loss
Of human lives. Those hardy Scottish men,

Have perils dared, which might perhaps have scared
South-nurtured ones.   For some poor grieving hearts,
Will view this work to 'mind them of their dead.
Those sacrifices of the toiling horde,
Will not be felt in generations hence;
When all have gone who bridged the smiling Forth;
And men and women yet unborn will then
With pride and veneration look on this
Fine noble span; in wonderment exclaim—
" In those days men were giants, who conceived,
And carried out, a mighty work sublime
And firm as this!"   Ah yes, they must possess
Gigantic minds, whose idealistic plans,
Grew from conception, more defined and clear,
Till they matured, and then assumed a form
More tangible, until by dint of time,
And persevering labour, they have grown
To these dimensions, 'neath man's sturdy hand!
Through all climatic changes he has wrought,
'Neath chilly skies, when beating blasts have swept
On every side; o'er swollen waters oft,
And brought his inborn courage to the fore.
And now in all its magnitude it stands,
Its firm foundations fathoms deep are sunk
Within those waters, where the complex work
Of vast proportions, now is mirror'd there.
The thundering engines with their pond'rous freights,
Will make its massive piers reverberate;
A thousand times the storms and winds may come,
And rack its girders, it will stand the test!
Wealth, skill, and northern energy, combined
With native genius, are embodied there:
And in its grandeur, man it seems has now
Himself surpassed!   For standing there he looks
But as a pigmy, to his hand's own work!
And while we gaze upon it, well we know
That those who reared its strong stupendous form,
Have done their country great and glorious good;
And with it surely they have stamped our times
For after ages:—placed for us withal
A record bright on the historic page.

Forget not those who built it: and inscribe
Some words of praise, to those who with their lives
Have paid their forfeit to the Bridge of Forth!
Just, was the royal mandate which conferred
Distinction on the leaders who survive:
And we would ask that each henceforth should have
A badge of honour to adorn his breast!

MORAL COURAGE.

"My Donald is so brave, Mother,
  Oh, why may we not wed?
For me he'd face the cannon's mouth,
  Nor once the ordeal dread;
Or dash into a seething sea,
  Another's life to save;
His fine physique, his flashing eye,
  Proclaim him strong and brave!"

"He may, Child, be a hero strong,
  Brave war thy love to win;
And yet a *moral* coward be,
  Weak, in resisting sin.
Brute courage, with brute strength, we know
  Performs herculean tasks;
Temptation tests our *moral* strength,—
  Our inner self unmasks.
If Donald be as good as brave,
  Nor weakly yields to vice,
Then wed him, Dear, he truly is
  A gem beyond all price!"

"FACES."

What a study are our faces,
  Yet are they beyond control?
Each one carries outward traces
  Of the inward mind and soul.

Every feature is a token
    Of the life that we have led ;
And reveals what is unspoken—
    Signs that are by others read.

Seals are set upon the features,
    To ourselves the most unknown ;
Faces are impressive teachers,—
    By our lives we mould our own.

We should sift ourselves, and cherish
    All the good traits of the mind ;
Foster them, or they may perish,
    Leave the evil dregs behind.

In our brows, our eyes, and noses,
    E'en the cheeks, the lips, and chin ;
Each of these in turn discloses
    All the strongest traits within ;

Shows us if refined, or clever,
    Intellectual, learned, and wise ;
Poets, and great musicians, never
    Can their soul's wealth there disguise.

Faces are of thoughts the debtors,
    Careful study tells us how
Men of science, men of letters,
    Bear the impress on the brow.

Sages, students, gospel preachers,
    Men of culture, men of mind,
These have all a type of features,
    Noble, beautiful, refined.

Eyes become the soul's reflection,
    Index to the mind within ;
Some betray the heart's affection,
    Through their depths the truth we win.

Some have faces full of gladness,
    Fond of life, and fond of fun ;
Some, that speak of care and sadness,
    Seem to wish that life was done.

Those who are to "drink" addicted,
   On the visage bear the trace :
Vice, we painly see depicted,
   On a villain's tell-tale face.

Those who let vile passions lead them,
   All betray it in their looks :
Sin and folly, we can read them,
   In their faces,—Nature's books.

Nature never once intended
   To dissemble in the face ;
In the countenance is blended
   Every failing, every grace.

May we gain, though 'tis but slowly,
   Nobler minds as years do roll ;
Till a light shines, pure and holy,
   Through the " windows of the soul."

If you'd have a face of beauty,
   Let your life be good and pure ;
Doing to God and man our duty,
   Lends a charm that will endure.

To the virtuous, there is given
   Beauty, e'en when youth is past ;
Till they see the gates of Heaven,
   They are lovely to the last.

TO A FRIEND LEAVING ENGLAND.

Take my heart's best wishes with thee,
   Far away across the main ;
God watch o'er thee, and protect thee,
   Till He sends thee back again.
If it is thy wish to leave us,
   We will let thee have thy way ;
Selfish thoughts we may not foster,
   We will never bid thee stay.

Other hearts will cling around thee,
   Newer ties will claim thy love;
In the land of thy adoption,
   E'en the skies will change above!
Northern stars will shine not o'er thee,
   Others will upon thee smile;
Yet awake the chords of memory,
   And forget us not the while.

If thy heart will let thee leave us,
   And to us seem as one lost;
We will seek not to retain thee,
   Whatsoe'er our parting costs.
We but ask that thou wilt cherish
   Thoughts of us, though thou mayst roam;
Love is deep, and ties are tender,—
   Think sometimes of those at home!

Will one pang of sorrow cross thee,
   Or remorse disturb thy mind,
When thou thinkest of the dear ones,
   Thou hast left in tears behind?
Yet I seek not to approach thee,
   Furthest be that thought from me;
Rather is my pity strongest,
   And affection true for thee.

Fare thee well! may God be with thee,
   On the sea, and on the land;
May He scatter blessings o'er thee,
   With His generous guardian hand.
Shield thee from the troubled tempest—
   Smooth the path beneath thy feet:—
Let thy precious charge be near thee,
   To afford thee comfort sweet.

Thou wilt see thine own dear country,
   Fade in distance from thy sight;
And the widening seas divide thee
   From our English cliffs so white;
See perchance, with misty vision,
   Beating heart, and quivering lip;
Then our parting words will haunt thee,—
   "May God speed that gallant ship!"

BIRTHDAY LINES TO MY AGED MOTHER.

My darling mother! in my filial love,
    While daily feeling thou dost grow more dear;
I call on thee a blessing from Above,
    And breathe a prayer that thou mayst long be here.

On this thy natal morning I would give,
    To thee the wishes of thy child's fond heart;
The fervent hope that thou for years mayst live,
    In peace and love, ere we are called to part.

Long may we revel in thy loving smile,
    Which has the power to chase away all gloom;
And may all good attend on thee the while,
    Thy presence sheds a light within thy home.

My earnest wish for thee upon this morn,
    Is that afflictions were not thine to bear;
Such in the past thou hast so meekly borne,
    Scarce with a murmur, or disheartening tear.

And oh! I ask my God to make them less,
    And if that may not be His holy will;
To grant they may not deeper on thee press,
    And give thee strength to meekly bear them still.

'Twill ever be my duty, Mother mine,
    To tend thy wants, increasing every day;
And to fulfil the slightest wish of thine,
    My joy to cheer, and light thee on thy way.

I 'mind the time, when lying on thy breast,
    I found my sweetest, surest, refuge there;
And at thy knee before I sought my rest,
    Thou taughtest me to lisp my evening prayer.

Thy fostering care around my childhood threw,
    A golden halo, formed of love-rays bright;
As flowers will grow bathed in the God-sent dew,
    My life expanded, neath its sacred light.

The loving words that thou to me wouldst say,
   Are all engraved upon my memory yet ;
And now at last, at thy declining day,
   I tremble lest thy sun too soon should set.

A smaller circle daily is thy bound,
   Thy life runs in an ever-narrowing groove :
And yet thy heart is close enfolded 'round
   With priceless love, which time can ne'er remove.

But ever strengthens with each passing day,
   And shows a richness all before unknown :
But deep as 'tis, it cannot once repay
   The pure fond love which thou to me hast shown.

God grant that it may long be mine to feel
   The greatest blessing sent us from the sky :
A mother's love ! for does it not reveal
   A spring of joy, whose font is found on High ?

BIRTHDAY WISH TO MY FATHER.

    Father dear upon this morn,
    From my heart to thee is borne,
    Loving wishes to adorn.
       Thy natal day.

    I would ask my God to shed,
    Blessings on thy hoary head,—
    Clear the path for thee to tread.
       From every thorn.

    Every good and precious thing,
    That the angels but can bring,
    May they on thy pathway fling,
       And make it bright !

    Unto Heaven I humbly pray,
    Long on earth to let thee stay,—
    Call not yet thy soul away,
       To dwell with Him.

Like an oak-tree past its prime,
Crusted with the silvery rime,
In the restful winter time,
    I see thee now.

Toil has long on thee been laid,
Ne'er I fear can be repaid,
Sacrifices thou hast made,
    For me, thy child.

'Tis my wish oh! Father dear,
To thy side be ever near,
There to solace and to cheer
    Thy agèd heart.

Thou hast bravely in the past,
Weathered through life's every blast,
Now thine evening brings at last
    Its rest and peace.

May it's tender glow so bright,
Like the summer's constant light,
Linger far into the night,
    Before its fades.

HAPPY MEMORIES.

Happy memories! how they haunt us,
    Sweetest moments lived and gone,
Rise before the mental vision,
    Till the heart feels not alone.
Clothed in subtle forms of beauty,
    Happy glimpses of the past,
Fill the soul with joys too fleeting—
    Gladdening gleams, too fair to last:
And illumes the living present,
    Till a spell is o'er us cast.

Happy memories! oh, we love them
    Treasures of the long ago:
But to see their sunny pictures,
    Makes the beating heart to glow:

While we revel in those visions,
    Memory brings like Hope, to cheer;
By its tender touch awakened
    Are the things we hold most dear;
Pleasant faces beam around us,
    Absent voices whisper near.

Memory throws up bridges golden—
    Spans the intervening time:—
Links the past unto the present,
    Chastened yet, and more sublime:
On the road, we since have traversed,
    All that was prosaic is lost;
Memory's gems, adorned by Fancy,
    Only have the chasm crossed;
Bringing balm unto the spirit,
    When with troubles tried and tost.

Happy memories! how they often—
    As the actual past we see,
In a mirror bright, reflected,—
    Thrill the heart, where'er we be:
Touch the spring, and they will show us,
    Moments all unknown to pain;—
Bring once more the sense of rapture,
    As we live them o'er again;
Brightest scenes will flash before us,
    In a vivid, golden train.

Happy memories! oh, we feel them,
    Grow more precious day by day;
Ever sweeter, more consoling,—
    Drops of nectar on our way;
Time but serves to make more mellow
    Loving memories true and fair,
And they come to us invested,
    With a rosy colour rare:
Memory but preserves the purest,
    Those for which the heart must care.

Even will one strain of music,
    Bring to us some vanished scene:-
Rouse to life some latent feeling—
    Place us where we once have been;

Through its power the old impressions,
    There received, again we feel;
And the past delights reviving,
    Softly o'er the senses steal.
Music thus enables Memory
    All its secrets to reveal.

Sweet are those associations,
    Oft it is some much-loved place,
Far away, that is remembered,
    Or some dear familiar face:
Locked in Memory's laden storehouse,
    There embalmed and laid at rest,
Are those thoughts, like priceless jewels,
    And when old, are loved the best:
Sent to solace and to cheer us,
    Happy memories, always blest.

A PAIR OF LOVERS.

With ardent gaze he scanned her face,
    With health and beauty all aglow:
And watched her youthful form of grace,
    Then spoke in thrilling accents low.

"Wilt thou be mine?" he fondly said,
    "For I have dearly loved thee long;
My constant thoughts of thee, have led
    To pure affection, deep and strong.

"I wear thine image in my heart,
    Thou art before me day and night;
And now I feel I cannot part
    From thee, my guardian angel bright.

"The more I see thee, more I feel
    My heart towards its ideal warms;
No other one shall ever steal
    My love from all thy soft'ning charms.

"There's beauty in thy golden hair,
 And in those truthful azure eyes;
Thou art so lovely, good, and fair,
 Like some sweet seraph in disguise.

"I cannot tell thee half the love
 That surges here within my breast;
My adoration now to prove,
 I ask that thou wilt make me blest,

"By being my own; oh! share my home,
 Let thy dear presence cheer my lot!
I'll promise that in years to come,
 By me thou shalt be ne'er forgot.

"I know thy love is mine, I've seen
 Its tokens in a hundred ways;
Thou hast betrayed thyself, and been
 The sunshine of my lonely days.

"I feel my offer well might be
 By one less noble, turned to scorn;
For one endowed with charms, like thee,
 A higher place would well adorn.

"I shall be proud to call thee mine,
 Thy beauty all the world will praise:
My wealth and fortune shall be thine,
 To keep thee from laborious days.

"Then, darling, be my loving wife!
 That bliss may fill my future store;
I'll shield thee from all ills of life,
 If thou'lt be mine for evermore!"

'Twas good, 'twas sweet, to hear him speak,
 His tender words her heart could move;
With downcast eyes, with burning cheek,
 She listened to his tale of love.

"I doubt not your affection now,"
 She softly whispered in his ear;
"'Tis sweet to hear your fervid vow,—
 To know that I have grown so dear;

"But when my beauty shall depart,
   And age shall stamp me with decay;
Shall I retain within your heart
   The place I feel I hold to-day?

"I fear you only worship youth,
   And when its transient charms are past,
Your ardour then may cool, in truth
   My image from your heart be cast."

"Nay, nay!" he cried, with burning gaze,
   While passion trembled in his tone:
"Come weal, come woe, through all my days
   I'll love, and cling to thee alone!

"Thy radiant beauty will not fade,
   Nor lessen with the lapse of time;
For those endearing charms were made
   To last when life is past its prime.

"E'en age can ne'er our love-bonds break,
   Thy heart on mine has deeper hold;
I fain would die for thy dear sake,
   For love like mine can ne'er grow cold!"

Thus she was won; while there he knelt,
   She gave to him her heart and hand;
And on their nuptial day she felt,
   The happiest lady in the land!

*   *   *   *   *

Years sped: a faded matron now
   Whose beauty long since passed away;
Sits lonely, with a time-lined brow,
   The locks that once were gold are grey.

Her ardent, trusted lover proved,
   False, faithless, fickle, and untrue;
Another's heart, alas! he loved——
   His early choice he lived to rue.

Too late the good fond wife was taught,
   That fleeting passion's vows ne'er last;
He but for youthful beauty sought,   [past.
   Then spurned her, when those charms were

Remained she constant unto him,
    Though all his love for her had flown ;
Her fascinations gone, and grim
    And cheerless had their home-life grown.

She bore for him no charms of mind,
    Though grown estranged, she ne'er would
Her spirit broke, her health declined. [chide ;
    A poor neglected wife she died!

ANOTHER PAIR.

"You tell me oft that I am fair,
    And say how much you love me now ;
You praise my glossy auburn hair,
    And what you call my "classic" brow.

"You tell me that my bright dark eyes,
    Are love-lit when they glance at you :
And while you seek their depths, your sighs
    Are like a lover's, warm and true.

"I know you deeply love me now,
    That to each other we are dear ;
Besides your oft repeated vow,
    I see you're happy when I'm near.

"You now admire what oft you call
    My graceful step, and sylph-like form ;
I see by every glance, that all
    These outward things, your senses charm.

"My soft white hands, the roses pink,
    That bloom upon my rounded cheek,
All please you now, but do you think
    The reason is so far to seek ?

"It is because I'm *young*, that now
    You love these beauteous signs of health ;
They're all that I can boast, you know,
    For I possess no worldly wealth.

"But when my beauty fades away,
  Oh! will you then my presence seek?
When these brown tresses all are grey,
  And when the rose forsakes my cheek?

"A faithful love, that time will test,
  Is what we women dearly prize;
I fear my own I have confessed,
  You've read it in my tell-tale eyes.

"From you I've thought it was concealed,
  Avowals ill become a maid;
A glance my secret has revealed,
  Or by a blush I've been betrayed.

"Stern time the ardent lover tries:
  When beauty dwells not in my face,
When dim shall grow these lustrous eyes,
  And when my form shall lose its grace:—

"*Then* if you show you love me, when
  I'm old, 'twill raptures bring to me;
I shall *believe* you're earnest *then*,
  Such love indeed would constant be!

"The mind, the heart, the soul, will all
  Outlive the beauty born of youth:
All these shall charm, and never pall,
  If filled with goodness, love, and truth.

"If these attract you now, then stay,
  And be my lover all through life;
Go! if they charm you not, I say,
  I'll ne'er consent to be your wife."

   *   *   *   *

He said he'd love through woe or weal,—
  Would all his fondest vows fulfil;
Though years her youthful bloom might steal,
  For her sweet self, he'd love her still.

A sacred promise, nobly kept;
  As time wore on he loved her more,—
Found virtues which in youth had slept,
  Soul-beauties, all unprized before.

Their mutual love grew year by year,
  The youthful flame was kept alive ;
Until at three-score years they were
  As loving as at twenty-five!

United were they, soul and heart,
  Shared all life's joys and sorrows were ;
Time's usage served but to impart,
  A deeper, stronger, love-bond there.

Though silvered now her hair has grown,
  Around her temples, once so white ;
And what though youthful bloom has flown,
  Her eyes retain for him their light.

Age brings her charms that will endure,
  That compensate for those of youth ;
That ripen but in years mature,
  A sweetness born of faith and truth.

And now in life's blest eventide,
  As early days they oft recall ;
They nearer, dearer, side by side,
  Wait calmly till the night shall fall.

THE PATRICIAN'S CURSE.

Within his old ancestral hall, one hallowed Christmas night,
Where, though 'twas cold and wild outside, the fires burned warm and bright ;
A proud patrician, tall and straight, in fierce defiance stood,
In all the pomp and boasted strength of rich and purple blood.
His hands were clenched, his black brows scowled, o'er dark and glittering eyes,
His attitude was one of scorn, that mocks while it defies.
A plebeian stood before him there, and craved his kind regard,
And offered him his large brown hand, with palm so rough and hard ;

He meekly asked that he might work for him, the noble
    lord,—
That he would help him rise by toil among his hirling
    horde.
And as a faith-pledge fain would greet the haughty
    white-palmed sire,
When "peace on earth, good-will to men," that day
    should all inspire.
"Keep back, keep back!" the despot cried, "and get
    thee hence instead,
I'll give thee work on my domains, wherewith to earn
    thy bread,
But never let thy toil-stained hand, in contact be with
    mine,
For if it does, my curse shall rest for aye on thee and
    thine!
A plebeian drew my son from home; and led his footsteps
    wrong,—
Caused him to forfeit all the rights that to his birth
    belong;
And when that ill-born villian plunged my home in deep
    disgrace,
I vowed that hand of mine should ne'er touch him, nor
    his low race;
Then woe be to the one who dares defy my stern
    command,
Nay, I would rather *die* than touch a finger of thy hand!
The servile wretch who breaks my law, that act shall he
    deplore,
Thus rouse my wrath, I'll curse both thee and thine for
    evermore!"

. . . . .

A week passed by, the new year dawned upon a wintry
    scene;
The snow-king with a spotless garb, enshrouded all the
    green :—
Transfigured with his wondrous wand, congealed the
    limpid streams,
That lay like tinted glass beneath the red sun's slanting
    beams.

And in the lord's sequest'red park, the erstwhile murmuring rill,
Was voiceless as the sun-kissed lake, that slept so cold and still;
The tall ancestral trees were decked with pendent crystals bright,
That ever and anon fell down upon the sward so white.
The proud imperious lord went forth, in warmest furs arrayed,
And down towards the lonely lake, his idle footsteps strayed.
All nature slept in solitude, as if it ne'er could wake;
There was but one poor hirling there, who swept the ice-bound lake;
The one whom just a week ago, he had rebuked in wrath,
And whom he now bade clear the snow from each surrounding path.
The proud patrician soon had skates upon his noble feet,—
Went skimming o'er the slumbrous lake, then was his joy complete!
He glided o'er its surface bright, for be it understood,
His lordship loved the pastime well, that warmed his frigid blood.
A crack, a crash, and lo! the treacherous ice began to break,
A moment more, the autocrat was struggling in the lake!
Immersed o'erhead, he raised a loud and frantic cry for aid;
The potentate when safe so bold, in danger was afraid.
Then for support he madly clutched the jagg'd ice o'er his head,
It only broke, and left for him, a wider gap instead;
The cumbrous garment donned that day, to keep his lordship warm,
Now only served to downward drag the massive portly form;
And as he loved secluded haunts, thus none were standing by,
To watch his battle fierce for life, or hear his desperate cry:—

None but the plebeian's ear had caught the mournful gurgling sound,
He hurried on toward the spot, despite the slippery ground.
"Come fellow here," the rich one cried, "lend me thy sturdy hand,
Assist me quickly, or I sink, oh! pull me on to land."
The poor man watched him in despair, his heart with pity stirred,
He saw the pleading up-turned eyes, the hoarse appeal he heard;
He fain had seized the out-stretched hand, but of that vow he thought;
Not just on him, on all his kin, a curse would then be brought.
He threw his neck-scarf, it was grasped, numb fingers clenched it fast,
He pulled with all his might, but lo! it broke in twain at last;
"Give me thy hand," came feebly then, "for I am sinking now,"
"I dare not sire," the poor man cried, "I fear thy wrathful vow;"
"Good heavens! and does my vow now stand between grim death and me?
I perish if I may not cling this moment unto thee!
For mercy's sake give me thy hand! my rash words I recall;
When face to face with death, I find, that we are equals all;
My limbs are stiffening fast, oh come! my curse I now revoke;
Too late! his face grew livid while with gasping voice he spoke;
For when the friendly plebeian hand reached out to him at length,
It touched a numb and listless palm, that now had lost its strength;
A moment more, the drowning man had drawn his dying breath.
The ghastly up-turned face had sunk in cold relentless death!

DREAMS.

Ye phantoms of thought that arise in the sleep,
    In colours so vivid and bright;
The while the moon's ray floods the blue mountain steep,
    Enhancing the beauty of night.

Ye visions of fancy, sometimes so obscure,
    On Morpheus' wings ye are borne;
And often so flimsy ye cannot endure
    But fly at the dawn of the morn.

Sometimes ye are strangely unreal and absurd,
    Grotesque are the pictures we see;
Ye tell us of things that we never have heard,—
    Show places where ne'er we shall be.

At times ye're so vivid and weird, that we think
    A yawning abyss we are near,
So awful our danger, we quail on its brink,
    Then wake, as if falling, in fear.

Then take ye the form of a lingering charm,
    And haunt in the light of the day;
Impressions that soften, the senses will calm,
    When Somnus has drifted away.

How often ye quiet and comfort the soul—
    Transport us to happier scenes;
Ye flights of the vision, we cannot control
    But yield to the spell of our dreams!

Oft-times we imagine the voices of friends
    Are whispering close to the ear;
Things transient and lovely the god of ye sends,
    Romantic, compared with aught here.

Perchance may some vague unconnected idea
    Come over our thoughts in the day—
Ideas, that no sooner conceived, than appear
    To vanish as quickly away.

We seem to have acted, or spoken, before,
   (But cannot recall it to mind);
Such actions, or words, we're repeating them o'er,
   'Tis part of a dream undefined ;—

Been hid in the deepest recess of the brain,
   And all but forgotten had been ;
An incident called them before us again,
   We feel in a shadowy dream.

And oft the dear faces of those who are gone,
   Appear in our slumbers so deep ;
We meet them in ecstasy—feel not alone,
   But speak with them sweetly in sleep.

'Twould seem they descend from the Home of
   Afford a significant theme :   [the Blest—
And scenes of the past will assume in our rest,
   The form of a beautiful dream !

And figures fantastic will lead us away,
   In dark lonely depths of the night;
The freaks and the pranks that the vision will play,
   That go with the first gleam of light.

The fairies seem waving their magical wands,
   They mystic and intricate seem ;
Our spirits are roving to far away lands,
   Oh ! such is the power of a dream.

TO A YOUNG LADY ON HER TWENTY-FIRST BIRTHDAY.

This morn from my heart I greet thee,
   On reaching thy twenty-first year ;
And heartily wish in the future,
   Thou many may'st see, and as fair.
When Spring with a lovely diadem,
   In the glorious month of May,
Stept forward to crown sweet Nature,
   And bade her the sceptre sway :—

Bedecked her with wreaths of blossom,
   Begemmed with the diamond dew,
That flashed with her slightest motion,
   And with every breath she drew.
'Twas then that thy loving parents,
   First looked on their dark-eyed child;
As welcome as were the May flowers,
   That bloomed in the dingle wild.
Long summers since then have glided,
   And standing thou art to-day,
At the door of the woman's epoch,
   Thy girlhood has passed away.
I see thee a merry maiden,
   The pride of a happy home;
Thy voice is the household music,
   As gaily thy light steps roam.
Thou'rt now in thy life's rich Maytime,
   Enjoying its gifts so sweet;
And treading a rosy pathway,
   With beauty and mirth replete:
With garlands of love's own weaving,
   To gladden thy fresh young heart;
And unto thy sweet girl-nature,
   A grace of their own impart.
Now basking in life's bright morning,
   The world is to thee yet fair;
But deem not 'tis made for pleasure,
   Unmingled with grief or care.
Thou seest not its sober aspects,
   Oh! prize it while youth is thine;
So live it, that sweet blest memories,
   May long through its evening shine.
God shield thee from all temptations,
   From aught in the world defiled;
Give thanks that He long has lavished,
   His blessings on thee, His child:
And use for His good, my dearest,
   The gifts that are thine in trust:
So give to thy name a lustre,
   When beauty shall sleep in dust.
Give thoughts unto those less favoured,—
   Whom fortune has ne'er caressed;

The thankful and humble spirit,
    Is ever the truly blest.
Live nobly, whate'er be thy portion,
    In woman's revered estate:
As maiden, or wife, or mother,
    Whatever thy destined fate.
By keeping to lines of duty,
    Wherever our lot is cast:
We win for ourselves that hearts-ease,
    That cheers us when youth is past.
It may be a minor cadence,
    Vibrates through this natal song;
'Twill into the heart sink deeper,
    And cling to the memory long.
When years shall have brought reflection,
    These words that seem worthless now:
To thee will have graver import,
    When time shall have stamped thy brow.
God bless thee, and guard thee always!
    And may'st thou enjoy through Him,
A long and a happy life Dear,
    That never a cloud may dim!

DEJECTED.

To-day I am sad and dejected,
    The beautiful sun will not shine;
I feel that the sky has reflected
    Its gloom in this bosom of mine.

The clouds are incessantly shifting,
    In majesty moving away;
Like icebergs they onward are drifting,
    O'er skies that are sullen and grey.

I fear that a storm is impending,
    The sky is o'ershadowed again;
Those ominous clouds are extending,
    To pour out a deluge of rain.

By southerly winds they are driven,
   In volumes are sweeping along;
While others are scattered and riven,
   And silently gliding among.

All nature seems brooding in sorrow,
   So dreary, and downcast, and sad;
And waiting a brighter to-morrow,
   In hopes to be sunny and glad.

So sad, and oppressive, and dreary,
   The heavens look down upon me;
My heart is so lonely and weary,
   Sweet Muse, I am yearning for thee!

I long for thy presence to cheer me,
   Come down from the heights, on thy wing;
I'm happy when thou art so near me,
   To soothe me, and help me to sing.

My soul is beset with depression,
   I want to unburden my heart:
My thoughts cannot find their expression,
   Why did'st thou so rashly depart?

In solitude often I ponder;
   Come down from thy beautiful home;
And join me as lonely I wander,
   Come hither, sweet comforter, come!

Descend through the portals of Heaven,
   Come down in thy freedom so wild;
The gift that my Maker has given,
   To comfort His poor humble child.

For oh! I am sad and desponding,
   All seemeth so formal and cold;
I speak to a world unresponding,
   And silent as yonder dark wold.

The sky seems to pity my feeling
   Have sympathy with the oppressed:
And night o'er the great world is stealing,
   To lull me to slumber and rest

ANSWERED.

Jesus, in the hour of midnight,
   Shaking with a dreadful fear,—
Threatened with a sore bereavement,
   Greater than my heart could bear,—
Yet amidst my bosom's anguish,
   Felt I then that Thou wert near.—

There, to hearken my petition,
   There, to aid and comfort me;
Close beside me, as I pleaded
   Humbly, on my bended knee;
There I, in my hour of trouble,
   Sought and found relief in Thee!

Blessèd Jesus! Thou didst give it
   Freely to this child of Thine;—
Granted me direct from Heaven,
   Mercies precious and divine;—
Caused within my darkened chamber,
   Peace and hope again to shine.

Jesus, can I e'er forget Thee?—
   Soother of my midnight grief;
Jesus, when I called upon Thee,
   Thou didst make my trouble brief:—
In my hour of tribulation,
   Thou didst give my heart relief.

Jesus, never Thou forsake me,
   Be Thou near me every day,—
Near to guide me in my actions,
   Near to light me on my way;—
Near to be my stay and comfort,
   Near to hear me when I pray.

Jesus, what were I without Thee?
   Oh! attend me everywhere;
Love me, oh, my soul's Redeemer,
   Keep me 'neath Thy watchful care;
What were earth without Thy teachings,
   What were life without a prayer!

A SILVER WEDDING GREETING.

The years have passed, and I greet you now
On the silver day of your wedded life,
But time has lovingly kissed the brow,
    Of husband, and of wife.

Though years have sped, yet their only trace,
Are the silvery streaks in your plenteous hair;
The rose still clings to the rounded face,
    And Care sits lightly there.

Love made you happier with its light,
As hand in hand you have glided on ;
For softly over your head its bright
    Fair nimbus long has shone.

What silvery music around I hear!
The wedding bells, with a silvery ring ;
While friends with silvery voices clear,
    Their silver offerings bring.

One backward glance at a long past day,
When bridal blossoms were strewn with zest ;
And loving hearts that were bright and gay,
    Your future journey blest.

God blest it too, with a wealth of joy,
Flowers graced your pathway by His command,
But lest earth's pleasures unmixed should cloy,
    He touched with chast'ning hand.—

For Death and Sorrow were not unknown,
Their shadows fell on your sunny ways,
Whene'er our Father would claim His own,
    In those sad bygone days.

Grief made a void in your youthful hearts,
God saw the chasm, and bridged it o'er ;
Faith made you stronger to bear your parts,
    With Hope, it can restore.

The springtide's blossoms have passed away,
But now the fruits of your union blest,
Are growing 'round you each passing day,
    Made richer by love's test.

Oh, happy pair!—for what untold joys
Unto their parents your off-spring brings,—
Fair blooming maidens, and noble boys,
    Reward with love that clings.

They cherish their home of childhood yet,—
Are bound to it by affection's ties ;
Your tenderest care they will ne'er forget,
    For such pure love ne'er dies.

Those dearest treasures be sure were sent,
To comfort you in life's evening time ;
To cheer its shades when noon is spent,
    Lead you, when past your prime.

The nuptial knot that was tied in youth,
Is now a sacred and silver bond,
Cemented closer by love and truth,
    'Twill last this life beyond.

'Twill ever deepen, and richer grow,
Till in the future afar 'twill wear,
A holier, mellower, golden glow,
    The path of age make fair.

You've reached life's summit, now in your prime,
Beside each other so true you're found ;
May you so live till the *golden* time,
    With every blessing crowned !

TO AN AFFLICTED ONE.

Gentle sister, 'biding there,
Meek and patient, frail and fair :
Being aloof from active joys,
Thy pure spirit ne'er annoys.

Sore-afflicted, sad thy lot,
Yet we hear thee murmur not;
Bowing to God's chastening hand,
Knowing 'tis by His command,
That thy life should crippled be;
Yet my heart goes out to thee
When I gaze upon thy face,
Where we can thy suffering trace.
Tended in thy restful bower,
Like a tender hot-house flower;
Growing lovlier day by day,
As earth's day-dreams melt away;
As thy soul-bonds loosen now,
Peace sits radiant on thy brow.
Gently nurtured, loved of Heaven!
Compensations it has given;—
Noblest souls we ofttimes find,
In frail structures are enshrined;
Through its mortal cage thine glows,
Consentrated, richer grows.
Earth's vain longings touch it not,
Chastening for a brighter spot:—
Basking in God's sheltering love,
Training for His crown Above.

MUSIC.

Oh! the mystic power of music,
   Thrilling every nerve and vein;
Makes us feel as though we're living
   Through life's happiest hours again:—
Every fibre is pulsating,
      With its sweet strain!

'Tis the soft'ning charm of music,
   Falling sweetly on the ear,
Lulling us as if in dreamland,
   Bringing all our loved ones near:—
As the notes we hear vibrating,
      So soft and clear.

Ah, the hidden soul of music,
    Thousands bow before its shrine ;
With its deep and tender pathos,
    Who loves not the art divine?
With old masters' inspirations,
    What joy is mine!

Hear the thrilling voice of music,
    Waking memories of the past;
As the melodies come stealing,
    Low and sweeter at the last :—
Noble and sublime creations,
    A spell have cast.

Hark! the harmony of music,
    Chords and grand vibrations made ;
What can touch the heart so tender
    As sweet music, softly played?—
With true sympathy revealing
    Each light and shade.

When the heart is sad and lonely,
    Then we feel the greatest charm ;
As its melody so cheering,
    Sheds a pleasant, soothing balm :
Till we grow 'neath each cadenza,
    Serene and calm.

Music is the soul's fine language,
    Understood in every part ;
A medium, that when waken'd, makes its
    Impress on another's heart :
And beneath its influence often,
    The tears will start.

Cultivate the gift of music,
    It will brighten many an hour,—
Cheer thee, when in deep depression,
    Soothe thee, with its mystic power :
It can make the humblest cottage,
    Like Orpheus' bower.

Oh! I love the charm of music,
   Love it more than words can tell;
All subdued I list' enraptured,
   As the sweet tones float and swell :—
They hold me, and my thoughts lift higher,
   With magic spell.

"BLACK DIAMONDS."

Tell me not there are no heroes,
   But those in battle's fierce array;
There are daring, manly fellows
   At work around us every day:
Clad albeit, in toil-stained garments,
   What does outward vesture matter?
Cannot hearts be just as noble,
   Just as true, 'neath dirty tatter?

Since the tender age of seven,
   Some men have toiled in deepest mines;
Where there blows no breeze from heaven,
   And where the bright sun never shines:
Toiled till they're of stunted stature,
   Bent and cramped as they are mining—
Form is sacrificed for labour,
   Yet we hear them not repining.

Men and boys set forth at morning,
   To work beneath the cold damp earth;
Each a woman's son, or husband,
   And is to her of priceless worth:
Bold, and fearless of all danger,
   Cheerfully they go unbidden;
Fearing not that Death in ambush,
   In the coal-mine may be hidden.

Waiting, when they're most unwary,
   In darkest depths he oft will lurk;
Then, without a moment's warning,
   He takes them when they're hard at work.

Who can tell the noblest natures,
   Toiling in the darksome measures?
Danger tests who are unselfish,—
   Proves that mines hide *human* treasures.

Who can paint the heart's deep anguish,
   When women hear the awful sound
Of the foul air, when exploding,
   Within the coal-mine underground?
Like the deaf'ning roll of thunder,—
   'Tis as if the earth were groaning,
When the fire-damp is escaping,—
   Followed by the victims' moaning.

To the scene of devastation,
   Men ever willing are to go,
To explore the mines undaunted,—
   To face the after-damp, their foe:
Face it for their dying comrades—
   This their cruel foe defiant:
Yet they promptly do their searching,
   Brave of heart, and self-reliant.

Touching tales we hear related,—
   How in the mine one dying man,
Wrote these words, "Good-bye dear Betsey"
   And, "You must do the best you can:"
Then with trembling hands the miner
   Added, "Pray God help us all;"
On his "corve" he traced the message
   Feebly, when he heard God's call.

And his final words we echo,—
   That God would help them all we pray:—
Grant His peace to those poor fellows,
   When in Death's strong embrace they lay:
And their dear ones now in sorrow,
   Pray we for their welfare too,
Aid them till their blest reunion,
   With their lost ones, loved and true.

Once there died a youthful hero
   A " hurrier " boy, who toiled below,
When the deadly gas was vented,
   And Christ methinks has claimed him now;
Others sought the path of safety,
   Called him, yet he went another;
Saying " No! I cannot join you
   Till I've found my darling brother."

Though a little rough black diamond,
   We know he died a noble death:
While these words, " I'll save my brother;"
   Were ling'ring on his dying breath:
Sacrificed his life in boyhood,
   Grieving now will not restore him:
Angels deck his brow in Heaven,—
   Why should earthly friends deplore him?

TO AN AMERICAN WRITER OF SOME EULOGISTIC VERSES TO THE AUTHORESS.

HARK! my lyre has roused an echo
   From the New World, far away,
Comes to me a chord of music,
   On the Old Year's dying day.

From those tender notes that reach me,
   Whispers from a distant shore,—
It would seem to me the minstrel
   Must have touched the lyre before.

Stranger, from my heart I thank thee!
   For thy sweet and cheering song
Wafted hither o'er the waters,
   Prompts me in my purpose strong.

If my songs have given comfort,
　　Even to one single breast,
By the gracious God who gave them
　　Are my efforts truly blest.

All my lays are free and simple;
　　As the wild-bird's song they flow,
From the heart, and thus it seemeth,
　　Into other hearts they glow.

Through the gift that God hath gi'en me
　　All my pent-up feelings gush;
I will sing while He permits me—
　　Till His voice shall bid me hush.

TO E.J.H. ON HER SEVENTEENTH BIRTHDAY.

Sweet gentle maid, thy friend's best wishes take
　　Unto thy heart, for they are all sincere:
My love is thine, and for thy own dear sake
　　I hail this day, what though thou art not near.
　　　　For I have seen
Thy childhood and thy girlhood pass away;
　　Bedimmed alas! by one dark mournful cloud;
But that has passed, and now thou hast to-day,
　　Attained that age of which we all are proud,—
　　　　Sweet seventeen!

Past are the first two epochs of thy life,
　　And standing on the threshold of the third,
Thy spirit finds there woman's cares are rife,
　　And trembles in its cage, like some poor bird.
　　　　But falter not:
Reared in the atmosphere of home, to shield
　　Thy charms unfolding, like a tender flower:—
As modest as the daisy in the field,—
　　Pure as the lily in its native bower,—
　　　　Blest be thy lot!

A MOTHER'S LULLABY.

Sleep, my child, for I am near.
   Close beside thy bed;
To wipe away that fretful tear,
   And soothe thy aching head.
Twilight shadows now are cast,
   Upon the cottage wall;
Sleep, for night is falling fast—
   And God is over all.

Rest, my precious darling, rest,
   Thy little troubles calm;
Mother sits beside thee lest
   Aught should do thee harm.
On thy little curly head
   The silv'ry moonbeams fall;
Angels hover round thy bed,
   And God is over all.

All thy childish sports are o'er
   Thy playthings put away,—
Folded is yon pretty flower,
   Until another day.
The little bird has gone to sleep,
   And ceased its plaintive call;
Silence reigns around thee deep,—
   And God is over all.

Then hush that peevish, fretful sound,
   And close those pretty eyes;
Oblivion reigneth all around,
   The wind has hushed its sighs.
The sun has lowered in the west,
   'Twas like a golden ball;
The weary world has gone to rest,—
   And God is over all.

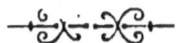

THE LOVER'S LAY.

Dearest, since I first beheld thee,
   Life is not the same to me;
Everything around is brighter,
   Tinctured with the thoughts of thee:
Life is fairer, life is sweeter,—
   Sweeter with the thoughts of thee.

Absence only makes thee dearer,
   And thine image 'gainst my will,
Comes before me, bright and radiant,
   Parted though, I love thee still;
Daily now my life grows sweeter,—
   Sweeter thoughts my day-dreams fill.

How I miss thy bright young presence,
   Here, away from thee and thine:
Yet thy spirit comes to cheer me,
   Oh! that I could call thee mine!
Since I knew thee, life is sweeter—
   Sweeter, as our hearts entwine.

Night and day thy bright orbs haunt me,
   And I seem to live again,
In the sunshine of thy presence,
   Could the vision but remain!
Life is fuller, life is sweeter,—
   Sweeter while such love-dreams reign.

Love has all things now transfigured,
   Glorified the meanest things:
Called forth tender, new emotions,
   Touched the soul's deep hidden springs;
Life is fairer, richer, sweeter,-
   Sweeter with a love that clings.

Oh! that I to-day might see thee,
   Meet thy lustrous, love-lit eyes:
Clasp thy hand in love's warm pressure:
   These, stern Fate to me denies.
Fond reflections make life sweeter,-
   Sweeter, while each moment flies.

But 'tis well to know that distance
    Cannot once our love-links break ;
Tender tokens, love's remembrance,
    Treasured are for thy dear sake :
Precious love-gifts make life sweeter—
    Sweeter thoughts of thee they wake.

Memory now the past illumines,—
    Those loved hours I've spent with thee ;
Burnished are like golden waymarks,
    Till they glisten, fair to see :—
Making present duties sweeter,—
    Sweeter, with the thoughts of thee.

Smiling Hope, with rainbow colours,
    Points our future, fair and light ;
From its ever flowing fountain,
    Brings me nectar day and night ;
Tells me life will yet be sweeter,—
    Sweeter with thy presence bright.

Sweet to know what though we're parted,
    Thou art thinking oft of me ;
Sweet to feel thou art responsive,
    True, as I shall ever be !
Not forgotten ! life is sweeter,—
    Sweeter to be loved by thee.

What a subtile touch of nature,
    Draws together heart to heart !
Soul is unto soul vibrating,
    Though so far from me thou art ;
Love-bonds strong have made life sweeter,
    Sweeter, though we dwell apart.

Would that thou wert mine for ever !
    Would that thou wert always near ;
Mine to keep, to love, and cherish,
    Mine to comfort, and to cheer ;
This is what I ask me often,
    Could I live without thee, Dear ?

THE FLOWER GIRL.

'Twas in the city's busy street,
   The air was keen and chill:
Benumbing was the fog so bleak—
   For winter linger'd still.

A little fragile form was seen
   To wander in the street:
A maiden selling flowers, and she
   Had cold and shoeless feet.

With timid, supplicating glance,
   The same words she would cry:—
"Who'll have a pretty bunch of flowers?
   Oh, come now, will you buy?—

"I've got some pretty crocuses—
   Daffodils of golden hue:
And here are lovely primroses,
   Snowdrops, and violets too."

And all day in the cheerless street,
   The strangers passed her by;
They heeded not her pleading voice—
   They heard not her low sigh.

Then tired and weary she sat down,
   Upon a window sill—
The poor and fragile little girl,
   So pale and gentle still.

She felt so cold and hungry then,
   And sighed in deep distress,
And drew more close around her form,
   Her little tattered dress.

A watchman passed, with measured step,
   And saw her sitting there:
He said: "My child, you'll go back home.
   You are not wanted here."

"Go home? I have no home," she said,
  "My friends are far away;
My mother, she is long since dead:
  Oh, please, Sir, let me stay.

"My master, he'll be angry if
  My flowers are not sold;
And oh! I dare not take them back,
  For fear that he should scold."

And then her eyes grew dim with tears,
  Her little heart was sad;
One solitary penny piece
  Alas! was all she had!

And when she tried to sell her flowers
  The passers-by would say:
"We do not want your flowers, my girl,
  Why don't you go away?"

And then the shades of eve crept on,
  And faded into night;
Then all the splendid shops were gay,
  With many a dazzling light.

And no one in the city cared
  For that poor wretched child;
Alone, in want, amidst the wealth
  And pleasures of mankind.

But ere another day had dawned,
  The girl had found a home;
A happy home! where all is love
  No more again to roam.

Her weary limbs found rest at last,
  Her spirit fled away:—
Fled from this dreary world of ours,
  Before another day.

For on a doorstep she was found,
  Her hand beneath her head;
Her flowers beside her: there she lay
  So cold, and white, and dead!

LINES TO A YOUTH ON ATTAINING HIS MAJORITY.

All joy to thee, on this thy natal day!
Though boyhood sweet for thee has passed away,
More dignified thou com'st before us now,
In all youth's ardour, with unclouded brow.
Upon the threshold of thy manhood we
Behold thee standing, buoyant bright and free:
With radiant smile thou meetst the coming years,
Unknown to sorrow, and life's withering cares.
Impulsive youth! with day-dreams fair and bright,
What though thy form has gained its manhood's height,
Thy soul will not attain, though e'er so pure
Its fullest stature, till in years mature.
Thou lookest back on this thy happy time,
And contemplat'st it, when in manhood's prime.
In gorgeous hues, all things to thee now seem,
Aglow with love; while Hope's inspiring beam,
Illumes the path where youth's impetuous feet,
Tread lightly now, on roses fair and sweet.
Though we no more shall know thee as a boy,
Yet may the fullness of all earthly joy
Attend thee ever, through life's mazy throng;
As good upholding, and renouncing wrong,
Thou keepest on with purpose firm and true,
And righteous ways, with rectitude pursue:
Bring honour, and with measure full and free,
Give back the love that erst has nurtured thee.
'Mongst fellow men to-day then start in life,
Put on thy armour, join the earnest strife;
Though strong temptations may beset thy way,
We fully trust that thou wilt "watch and pray."
Strong be thy faith, ask God to be thy guide,
And lead thee right, then will no ill betide.
Oh! may thy life like placid streamlet be,
That wends in peace so gently to the sea;
Unlike the torrent, tearing onward fast,
With mad impetus, all too quickly past.

Now thou hast reached that all-important age,
When thou must step upon life's busy stage;
The joyous youth the prologue but has been,
The curtain rises on the opening scene.
And thou henceforth must take a foremost part
In life's great drama, and where-e'er thou art,
Enact it nobly; make thy efforts shine,
And let a truly worthy part be thine:
Sustain it well, so that thy manly *role*,
Be emulated by a brother soul;
And when at length the final scene shall close,
The words "well done!" shall greet thee 'midst applause.

THE DYING CHILD.

Mother, I am going to leave you,
   I am going so far away;
I shall be in happy Heaven,
   Ere there dawns another day.

Mother, see the sun is setting—
   Sinking slowly in the west;
And my spirit too is fading,—
   I am sinking fast to rest.

Mother, you will feel so lonely,
   When I am no longer here;
You will miss your little Lucy,
   And you'll wish that I was near.

Mother, you will miss my presence,
   In our little cottage home;
You will never hear me singing,
   You will feel so sad and lone.

Mother, tell my little playmates,
   They will never see me more;
Tell them they will never see me,
   Playing at our cottage door;

Mother, I have loved them dearly:—
  Tell them that I said good-bye;
Jesus blest the little children,
  And he calls me up on High.

Mother, you have had to scold me,
  I have been a naughty child;
You have often had to chide me,
  But how gently, and so mild.

Mother, will you please forgive me?—
  Now my end is drawing nigh:
For I know I've often grieved you,
  Forgive me! now, before I die!

Mother, you must cease your weeping,
  Hold my little wasted hand!
I am going to dwell in Heaven—
  With the happy angel band.

Mother, it is hard to leave you,
  But you soon will follow me:
When we meet again in Heaven,
  Oh! how happy we shall be.

Mother, see the angels coming -
  Coming for your Lucy now;
Mother dearest, sit beside me,
  Wipe the moisture from my brow.

Mother, will you come and kiss me,—
  You have loved your little girl:—
Good-bye, I am going to Heaven,
  Farewell, Mother dear—farewell.

ODE TO THE POET LONGFELLOW.

Wilt thou take this humble tribute?
  As a token of my love:—
Love for all that thou hast written,
For the noble inspirations,
  Harder hearts than mine would move.

I have read thy soul's deep language,
    In the words on every page,
That thy pen has traced in boyhood,
And the sterner years of manhood,
    And when bowed with hoary age.

I have read them, and reflected,
    Felt the weight of every word;
And have found relief and comfort,
For thy thoughts have roused an echo,
    Touched a sympathising chord;—

That within my heart has slumbered,
    And awakes responsive now;
Yet my genius is as nothing
To thine, Western Star of beauty,—
    Now alas! fast sinking low.

Like the brooklet to the ocean,
    Like a shrub unto a tree;
As a molehill to a mountain,
And as moonlight unto sunlight,
    Such am I compared with thee!

Thou hast tuned the living lyre,
    Touched it with a master's hand;
Showing wisdom, meditation—
Minstrel loved among the people,
    Singing all throughout the land.

I have read the "Golden Legend,"
    And the wondrous, charming tales,
Of the "Fireside," and the "Seaside,"
And the beauteous "Birds of passage,"
    I would praise, but language fails.

They so pure and elevating,
    Take our thoughts away from earth;
Oh! I love thy brief effusions,
Softened by a shade of sadness,
    None can truly tell their worth.

I have read with deep emotion,
   Till my eyes have filled with tears,
At the pictures called before me,
Of thine own sublime creation,
   Soothing all our earthly cares.

I am but thy younger sister,
   In the Old World far away;
Through life's pathway toiling onward,—
And before me are thy footprints,
   Shining like a guiding ray.

Though I know these lines unworthy
   Of the subject of my song;
Yet the simple words are heartfelt,
And I trust thee, unknown brother,
   As the weak will trust the strong:—

For I know thy heart is tender,
   And will every fault forgive,—
'Tis in all thy works reflected;
Though the ocean deep divides us,
   Yet amongst us thou dost live.

Bard immortal! may good angels
   Ever hover round thy head;
Blessings on thy name for ever;
For thou still wilt speak unto us—
   When thy spirit shall have fled.

UNITED.

I SEE in the mirror of fancy,
   A picture so vivid and bright;
I cannot but pause and inspect it,
   'Tis glowing with rosy-hued light.

The figures within it are living,
   And two my attention beguiles;
For there are a pair of true lovers,
   Their faces enwreathed with sweet smiles.—

And there is a little winged cupid
    Just hovering 'tween the fond pair;
Through intricate paths he has led them
    To groves that are sunny and fair.

He leads them toward a bright temple,
    All sacred to prayer and to praise;
'Tis filled with a radiant glory
    That pierces the dim winter haze.

They enter, in dignified silence,
    The aisles where so many have trod;
And there at the beautiful altar,
    The two are made one, before God.

And thus both united and happy,
    They each give a warm nuptial kiss;
And there with my blessing upon them,
    I leave them to sweet wedded bliss!

"THE BATTLE IS OVER."

The battle is over, go look at the spoil,
And bury the poor mangled dead in the soil:
Go, see what a sickening sight is revealed,
Where thousands lie slain on the crimson-stained field:
Reflect what the war to the nation has cost,
And think of the anguish for those that are lost.

The battle is over, what good is achieved?
For still they believe as their fathers believed;
Our faith is unshaken, we think as before,
The warfare is over, the men are no more;
We sought to avenge what we fancied a wrong,
The strife was unequal, the weak with the strong.

The battle is over, the fighting was hard;
And if we have conquered, what is our reward?
We know not; and still it is taken for good,
That triumph, and honour, and glory, mean blood!
No guerdon is ours, we in truth were to blame,
Our passion is o'er, and we're burning with shame!

The battle is over, and thousands are slain,
We fain would redeem it,—restore them again;
Go, bring them to life on this earth if ye can!
And fill up the ranks as they were, to a man;
Ye cannot! then bury them under the sod—
Death may do man's bidding, but Life comes from God!

THE MAIDEN AND HER LUTE.

Sweet lute let us discourse again,
    As evening's twilight gathers round;
The wild west wind its minstrelsy,
    Will join, with sweet melodious sound.

The raindrops patter on the roof,
    The autumn day is waning now;
And all is peace within my cot,—
    The fading embers flicker low.

The missel thrush has hushed his song—
    Within the bush has gone to rest;
The scattered clouds are drifting on,
    The sky is heavy and oppressed.

The beetle swiftly buzzes by,
    As on its blind career it goes;
The rose-trees scratch the window-pane,
    And beat it with their briery boughs.

The objects 'round grow indistinct,
    Dim shadows rest against the wall;
A spell that I can not resist,
    Is softly creeping over all.

'Tis now the time I love to speak,
    To let my maiden heart o'erflow:—
To speak unto my treasured lute,
    And trill a song of mirth, or woe.

I touch a chord, and it responds—
    Reveals a tone, that I would seek;
It seems to sympathize with me,
    And softly to my heart doth speak.

If I am sad, a soothing strain
  I waken from its strings so sweet;
If I am glad, my touch is gay,
  My happiness is then complete.

I linger o'er it, till the light
  Has faded from the weeping sky;
The room is dark, and now the wind
  Has lowered to a moaning sigh.

I can no longer see its strings,
  Yet every touch it answers me;
My fingers, as by instinct make
  It speak, what though I cannot see.

And when I cease, a solemn hush
  Hangs o'er my dwelling, like a spell;
As Nature hearkens, all intent,
  Her favourite muse she loves so well.

To me it is beyond all price,
  Sweet solace of my leisure hour;
It is my friend in every mood,
  It has a deep soul-soothing power.

Give me my lute, I covet not
  The riches all the world may bring;
Let me in solitude at eve',
  Unite with it, and softly sing.

LINES TO AN INFANT.

Poor helpless babe! thou knowest not
  The world to which thou'rt born;—
That tho' life's path has roses sweet,
  Behind lurks many a thorn,—
And all the fairest flowers on earth,
  By biting blasts are torn;

But these are yet unknown to thee,
   A stranger to the world:
Yet if thy life be spared, its scenes
   Will be to thee unfurled:
As on the "Railroad of Old Time,"
Thou day by day art whirled.

Wrapped in thy little swaddling clothes,
   What is this land to thee?—
'Tis but a desert, unexplored,
   Encircled by the sea!
Yet who can tell, to see thee now
   What one day thou wilt be?

Who knows what hidden treasures lie
   Within that little brain:
And what these tiny hands will do,
   If life and strength remain?
We cannot tell thy course, ere age
   Makes thee a child again.

Thy voice in future will be heard
   Above that whimp'ring cry:
It yet may sway the people's minds,
   When it is lifted high.
God grant that all those folded buds,
   Expand before they die!

Thy share of trouble for thee waits,
   Upon thy future way:
May Mercy with its gentle hand
   Soon chase it all away,—
And ever may the light of Hope,
   Illumine with its ray.

And tho' life's path be rough and steep,
   It is not always night:
For here and there amid the shade,
   There beams a sunny light;—
An opening on the dreary way,—
   A glade, that gleams so bright.

A span of mingled joy and woe,
  The bridge that waits thy feet:
Thou sweet unconscious little one,
  Laid in thy crib asleep;
I bid good-bye, and leave a kiss
  Upon thy baby cheek.

RETROSPECTION.

When looking back on the bygone years,
The lights and shadows, the smiles and tears,
The joys and sorrows the heart has known,
And precious boons that have been our own:
The soul goes out in a song of praise
For mercies sweet that have blest our days.
There are no roses without a thorn,
And looking back on afflictions borne,
But seems to brighten and make more dear
The pleasant days that were fair and clear:
The rays of joy on the past we see
Like rainbow tints on a storm-lashed sea:
And faith has shone like a beacon light,
And soothed the spirit through grief's dark night.
Each natal day there's a sweet content
To backward look on a life well spent :—
On work performed, and on duties done,
On the good achieved, and the honours won.
Kind words and actions from day to day,
Fall sweet as flowers strewn on life's way.
A life well lived is the best enjoyed,
We measure time as it is employed:
In joy, on gossamer wings 'tis sped,
In pain, it passes on wings of lead;
And this must solace all hearts opprest
" Who labours hardest finds sweetest rest."
The thoughts turn back, and the past appears,
To dearer grow with the lapse of years;
And youth resembles, so soon 'tis flown,
The tender light of the dappled dawn;

The rosy glow of the orient skies,
That marks the place where the sun will rise;
The transient glow must too soon give way,
Before the glare of life's fleeting day:
And ere 'tis valued behold! we trace,
Time's footsteps left on the care-lined face;
And ere we know it, oft-times are there,
His gleams of silver amongst the hair.
Thus age creeps on, as the day will glide,
The sun must set at the evening-tide;
So one by one do our friends depart,
And links will break that must wrench the heart:
Each plays his part on the world's wide stage,
Some go when young, and some ripe with age.
Those whom in youth we have loved the best,
Have done their parts and have gone to rest:
Oh! strange it seems it should oft be so,
That hearts most cherished are first to go;
The true ones left, be they e'er so few,
Whose friendship came like the grateful dew,
That falls so fresh on the verdure parched,
They cheered the way as we onward marched;
Let such be prized while our path they cross,
Like grains of gold on a road of dross.
Till we in turn must obey the call;
And why should ever the grave appall?
Life's but the passage to higher things,
Before the spirit has found its wings;
And death is but our chrysalis state,
Whence winged we soar to the Glory-gate!
To enter There in our new array,
The perfect light of a fadeless day;
Nor eye of mortal can pierce the veil
That hides the Realms where no ills assail;
May each so live that as fresh years come,
We worthier feel of our Father's Home.

FAREWELL LINES TO DEPARTING FRIENDS.

Farewell, farewell! these cruel words,
　Whose import we but feel too well,
Must now be said, and in them lies,
　A depth of feeling none can tell.

May God speed on that gallant ship,
　And bear you swiftly o'er the brine!
For love and hope await you there,
　Their tendrils round your hearts to twine.

When dwelling where the southern cross,
　Glows all resplendent in the sky;
Oft may your thoughts be wafted here,
　As whispering zephyrs pass you by.

And scenes that you have left behind,
　Before your vision oft arise;
Like some fair picture they may come,
　And pass before your tear-dimmed eyes.

But one I know will haunt you most,
　And dearer be to you than all,—
Though sweet sad memories in its train,
　Unto your hearts it may recall:—

The picture of the dear old home,
　That ne'er will be the same again;
When all its circle was complete,—
　Ere death its links had snapt in twain.

And vanished voices you may hear,
　Upon the sunny southern breeze,
Of those who loved you long before
　You trod that land across the seas.

And when the heart's deep fount o'erflows,
　Recalling scenes long left behind,
We know that Love has forged a chain,
　Two Lands apart with it to bind;

So strong, that but by death 'twill break,
  What though 'twill stretch the seas across:
Love too will memory's tablet take,
  And keep it free from gathering moss.

Whatever gorgeous sights you see,
  Revere the Land that gave you birth,—
The many loving friends, who ne'er
  May meet your forms again on earth.

And where the southern clime its wealth
  Of bloom shall all around you shower,
Oh! may you never once forget
  The English little wayside flower!

Good-bye, sweet children, may you rise
  And live in goodness to adorn,
Your future home, yet always love
  The dear old Land where you were born!

You'll help to make Australia great,
  Our hope and pride; some future day
Its sons may see the Mother-land,
  With all her glory passed away.

Farewell, farewell! I leave you now,
  And this shall be my parting prayer:—
That God will guide you, and will drop
  His choicest gifts upon you there!

THE EVENING STAR.

Where art thou wandering, bright little star?
Up in the beautiful heavens afar;
Traversing onward, where e'er thou art seen,
To offer us guidance on earth with thy beam.

The first to appear in the clear azure sky,
Like an angel of hope thou art beaming on high;
Bursting forth softly, sweet vesper so bright,
Beaming so pale in the lingering light.

Smile in thy purity over the dell,
Twinkle serenely o'er water and fell;
Gem of rare beauty, so faithful and true,
Rising at eve in the firmament blue.

Thou heavenly lamp of the beautiful night,
We marvel on earth at thy clear steadfast light;
Unfading thy glory, thy destiny there,
Faith's beacon to guide us to portals more fair.

A comforting thought to a fond yet sad heart,
That must sever from loved ones— must wander apart
Is this sweet reflection, that each other's eyes,
Though distant, will see thee at twilight arise.

If one should be borne from this world to On High,
Far beyond thy domain in the lovely blue sky;
Thou'd seem then to beckon the other to rest
To follow their soul to the "Realms of the Blest."

A SIMPLE TRUTH.

A TRAIT there is in human nature weak,
In that we often crave the things that we
Do not possess; for such far-off we see
With rose-tinged vision;—set ourselves to seek
To gain an object; which, like sunlit peak,
Seems less ethereal on a nearer view.
'Twas even so in childhood; then we knew
The land looked fairer just across the creek;
Toys more enticing to our envious eyes,
In other hands. So be it understood
That what we own, we all too lightly prize;
And thus we err. Grand aspirations should
But be our aim; if we would nobler rise,—
Strive to attain that which is pure and good.

LINES ON THE OPENING OF HAROLD PARK, LOW MOOR,

SEPTEMBER 19TH, 1885.

What is this glad expectant throng?
    For what are all these banners gay?
The answer we can read ere long—
    That Low Moor is *en fête* to-day.

There's one whose memory still is green—
    Who lived a pure and blameless life ;
Has left a mark where he has been,
    With noble deeds his days were rife.

He died in manhood's early years,
    Yet not before much good he'd wrought :
We see to-day, midst smiles and tears,
    The outcome of his care and thought.

Who knows what good he might have done
    Had he been spared to riper years?
Laments are vain; his crown is won—
    He rests beyond all earthly cares.

He made "the wilderness to bloom"—
    The barren waste, a flowery spot :
His name through all the years to come,
    Revered will be, and ne'er forgot.

Thus is this happy grateful crowd
    Assembled here from many a home :
Awaiting those of whom they're proud—
    To-day his honoured parents come,—

To ope' the gates of "Harold Park,"
    And from the fountain raise the veil,
In memory of their son; but hark !
    With cheers the noble pair they hail.

For Lord and Lady Cranbrook move
    Amongst the throng, with stately mien :
And every heart exults in love,
    As now their welcome forms are seen :

The sun shines out ; the banners bright
   So gaily flutter in the wind ;
The music sounds ; and all unite
   To leave an impress on the mind.

Lo ! every murmur now is hushed
   In silence for each speech and prayer ;
And fervent words as ever gushed
   From heart, are now being uttered there.

When these are o'er, the silence breaks
   With one prolonged and heartfelt cheer ;
The key is turned ; the echo 'wakes,
   For children singing now we hear.

Their youthful voices all have vent,
   The music on the breezes float ;
A fine old hymn to heaven is sent,
   And silvery clear rings every note.

Now forward moves the eager throng,
   And enters at the gilded gates ;
And once more silence reigns among
   The happy crowd, that quietly waits,—

The lady mother's hand to raise,
   The veil from off their tribute there,
To her dear son, who spent his days
   Amongst his sturdy workmen here.

When earnest words have all been said,
   The cover see, she lifts away ;—
And as the ringing cheers are spread,
   Reveals the granite column grey :

A fountain of pure water clear,—
   A fitting tribute to his name ;
Pure thoughts sprung from his soul when here,
   And lofty was his every aim.

See ! how the people now parade
   Their park, where spacious walks abound ;
For toiling ones this gift was made,
   When labour's o'er, here they'll be found.

This day in fancy long they'll see,
　"The Park" will be the people's pride ;—
An earthly paradise 'twill be ;—
　A boon to all on every side.

TO KATIE ; ON RECEIVING HER PHOTO.

Little Katie, is this you dear?
　Now a lovely woman grown!
Unto you across the waters,
　Oft have I in fancy flown.

But I pictured you my darling,
　Just the little girl you were,
When you left the Mother-country,
　In your sweet child-beauty fair.

Yet I see my once wee Katie,
　Peeping through this woman's guise ;
There is here the child's glad spirit,
　Beaming from those mirth-lit eyes.

Oh, that I might, just a moment,
　Clasp your hand across the foam !—
See you, hear your sweet voice speaking,
　In your sunny southern home.

What would I not give to kiss you!
　If but for another's sake ;
For the love I bear your mother,
　Time, nor distance, cannot break.

May your future lot be happy,
　Winsome, loving-hearted girl ;
If we ne'er should meet again Love,
　Take my blessing, fare-you-well !

THE BLIND.

Oh, have pity on the sightless,
   You who have your every sense;
Hear the songs that they will sing you,
Listen to their touching music,
   Give them too some recompense.

Kindly lead them, gently guide them,
   For they know not where they go;
Help your sisters, and your brothers,
Who must live in utter darkness
   Ever while they're here below.

Let us try and make them happy,
   Give them all our care and love;
Some have never seen the beauties,
And the glorious wealth of nature,
   In the world in which we move.

All that is sublime and lovely
   Gladdens not the blind one's eyes;
They have never seen the ocean,
With its mighty white-capped billows
   On its bosom, fall and rise.

See they not the snow in beauty,
   Lying calmly on the land,—
Folding all in dreary silence,—
Clothing in a garb of crystal
   All beneath its cold white hand.

Nor the flowers in all their freshness,
   Blooming in the fair sunlight,
With their perfect forms so lovely,
Slender stamens, softest petals,
   Chastely coloured, rich and bright.

See they not the stately forests,
   With their varied shades of green;
Nor the soft and verdant meadows,
Or the rippling stream and fountain—
   All these some have *never* seen.

Never seen the golden sunlight,
   And the heavens' brilliant blue;
Nor a gorgeous crimson sunset,
When the clouds are softly tinted,—
   Streaked with many a vivid hue.

Never seen the bright moon shining,—
   Lighting up the midnight sky,
Earthward ever softly beaming;
And the thousand stars that quiver
   In that mighty space on high.

These, and many other beauties
   Cannot ever charm the blind;
They have never seen the moorland,
With its sweet wild purple heather,
   Gently waving in the wind.

Sights that are to us impressive,
   By the blind are ne'er enjoyed;
Busy, moving life around them
Is beyond their comprehension—
   All to them is blank and void.

Yet in their imagination
   Things described to them must dwell;
Faces of their friends familiar,
They must paint as ideal pictures,
   And the spots they know so well.

Who would walk in total darkness,—
   Be as in perpetual night,
Seeing not dear kindred faces?
Pity all then thus afflicted—
   Comfort those devoid of sight.

Ah, it must be dark and dreary!
   Life to them be like a dream;
One from which they cannot waken,
Till their happy souls, immortal,
   Wake in Heaven's golden gleam!

REMEMBRANCE.

When those we love are far away,
    Across the mighty main;
Oh, how we yearn so for the day
    To see them once again.

In fancy, we can hear them speak
    As once we used to hear;
When last we kissed them on the cheek,
    And dropt a parting tear.

And they will haunt us in a dream,
    Though far from us they are;
Their much-loved forms, around us seem
    Like spirits from afar.

'Twas hard to say the last "good-bye,"
    When parting from their side;
And yet they took our heart-felt sigh
    Across the ocean wide.

Oh! if we could but see them now,
    If only for a day;
To press a kiss upon their brow,
    Or cheer them on their way.

We love the spots where they have moved
    Though now so far they roam;
We treasure things we know they loved,
    When they were here at home.

We prize the books they used to read;
    And love their vacant chair,
That tells a silent tale indeed,
    Of one who oft sat there.

'Tis sweet to think of those we love,
    And sweet to know that they
Are watched, like us, from Heaven above,
    Though far from us away.

The one great Father of us all,
   He guards them over there;—
Who watches every sparrow fall,—
   We trust them to His care.

WORDS OF CHEER.

Oh! friends in affliction, the winter departs,
   The bud has appeared on the tree;
Though darkness o'ershadowed, and all but o'er-
   A rift in the clouds we can see: [whelmed,
The brunt of the tempest has passed o'er your heads,
   But fairer the future will be.

You've been in distress, but the ordeal has shown
   That sympathy yet is awake,
And proved you have friends where you little had thought,
   Whose prayers have been breathed for your sake;—
Compassionate hearts, who so freely have tried,
   A share of your burden to take.

It may be the weight of your sorrow or pain,
   Seems more than your spirit can bear—
But tell it to God; He will never, I know,
   Permit you to sink in despair;—
For He, in His infinite goodness, has ne'er
   Been deaf to a genuine prayer.

Then tenderly, lovingly, Mercy will come,
   And lift up the curtain of gloom,
And let in the light from the glory beyond,
   To brighten each sufferer's room—
She always is ready to soften for us
   Our passage from birth to the tomb.

It may be that now she is close at your side,
   Her figure but veiled by a tear;
Whenever misfortune assails us we find
   That angel's sweet presence can cheer,
And ever when darkness is densest we know
   The dawn of the morning is near.

And listen, my sisters, the springtime has come,
   With promises rich as of old ;
And think how the whole world of nature revives,
   That erst seemed so withered and cold :
The flowers of summer will flourish again ;
   The moors wear their purple and gold.

Hope peeps through the chinks of the barriers grim,
   That woe has erected around :
They'll crumble away, and its sweet smiling face,
   Once more at your side may be found :
The crocus but waited the snow-wreaths to melt,
   Then broke through the frost-crusted ground !

I know it is hard to in meekness submit,
   Whenever great troubles befall :
But strive to be cheered, for howe'er we lament,
   We cannot the lost ones recall.
May God in His love the afflicted restore,
   And give His sweet peace to you all.

"DRIFTING APART."

We are drifting apart now, my darling,—
   Each going on our separate way :
     For the beautiful past
     Was too dream-like to last,
   Too fraught with sweet visions to stay !

In our youthtime we wandered together,
   Each deeming the other most dear ;
     But a hard cruel fate,
     Came between us of late,
   Our love must be laid on its bier.

We were destined while young to be severed,
   Though life was all sunshine with thee ;
     Though we thought side by side
     Through our journey to glide,
   It seems it was never to be !

Though long years we have glided serenely,
   Our paths are dividing in twain;
     Thy life is before thee,
     Oh! now I implore thee,
Go forth, and be happy again!

I can never forget thee my darling,
   Nor yet those bright days that have fled;
     In Arcadian bowers,
     We gathered sweet flowers,
Now scattered, and scentless, and dead!

My bark near to thine sailed life's river,
   With hope buoyed each merry young heart;
     But mine with the surges
     From thine now diverges,
Alas! we are drifting apart!

We can never again be united,—
   For youth with romance comes no more;
     Yet 'twas lived not in vain,
     For sweet mem'ries remain,
Of halcyon days that are o'er.

"I LOVE TO KISS THAT FADED CHEEK."

I love to kiss that faded cheek,
   And press it gently 'gainst mine own;
And those sweet eyes I love to seek,
   Whose lustre now alas! hath flown.

For I have seen them beam in mine,
   Whilst on thy breast my head hath lain;
Now Mother, as I look in thine,—
   I wish myself a child again.

Oh! vain the wish, it may not be,
   That precious time will come no more;
And yet another waits for thee,—
   The childhood next the Golden Shore.

As Time speeds on, with ceaseless wings,
    It leaves the trace where it hath been ;
The changes in its course it brings
    With ruthless hands, are ne'er unseen.

The tide of years may roll along,
    And drift us into channels new ;
Yet can I e'er forget thy song ?—
    The loved, the beautiful, the true !

Though time hath changed us Mother dear,
    Yet Memory keeps the treasured past ;
They're golden hours whilst thou art near,
    Oh! would that they might always last.

Now I must be what thou hast been,
    We're changing places day by day ;—
I leaned on thee, now thou dost lean
    Upon me, I am now thy stay.

My will is thine, thou leavest to me
    Life's burdens that on thee have prest ;
The noontide's labour mine must be,
    For thee—the evening's peaceful rest.

Now I must lead, who once were led
    By thee, in balmy days gone by ;
When golden dreams my fancy fed,
    In youth, beneath thy watchful eye.

Thou'rt passing from before mine eyes,
    As dreams have passed, I felt were sweet ;
Dark grief will cloud my sunny skies,
    When I thy form no more may greet.

Thy path to brighten to the tomb
    I hold o'er thee a torch of love ;—
To cheer the way, dispel the gloom,
    Till light bursts on thee from Above.

Far be the day when thou must go ;
    Why Time advance with step so bold ?
Oh! grief of heart, oh! bitter woe,
    When I shall see thee dead and cold !

And thou no more to me wilt speak,
  Nor pass thy fingers through my hair
Caressingly; and on my cheek,
  Imprint a sacred love-kiss there.

To God in Heaven I leave our fate,
  For Mercy He will first dispatch,
To bear His summons through the Gate,—
  And raise with gentle hands the latch.

THE BEGGAR GIRL.

She gently knocked at a rich man's door,
  Then she meekly asked for alms;
Her face was sweet, but of pallor hue,
Her dark-fringed eyes were of azure blue,
  And her voice had a tone that charms.

The snow fell thick from a murky sky,
  And the keen night wind blew strong;
She was thinly clad, and with cold she shook,
In her upturned face was a sad pinched look,
  As she stood and pleaded long.

The servant listened her lowly plaint,
  And stared but with proud disdain;
Then when her piteous tale he'd heard,
Informed his master, who gave the word,
  "Oh! tell her to call again—

"They *are* a nuisance, those tramps," he said
  To his company 'round the board;
"I've heard those pitiful tales before!"
And he stamped his foot on the bright oak floor,
  And scowled like an angry lord.

"Dismiss her James! I'm engaged to-night;"
  He roared from his velvet chair;
"But tell her to call in a day or two,
I'll search her story, and if 'tis true,
  I'll see if I've aught to spare."

The man this message, with lofty air,
    To the beggar maiden took :—
"The master says you may call again."
She turned away with a throb of pain,
    And a yearning wistful look.

She went no more. At the cold grey dawn,
    When the streams with ice were bound;
With a crystal snow-drift 'neath her head,
The rigid figure, so white and dead,
    Of the beggar maid was found!

The angels pitied her weary soul,
    And bore it beyond the storm ;
They softly came in the solemn night,
And scattered the snowflakes pure and white,
    On the poor child's sleeping form.

And there she lay, in her heavenly shroud,
    Where nature was all at peace ;
Her thin hands clasped on her childish breast,
The little pilgrim had found her rest,—
    Her spirit its glad release.

"BROTHERS AND SISTERS."

Brothers and sisters, come let us arise,
Go to our labour, while bright are the skies;
Dusk will come o'er us, the day will soon close,
Night will o'ertake us, when we can repose.

Brothers and sisters, now let us away,
Each to our calling while yet it is day;
Fortune awaits us, our efforts to bless,
Good honest workers will meet with success.

Brothers and sisters, then let us be brave,
Use to advantage the talents God gave;
Start in good earnest, and work with a zest,
Ere the sun enters the gates of the west.

Brothers and sisters, dark shadows may lurk,
O'er and around us, but still we must work ;—
Work with a purpose, and each take a part,
Help one another, with courage of heart.

Brothers and sisters, oh ! let us from youth,
Strive to be foremost in virtue and truth ;
Lift up the fallen, and give them a hand,—
Aid them with honour to pass through the land.

Brothers and sisters, how vast is the field !
Rich is the harvest each acre will yield ;
Strive who can work for the Great Master best,—
He will reward us with comfort and rest.

THE LOVER'S LAMENT.

When the summer time was waning,
    And trees their leaves began to shed ;
Then my weary footsteps wandered
    Towards the spot where rests the dead :
Dear to some are all the sleepers,
    Where lisping willows round them wave ;
But to me one mound is sacred,—
    My heart lies in that little grave.

Though the snows of many winters,
    Have placed a covering pure and bright ;—
Spread by angels fair, as emblems
    Of my beloved one's soul so white :
Yet I cannot once forget her,—
    Still for her my soul will crave ;
All my dearest hopes there sleepeth,—
    My heart lies in that little grave.

Now my life is cold and lonely,
    And oft my spirit longs to go ;
Yet it were not well to murmur,
    For God, it seems, has willed it so ;—

Willed that I should linger hither,
    And but one thought will make me brave;
'Tis that she must know in Heaven,
    My heart lies in that little grave:

Know that I revere her memory,
    And love the earth where she is laid;—
Know that when her spirit left me
    A void within my life was made:
Never will her trust be broken,
    Nor once revealed the love she gave;
None may know my silent sorrow,
    My heart lies in that little grave.

Only once I've seen her semblance,
    And like a light from heaven it flashed,
As a soul to mine responded,
    For one brief moment, then it passed:
Passed me like an inspiration,
    Within the old cathedral nave;
Beamed on me with tender pity,
    Whose heart lies in that little grave.

Time but makes the past grow dearer,
    For Memory weaves a fadeless charm;
Shows her as she stood beside me,
    And blest me with her love so warm:
Oh! to see her living presence!
    But it were vain to madly rave;
While for her my soul is yearning,
    My heart lies in that little grave.

True to her who yet was truer,
    For ne'er her like will live again;
Oh! that I were laid beside her,
    As free from sorrow, sin, and pain!
She has passed the narrow portal,
    As dark as some unfathomed cave;
Till our souls shall meet in Heaven
    My heart lies in that little grave.

Meekly I must bear my burden,
    And though to rest with her were sweet,
I must do my Father's bidding,
    Nor leave my labour incomplete;—
Wait awhile till He shall call me,
    Nor let the vanished past enslave:
But for me the days are cheerless,
    My heart lies in that little grave.

Though the waiting-time be weary,
    And none my deepest grief may know;
Memories of the past are mingled,
    With visions born of joy and woe:
If I strive One will in mercy,
    A place for me beside her save;
Till we are in Heaven united,
    My heart lies in that little grave.

GRIEF.

When grief assails the tender heart,
    For some departed soul:
How vain, till tears have had their fling,
    To seek to such console.
And falling on impressive youth,
    That measures time so long,
It crushes all aspiring hopes,
    That once were hot and strong.
They mourn intensely, and despair
    Oft blights the trusting heart:
They think their grief will always last—
    That it can ne'er depart.
They cannot see beyond the cloud,
    That shades the present hour;
They know not that their future path
    May teem with many a flower.

When sailing on the sea of life,
   We meet a friendly bark;
And greet it only for a time,
   Then lose it in the dark:
And we henceforth must drift apart,
   By many a storm be tossed;
We may not pass that bark again,
   Its track no more be crossed:
And yet its 'semblance we retain,
   When it has passed away;
To memory's chamber oft it glides,
   To linger day by day.
And why should heart so cling to heart,
   That for a time have met?
And why should memory cherish them,
   And parting cause regret?

When sorrow bows the gentle heart,
   A gloom seems over all;
And things that once had looked so bright,
   Before our sorrows pall.
Then nature's charms seem all subdued,
   It smiles for us in vain;
What though its beauty beams around,
   It seemeth not the same.
The flowers still will bloom as sweet,
   Upon a summer's day,
Yet something mars their fresh perfume,
   And blights their colours gay.
The gentle moon will shine the same
   The Empress of the night;
Yet o'er its brightness there's a gloom,
   That dims its silvery light.
The evening wind will still breathe low,
   Along the silent plain;
There's sadness in its music, when
   The heart is full of pain.
When those so near are called away,
   We deepest sorrow feel;
'Tis vain to soothe the wounded heart,
   That time alone can heal.

We miss a faithful, kindred one,
  That we could fondly trust—
That beat in unison with ours,
  We grieve when it is dust.
There is a grief for dearest ties,
  Or loving, long-tried friends,
That rends the sympathetic heart
  It breaks, before it bends.

A WELCOME HOME.

Welcome dearest, oh! we meet thee,
  With what joy from o'er the main;
Loving hearts so fondly greet thee,—
  Welcome! dear one, back again!

Welcome here amongst us gladly,
  For the sake of long-past days;
Time has changed us all so sadly
  While we've walked our separate ways.

From a sunny land of brightness,
  England first would meet thy sight,
Clothed in robes, which from their whiteness,
  Showed 'twas drest for winter's night.

Coldly sleeps our Isle, no colder
  Is far Greenland's ice-locked strand;
Never did the Frost-king bolder,
  Wield his sceptre o'er our land;—

Yet our northern race is fearless,
  And he bears for us a charm;
For 'neath skies so dull and cheerless,
  English hearts beat true and warm.

If our skies had been all cloudless
  When thou stept upon the shore;
Had thy native land been shroudless,
  Couldst thou then have loved it more?

Thou wilt miss familiar faces,
   Sigh for those who are not near;
Youth steps up to fill their places,
   They, with time, will grow as dear.

On one spot I see thee weeping,
   O'er those dear ones loved and true;
Like our flowers, they are but sleeping
   Till they're called to bloom anew.

Those still left must be the dearer
   Now the older ties are gone;
Death but draws the living nearer,
   Till he claims us, one by one.

We have waited to caress thee,
   While from us thou still didst roam:
Oft we've prayed for God to bless thee,
   Guide thee safe to friends and home.

OLD FRIENDS.

'Tis sweet to meet the dear old friends,
   The good old friends of long ago;
Who stood by us in adverse years
   Proved true in hours of deepest woe.
Who constant were through changeful years,
   And felt with us in every mood;
Through beaming eyes, and clasp of hands,
   Our kindred hearts have understood
The tokens of a friendship firm,
   That yet will bear the strongest test;
When faith, goodwill, and sweet accord
   Abounds in each, then all are blest.
And life glides like a happy dream,
   When of our friends affection sure;
Who freely offer help unsought,
   And but from motives good and pure.

Who cling to us where'er they be—
　　Keep loyal though we dwell apart;
A bond unites us, which we feel
　　Is anchored fast within the heart.
We dearly prize the tried old friends,
　　And welcome them whene'er we meet:—
In memory cherish happy hours
　　We've spent with them in converse sweet.
Their genial tones, their fervent words,
　　Go with us through the lapse of years;
Recalling such, retains the power
　　To call up smiles, or move to tears.

LINES:

On hearing of the intended demolition of Haworth Old Church, the burial place of Charlotte Brontë.

Hold! your sacrilegious hands;
Touch not that venerated pile;
Let it stand, so quaint and ancient,
For its dear associations,—
Think of those who trod its aisle.

Pause and think; then touch it not;
For 'neath that sacred tomb there sleeps,
One whose memory still we cherish,
She whose life-work ne'er will perish,
And for whom the world still weeps.

From that ever fertile brain,
Emanated thoughts sublime;—
Gave the world a priceless largess,—
Twined a mighty wreath immortal,
'Round that temple, marked with time.

Noble inspirations grand
Flowed with vigour from that pen;
Gave her works a soul-born pathos,
Tinged anon with fiery spirit,
True to nature, and to men.

And her sister rests with her,
Gifted with a talent rare:
Lived their separate lives for others,
In one grave beneath that tablet—
Slumber now the sisters there.

Once within this village quiet,
The light of genius shone around;
Now it woos the world unto it,
Where their mortal dust reposeth,
Underneath that hallowed ground.

Sparks of genius kindled here,
Won them all a world-wide fame;
Near that sacred pile abiding,
Yonder moorland wild with heather
Fann'd them to a shining flame.

Honoured as their resting place,
Spare, oh! spare it to the last;
Guard it, save it, from destruction;
Hold it yet in veneration—
Treasured relic of the past:

Let not ruthless hands destroy,
That sacred edifice so grey;
'Tis the one our country loveth,
Emblem of the bygone ages,
Built by hands long passed away.

Once upon her bridal morn,
She knelt before that altar there;
Gave her hand to him who loved her,
Genius then her brow encircled,
While she breathed the holy prayer.

Then alas! within a year,
In sable garments moving slow;—
There was seen a sad procession
Seek that place so dim and solemn,
In the tomb they laid her low.

Keep it, for the love we bear,
None again her place can fill;
There the dead in peace reposeth,
Softly tread, thy voice subduing,
Hold that altar sacred still.

All the village worthies old,
Ever prize it more and more;
Monument of their ancestors;
Spot wherein they love to worship,—
Their forefathers went before.

Many have been baptised there,
Wedded at that altar old;—
Then in other years were carried,
In that peaceful churchyard buried
In the earth so damp and cold.

Oh! retain it for their sake,
Let not hands its walls efface;
Let not then their every vestige,
Dwell alone in memory's vista,
Leave us yet that single trace.

Let it but decay with time,
'Tis the wish that thousands crave:
At the shrine of genius bowing,
Bending low with softened feeling,
Paying tribute o'er that grave.

Sacred to her memory dear,
Who liveth, tho' her soul is fled:
Precious is the spot she haunted—
Save it;—for the love of Heaven!—
Hear the voice that mourns the dead.

SORROW'S SEAL.

When sorrow comes with its chastening hand,
Upon the features it leaves its brand;
The heart is never again the same,
So prone to hope, as before it came;
Nor yet so buoyant, subdued it lives,
And bears the mark that a great grief gives.
When sorrow's seal we are bound to wear,
It tempers joy, till it gleams less fair.
But tearless anguish the most of all,
The spirit saddens, and casts a pall
O'er all earth's beauties; and leaves its trace,
Imprinted deep on the furrowed face;
The heart may break with a dry-eyed grief,
When tears gush not, to afford relief;
The voice may laugh, and the lips may smile,
But only a mask is worn the while.
We meet such faces in every mart,
That always speak of a blighted heart;
That still must live, though it be opprest—
In patience wait for the promised rest.

THE BLIND MOTHER.

Come here my child, I cannot see thy face,
Yet o'er thy features I can pass my fingers;
And as on them my touch so fondly lingers,
    Their form I trace.

'Tis sweet to have thee nestle close to me,
To hear the voice of one I love so dearly
As thou wert once, in fancy still I clearly
    Can picture thee.

With gentle hand I love to stroke thy hair,
And solace find while I am thee caressing;
For then I breathe upon thy head a blessing
    A voiceless prayer.

I who have watched thy childhood's rapture wild;
May never more behold thy outward semblance:
Yet thou wilt ever dwell in my remembrance,
    My precious child!

'Tis sad that I who bore thee, may not mark
Thy progress; who once gloried in beholding
Thee daily, like a tender bud unfolding,—
    For all is dark!

Why should I murmur till the teardrop starts?
Oh, why from me should come this vain repining?
Affliction only is my soul refining—
    Ere it departs.

And sorrow teaches; as life's sun goes down.
We learn to know that while we are enduring
Our earthly crosses, we are thus securing—
    The promised crown!

This source of joy within my heart still springs,
And makes me meeker bear affliction's chastening,
That I have power to note thy *soul's* awakening
    To higher things:

'Tis granted me to help it to expand,
And this I find my sweetest consolation,—
To point for thee, beyond earth's tribulation
    The Better Land.

Where, with the veil uplifted from my eyes,
Our earth-life finished, like a well-told story:
I shall again behold my child in glory,—
    Beyond the skies!

DESPONDENCY.

One by one, the leaves are falling,
    Lifeless, from that old ash tree;
Sweeping earthward, with a rustle,
    Bringing mem'ries sad to me.

One by one my hopes are fading,
   Like a glorious summer day
Hopes that once so fondly beckoned,
   Melt in shadows far away.

One by one my dreams are dying,
   Dreams that wrapt my girlhood's years,
With a mantle bright and spotless,
   Now alas! dissolve in tears.

One by one have friends departed,
   They the Golden Gates have won;
Left me on the dreary roadway,
   Toiling 'neath the mid-day sun.

Year by year my youth is passing,
   Age is waiting for me now,
With his shining locks of silver,
   And a furrow for my brow.

Things that I have treasured dearly,
   All that I once used to prize,
Like the morning mists have drifted
   Floated from before mine eyes.

I have hugged them fondly to me
   Nursed them long, but they have fled;
All my day-dreams are illusions—
   Numbered with the silent dead.

Has my life been blank and aimless,
   Have I lived, yet lived for naught?
Has Ambition mocked my footsteps,
   Has it raised one lofty thought?

Does it pave the road to fortune?
   Once I used to think it must;
Now methinks its light misguiding,
   It but sprinkles glittering dust.

Yet 'tis sweet to life's dull palate,
   If some good it but achieves;
I will forward look, and upward,
   Heavenly trust all pain relieves.

PICTURES IN THE FIRE.

"What see you in the fire?" he said,
  "What see you in the fire?"
The maiden looked at the embers red,
She paused a moment then smiled, and said,
  "There is much that I admire.

"I see the form of a maiden gleam,
  She is wearing a bridal crown:
I see the sheen of a liquid stream,
And the flowers that grow beside it seem
  To form her a beautiful gown.

"The path before her is gay and wide,
  It glows with an amber light:
And jewels are scattered on every side,
That are borne along by the streamlet's tide,
  And glitter resplendently bright."

"What see you in the fire?" said he.
  "What see you in the fire?"
From the maiden he turned to a boy at his knee,
Who steadfastly gazed, then a picture could see,
  When he answered the old grand-sire:

"I see amidst the ember's glow,
  The form of a battle-field;
I see the quiver of lance and bow,
The friend and foe are there laid low,
  And each soldier is wearing a shield.

"I see a ship upon the main,
  Bearing the brunt of a gale:
'Tis tost and lost, then seen again,
And I see the splash of hail and rain,
  As it beats on every sail."

"What see *you* in the fire?" said they,
  "What see you in the fire?"
They asked the old man bent and grey,
He scanned the fire with ruddy ray,
  Then gravely spoke the sire:

"I see a dark, slow-moving band,
   Bearing a burden in woe;
A life has run its golden sand,
I see the spot of sunny land
   Where they will lay it low.

"And I can see the sable pall—
   It droops in a shadowy wave;
While sunbeams linger over all
And weeping willows o'er it fall—
   Around the lonely grave."

A SONNET.

Only a half-blown rose, and drooping now;
What is its life? a frail ephemeral thing;
Delicious scent to those soft petals cling,
Though in its moss-sheath its sweet head doth bow.
The odourous essence it exhales e'en now,
Must be its spirit,—that which we conserve,
Like our soul's inspirations; we preserve
Live thoughts for future minds, when we sleep low.
Sweet dying rose! plucked from its parent stem,
Its brief life filled a purpose; it conveyed
Joy into two young hearts; and thus to them
'Twill dear remain, when beauty has decayed.
Besides the perfume in its crimson folds
This rose the secret of a life's love holds!

A MARRIAGE ODE.

So fresh and sweet breaks the summer morning!
   An index bright of the opening day;
The dawn-tints linger above the hill-tops,
And perfume rich of the new-born flowers,
   Is wafted 'round, as the zephyrs play.

Two loving hearts, that are interwoven,
    Shall ere the sunset, no more be twain :
When once united in love-bonds holy—
Their nuptials loyally celebrated,—
    No separate ways may they know again !

The love-shafts sent from the bow of Cupid,
    Have deeply pierced to each fond young heart ;
By mystic tendrils they're drawn together,
As time glides on may they cling still closer,
    Souls in affinity ne'er can part.

Each full of trust, they have trod one pathway,
    Through fair elysian bowers of bliss :
Their troth is plighted, now they to Heaven,
Before the altar will vow allegiance ;
    And seal the compact with love's own kiss.

Behold they come in their youthful glory,
    True love encircles the happy pair ;
The sweet young bride in her maiden beauty,
With graceful form, in her bridal raiment,
    Of lovely texture, as rich as fair.

Forth from the home that has known her girlhood,
    She gaily steps, and with fearless feet ;
No more as maiden to cross its threshold,
With heart o'erflowing with memories tender,
    Oh, may her wifehood hold joys as sweet !

A love alliance, with Heaven's sanction,
    For white-robed Honour is with them there ;
The smiles of friends with their sweet approval,
Conveyed through gifts, with their heartfelt blessing,
    Enhance the joy of the hopeful pair.

Their rosy dreams will be consumated,
    On paths untried they will henceforth tread ;
All looks propitious, then may their future,
Be all translucent, and both be faithful,
    With never a cloud to loom o'erhead.

But oh, no pathway is paved with roses,
   Some briers may spring that we may not see ;
But each the other must ever cherish,
May both prove worthy in trust and honour,
   That golden circlet the pledge must be.

At Hymen's throne as the pair are bowing,
   Two fair-browed cherubs upon them wait ;
Sweet Love and Hope, and they're linked together,
May these, when o'er is the solemn service,
   Be staunch attendants what-e'er their fate.

Oh ! joyous bride, in his love confiding,
   May naught the peace of thy heart destroy :
On him who won it thy hand bestowing,
He will endow thee, and claim thee proudly,
   May both drink deep from the font of joy !

A good man's love is a rich possession,
   Such has been won by the pure young bride :
She charms us all ; and her fair young bridesmaids,
And favoured guests, on this marriage morning,
   Regret that now she must leave their side.

Those who have nurtured their dark-eyed darling--
   The loving mother, the father dear ;
The noble brothers, the gentle sisters
Who love her fondly, we know will miss her,
   For all looks brighter when she is near.

God guard you both ! He will ne'er forsake you,
   If you but trust in His boundless love :
Walk in His ways, through the opening vista,
He'll crown your happiness, bless your union,
   Nor part you e'en when in Courts Above !

MY CHILDHOOD'S HOME.

   I'VE seen the home, the old, old home,
     When once I used to dwell ;
   The same lov'd house of long ago,
     That knew me as a girl.

I've been within that dear old place,
   So sacred unto me:
And thoughts that time can ne'er efface,
   Crowd on my memory.

Imprinted deeply on my mind,
   Remembrance of the past:
And little childish incidents,
   Will haunt me to the last.

Each little nook recalled to me
   Some long past, childish scene,—
I seemed to live it o'er again,
   Though years have rolled between.

Though others call it now their home,
   And will in future time,
It is the same old place to me,
   And still I call it mine!

The garden where I used to play,
   Where Mother sweetly smiled;
Oh! what would I not give to-day,
   To be once more a child.

Come back, come back, ye days of old!
   Come back, my childhood's hours!
And let me wander once again
   Among the sweet wild flowers;

And feel as once I used to feel,
   When all the world seemed bright:
And day would come, and day would go,
   And all was love and light.

Oh! that I were a child again,
   Within that dear old cot;
Untutored by the hand of Time,—
   And by the world forgot.

THE OLD MAN'S SOLILOQUY.

Where are the friends I used to know?
The dear old ties of long ago;
In yonder churchyard sleeping low,
          Passed away, passed away.

When I was young, my heart was light,
All things have changed that once were bright,
And joys that then were my delight—
          Passed away, passed away.

I pictured life without a care,
In glowing colours everywhere;
Now all that once seemed sweet and fair—
          Passed away, passed away.

Brown was my hair, and smooth my brow,
My form was straight, I stooped not so
When I was young, but youth has now
          Passed away, passed away.

And now my locks are white as fleece,
And soon my life on earth will cease,
Then you will see me laid in peace—
          Passed away, passed away.

Say, who will shed for me a tear,
When I shall be no longer here?
Not one! for those that were so dear
          Passed away, passed away.

I've seen the ups and downs of life,
Have known its troubles, cares and strife,
Long since my faithful, loving wife,
          Passed away, passed away.

My friends have left me, one by one,
I'm in this dreary world alone;
For all those I have loved are gone,
          Passed away, passed away.

How oft in evening's twilight gloom,
When I am sitting all alone,
The forms of loved ones 'round me come—
          Passed away, passed away.

Then if I listen I can hear
Sweet voices whisper in my ear,
Familiar tones, so soft and clear—
          Passed away, passed away.

I know my life will soon be o'er,
I'm ready for the other Shore,—
To leave this earth for evermore,—
          Pass away, pass away.

Yet I will trust my only Friend—
Wait in submission for my end,
When a good angel He will send,
          To bear me up to Heaven.

MERIT REWARDED.

Upright, brave, and persevering,
    Doing what good where-e'er he can:
Willing to assist his brothers,
    There we see a noble man.—

Faithful in his every duty,
    Prompt in acts of kindness, too:
Swayed by every generous impulse,
    Steady, trusty, courteous, true.

Such a man is well respected,—
    Wins his fellows' deep regard:
And we find that he is honoured,
    Merit gets its due reward.

If, for sterling worth, no guerdon
    In return, on earth were given,
God will see that every virtue
    Has a just reward in Heaven.

THE HORSE.

Oh, noble creature, friend of man,
    With thy bold prancing step;
He loves thee, with thy coat so sleek,
    And arched and glossy neck.

Tho' liberty may not be thine,
    Yet where thou art not free,
May Mercy ever guide the hands
    That hold a rein o'er thee.
Thou servest man, in peace and war,
    Ye are oh, gallant steed,
Companions in the battle field,
    Where ye together bleed.
Sagacious, patient, docile beast!
    These attributes are thine;
Permitting man to curb thy will
    Imperious and fine.
Thy beautiful and flowing mane,
    Falls down like silken bands;
And decks thy graceful head so high,
    Smoothed by thy master's hands.
Thy quiv'ring nostril now I see,
    And wild, dilated eye,
That speaks of slumb'ring fire within
    A spirit firm and high.
Of all dumb creatures thou dost best
    Befriend the human race;
Man's favourite, except his dog,—
    Thou hast the foremost place.
And while with proud, majestic mien,
    It ever is thy plan,
While conscious of superior strength,
    To still submit to man.

"I DREAMT SHE DIED IN CHILDHOOD."

I dreamt that she died in childhood,
    When her cares had not come near;
But her fair young cheeks were daily
    Bedewed with a childish tear;

Called forth at the little troubles
    Which sensitive children feel;
By the heartless harsh rebuker,
    Who can wound but cannot heal.

In the springtime of youth and beauty,
   Her life like an April day;
Ere childhood had merged into girlhood,
   I dreamt she had passed away.

With no one to sit beside her,
   To watch the sweet spirit go:
Upward, to beautiful Heaven,
   As pure as the falling snow.

She had died alone, uncared for,
   And left not a message for me ;
But they showed me her broken playthings,
   And the cup she had used for her tea.

But they only heightened my sorrow,
   And filled me with vain regret—
The grief at the separation,
   When kindred hearts have met.

But I knew that her little sisters,
   Who loved her with simple trust,
O'er her lowly grave would linger,
   To weep o'er their sister's dust.

For one by one she had nursed them,
   As she sat in her little chair;
And I knew they would miss their sister,
   With her tender, motherly care.

For I dreamt that the child was sleeping—
   That in Death's cold arms she lay—
And gone was her animation—
   For her soul had flitted away.

I should never see her near me,
   With gentle childish grace ;
Nor watch the light and shadow
   Pass over her sweet young face.

For I've often watched her features,
   When she thought I did not see;
While her little hand so slender,
   I had clasped upon my knee.

And every fresh expression,
    I could read as in a book ;
One moment she was sullen,
    With a pleading pouting look :

And then a smile so transient,
    O'erspread her thoughtful brow ;
And lit up every feature,
    Till her face seemed all aglow.

Thus I grew to love her dearly,
    Yet I dreamt that she was dead
To the Land of the white-robed angels,
    Her soul had for ever fled.

THE ITALIAN BOY.

A CHILD from *Italia* stood in the gay throng,
I noticed him there as I saunter'd along ;
He fingered a harp as he sung a sad lay,
Of his own native country, so far far away.

And then he repeated the song once again,
In his own native tongue, in a sweet childish strain ,
And beseechingly looked up to all passers-by,
With lustrous brown eyes, that were pensive and shy.

When he got no reward, then he sung it once more,
Till his voice became husky with singing it o'er ;
How he longed for a hand that would drop him a mite,
For perhaps he had nought with to purchase a bite.

Then he played a sad plaintive Italian air,
And his face wore a look of distress and despair ;
His hopes were all fled, and his heart knew no joy,
For they passed by unheeded the poor little boy.

They said that his harp was discordant to hear,
That his voice sounded hoarse as it fell on the ear ;
They ne'er gave a thought that all day he had sung,—
That his harp so untuneful was old and unstrung.

He looked so forlorn, in the grand busy street,
He could not with hope or with sympathy meet:
And ere the song ended they wished him from there—
And told him they surely had "nothing to spare."

I pitied the child, from the depths of my heart,
For I saw how his tears were beginning to start:
I gave him a trifle, he brightened with joy—
For it gladdened the heart of the poor little boy.

And then I was happy, my heart felt so light,
I wished that some others would each give a mite:
God notes them, and blesses each mite that is given,
For surely such acts are recorded in Heaven!

SMILES AND TEARS.

I saw her smiling through her tears,
   Like sunshine after rain;
She'd cast aside her passing fears—
   Was happy once again.

A cloud of grief had made them start,
   Those gushing, pearly tears;
They had their source at her young heart
   O'erwhelmed with doubts and fears.

Her eyes then glisten'd, like the flowers
   With dewdrops covered o'er,
That nearly dimmed her youthful sight,
   But soon she wept no more.

A gleam of radiant hope she felt,
   The darkness turn'd to light,
Her sorrow then began to melt,
   She once again was bright.

I thought it was a lovely sight,
   Those smiles and tears combined;
Like day that follows after night,
   And clouds with silver lined.

How soon again the young are gay!
    And soon forget their grief;
The smile had chased the tears away,
    And hope had brought relief.

A GOOD SON.

Oh, where is there a holier sight
    Than a mother and her son,
Whose hearts in fondest love unite?—
    I answer, there is none!—

There is no sweeter sight on earth
    Than a kind attentive boy;
Who appreciates his mother's worth,
    He is her heart's best joy.

I know a good, devoted son,
    Who loves his mother dear;
For her would give his life so young,
    She loves to have him near.

'Tis sweet to see him bending o'er
    To kiss his mother's cheeks;
As years steal on, he loves her more,
    Her presence oft he seeks.

Anticipates her every wish,
    And helps her all he can;
Know, when you see a boy like this,
    He'll make a noble man.

'Tis pleasing in the sight of God,
    Such tender, filial love;
Such boys will find a just reward,
    In happy Heaven above.

OLD LETTERS.

I sat alone in my parlour to-day,
The wind wailed low, and the sky was grey:
I felt despondent, and weary, and sad,
And thought that nothing could make me glad.
Then Memory conjured up for me,
Old faces I never again may see:
For I thought of every absent friend,
And of the missives that kind hearts send.
I sought a pile of my letters then,
Written by many a friendly pen;
I had them carefully treasured away,
And oh, they gladdened my heart to-day!
Though only a packet of letters old,
They'll speak when the hands that traced them are cold;
What though the paper is yellow and worn,
And every fold is now soiled and torn:—
What though the ink is faded and grey,
I'll cherish them still, for many a day.
As I read, vague figures seemed stealing near,
The forms of my friends, that are loved and dear:
I felt not alone in the parlour dim,
For Fancy had summoned their spirits in.
One note that I prize, and have not its compeer,—
Was sent by a Lady we all must revere:—
So noble and good, exhalted and grand—
Whose name is honoured in every land.
There is one that came from a lowly cot,
I value it too, and would part with it not:
Though but from a peasant of humblest birth,
Its every word is of comfort and worth.
Some bring the writers before my eyes,
The thoughts they have written I dearly prize:
And some by strangers to me were sent,
Whose hearts on the kindest thoughts intent.
Dictated those missives I proudly own,
What though their writers I never have known.
Some letters a masculine hand betray,
The characters bold, a freedom display:

Some from their grace and their beauty are such,
That reveal a feminine, delicate touch,
And some in a well-formed hand refined,
Bear words that came from a master mind.
While some are traced in an unformed hand,
Uncertain, unsteady, the characters stand;
Some being too large, and others too small,
A child's frail trembling, and blotted scrawl.
Some came from the other side of the globe—
From a land that wears a flowery robe;
Where the southern cross hangs high above,
And brightly beams upon one I love:
They form the links of a precious chain,
Across the blue and expansive main,
Connecting one in that beautiful clime,
Though far away, with this bosom of mine.
And some in a friend's confiding strain,
Seem seeking solace as they complain;
Sad thoughts and feelings to me they impart,
And lay before me a grieving heart.
And some are full of glad words of cheer,
To help me along life's pathway drear;—
A sweet reward for some effort of mine,
That made the light of their friendship shine.
Who says that a letter is a worthless thing?
Ere I tied them again with a silken string,
In the gloom of my heart they had cast a ray;
And I stored them again for a future day.

NOT FORGOTTEN.

I miss a form that once was wont,
    To greet me in a tender tone;
A gentle girl with serious face,
And none can ever fill her place
    Who died and left me here alone;
Of all my hopes she was the font,
    I miss her still,—I miss her still.

Had she but lived! oh, who can tell
    The joys my later life had known?
A happier fate mine then had been:
Oh! could my angel but have seen
    My sorrow now, she had not flown;
If she had lived all now were well:—
    Oh! had she lived,—oh, had she lived!

Could she have lived and known the love,
    I bore for her, and still must bear;
She cannot see this stricken heart,
Nor know what pain it cost to part,
    And this is now my daily prayer,
That I may meet with her Above,
    And live for aye,—and live for aye.

Why did she go? when her young life
    Was just expanding to our view;
When in her first fresh glow of youth,
The sweetest child of faith and truth,—
    To whom the world was fair and new;
Nor recked she of its sin and strife,—
    Why did she go,—why did she go?

I love the mound where she is laid,—
    A sacred link 'twixt me and Heaven;
Too early she was called to rest,
But sorrow all too soon had prest
    Its seal upon her heart, and riven
Her cherished hopes, oh! had she stayed,—
    What joys were mine, what joys were mine!

The changing seasons come and go,
    And still this saddened heart must beat,
Through Springtime with its buds and showers,
And Summer with its wealth of flowers;
    Through golden Autumn, rich and sweet,
And dreary Winter white with snow,
    I must live on,—I must live on.

She cannot come again, and yet
    Her spirit sometimes hovers near;
Her soul and mine a moment meet,

And seem to hold communion sweet,
   Which only makes the past more dear,
In sacred, loving memories set,—
   To come no more,— to come no more!

And though she ne'er will bless my sight,
   'Tis vain to question God's decree;
The children's Kingdom holds her now,
And garlands wreathe her sainted brow,
   Such bliss as hers is not for me,
Till I shall see Eternal light,
   And join her There,—and join her There.

THE POET'S PLEASURE.

Oh! who can rob him of that inward power
   A gift of Nature to a favoured few;
   They pity him! ah, if they only knew
His pleasure in one single lonely hour!

Then they would pity not, but rather crave
   The independence of the poet's life;
   Removed apart, nor mingles with the strife,—
His years one dream from cradle to the grave.

His Muse attends him through life's varied page;
   Set in the soul, and like a shining star,
   Diffuses light—thus he can see afar,
And stamp his ideals for an after age.

If all the world is cold to him; he finds
   In solitude a secret solace, where,
   Renouncing all things worldly, calmly there
Pours out his pent-up feelings to the winds.

The lofty inspirations of the soul
   Surround him at the silent midnight hour;
   As there, within his solitary bower,
His genius spreads its charm 'neath his control.

Sublime interpreter of Nature, he
   Brings forth her beauties to the common eye;
   Her praise to unobservers singeth high, -
Ethereal charms that none but bards can see.

What though aloof, unto the world he sings—
   Unto a thousand of his fellow-men ;
   The heart unburdened speaketh through the pen,
The inmost feelings of his breast he flings,

On every side, nor cares he what we think,
   Descries a treasure in his path each day ;
   His thoughts o'erflow, his vision soars away,
He finds relief in paper and in ink !

And thus he lights the weary gloom of night.
   He toileth with a pleasure unalloyed ;
   What strikes him then to be by us enjoyed.
Henceforth indelible, when he hath ta'en his flight.

When he departs—and not till then—we see
   The precious gift that he hath left behind :
   A legacy immortal is enshrined
In all his works,—we bless his memory.

Ambitious not for riches or for fame,
   He loves his art, and there his pleasure lies—
   In doing his work, and only when he dies,
A glorious halo clings around his name.

OUR GALLANT FIRE BRIGADES.

God bless the firemen of our land,
   Where ever they may be :
These men to whom we owe so much,
   Whose daring deeds we see :
They quench the flames so fierce and grand,
The dauntless firemen of our land.

Who, when the awful signal sounds,
   Are ready at the call,
To face the furious scorching fire,
   Which others would appal—
They quench the flames so fierce and grand,
The dauntless firemen of our land.

In buildings, when the curling flames
    Would soon destroy the spot.
The service rendered by these men,
    Will never be forgot.
They quench the flames so fierce and grand,
The dauntless firemen of our land.

They snatch us lives and property
    From out the lurid blaze;
They cope with that great element,
    Oh! let us sound their praise:
They quench the flames so fierce and grand,
The dauntless firemen of our land.

With daring agile steps, they mount
    To places insecure ;
'Mid suffocating smoke and steam,
    Are trials that they endure :
They quench the flames so fierce and grand,
The dauntless firemen of our land.

And oft with danger to themselves,
    That tries the valiant heart :
As flames advance, each gathers strength,
    And does his noble part.
They quench the flames so fierce and grand,
The dauntless firemen of our land.

What gratitude must fill the hearts
    Of all whom they have saved !
For those who snatched them from the blaze,
    For them the danger braved !
They quench the flames so fierce and grand,
The dauntless firemen of our land.

Yes, many fellow creatures' lives
    Are to the firemen due,—
What could we do without the brave,
    The noble, and the true ? —
Then let us swell the chorus grand,
God bless the firemen of our land !

LINES ON SEEING AN ARTIST AT WORK.

Behold it forming, by his skilful hand,
    As if by magic, how it grows beneath
That master's touch: till forms and figures stand,
    As if in life, upon the purple heath:

Till on the canvas, once so blank and bare,
    That waited for a genius to adorn,
Appears a host of men, who gazing there,
    Await the opening of the rosy morn.

Each one instinct with life, the picture glows
    With warmest tints, and all to nature true:
While yonder stream that in the background flows,
    Reflects the sky's own brilliant azure hue.

And when 'tis done, we gaze with wonder on
    The mighty work, that eloquently speaks:
Our lips unsought, will frame the words "well done!"
    To see the life-blood seem to tinge the cheeks:

And Raphael's power could not more beauteous make,
    Each well-formed face, defined with shade and light;
And lustrous eyes, that gazing, seem to wake—
    And look out from the canvas, warm and bright.

To life so faithful—subject fully grasped:
    Each face consulted, tells its separate tale:
True genius close to Nature's self is clasped—
    Its power can charm when other arts will fail.

O painter toil! reflect the human heart,
    In all its phases on the canvas there,
Pourtrayed in visage, and display thine art,—
    Depict us scenes with all thy grace and care.

SKY-TINTS.

Blood-red the sky at sunset shone:
'Twas one immense illumined field
Of splendour, stretched from East to West,—
A gorgeous ruby. Flaming wreaths

Spread bright o'erhead, like rippling waves,
Then melted soft in distance dim,
In one grand lurid, vast expanse,
Of boundless firmament. Until
The whole grew crimson-tinted far
As eyes could see. Then came a change:
A brilliant amber light appeared,
That mingling with cerulean hue,
Formed brightest green. These rainbow tints
Shone in the West, so clear and bright,
Like gleaming bands of vivid shades.
The western sky resembled then
A beautiful emblazoned plain;
With colours rich together blent,
That seemed to cast a glow on earth;
A few brief moments, then they grew
Less vivid as the night stole on,
Soft and fainter still, then merged
Into a dusky golden-grey;
The opal-tinted light had gone,—
Died in the heavens, like a sweet dream;
We know not whence it came, nor know
To where it goes. We only know
It fades away all unperceived,
Into the deep mysterious realms
Ethereal bright. Such brilliant skies
Are eloquent; for they portend
That tempests soon will smite the earth!

MODERN SOCIETY.

The more I see of this strange world,
  The more a mystery 'tis to me;
All worldly people whom I meet,
  Unsolved enigmas seem to be.

I cannot understand their ways,
  Their aims are all outside my reach;
Amazed, I watch the far-off throng,
  Learn lessons stern, some lives can teach

Upon the surface things appear,
    To be so honest, fair, and bright;
But underneath it, lurks I fear,
    A depth of sin, ne'er brought to light.

A charming, pleasant, winning front,
    Towards our view too oft is turned;
Behind the outward guise sometimes,
    Lie hearts, that if laid bare, were spurned.

The fleeting glimpses I can get,
    Of modern life, reveal to me,
That where one would the least expect,
    Are grave defects, so hard to see.

Smooth-tongued dissemblers smile at wrongs,
    And smother conscience in their youth;
They freely flaunt at Pleasure's feet,
    Unknown to guileless realms of truth.

I sadly fear that in our midst,
    Some uncurbed social evils sleep;
All winked at by the world at large,
    O'er which strict Virtue well might weep.

My nature cannot keep in touch,
    With those I find are insincere;
While frivolous ones I would avoid,
    Commend me to affection's tear.

False pride, and artificial show,
    The worldly ways of life beset;
With empty cant are others marred,
    What class were all found perfect yet?

The world consists of sharps and flats,
    All complicated airs to me,
In minor strains; I would that more
    Were in a simple major key.

With no discordant blatant tones,
    The sweet harmonious notes to mar;
All cheerful strains of peace and love,
    That on the senses never jar.

I. unsophisticated — search
   Some "worldlings'" faces I have met
And there I try to read their hearts,
   But ne'er have been successful yet.

Both good and ill are always blent
   In human nature, know we well;
In some proportion; but sometimes
   The gilt from gold is hard to tell.

I seek for *real* good sterling worth,
   This would I ever fain pursue;
Kind, constant, faithful, trusty hearts,
   That in grief's hour are staunch and true.

And these sometimes I've thought I'd found,
   While fondly in them I believed,
And prized them till my hopes were crushed,
   On finding I had been deceived.

The gravest faults sometimes lie hid,
   'Neath thin veneering, all for show;
Deceit, vainglory, artful shams,
   Some fair exteriors lay below.

A heart wherein one could repose
   The fullest trust, I fain would find;
But selfish, hollow, and untrue,
   The worldly are, soul, heart and mind!

If folks were only what they seem,
   I'd cling to those I thought the best;
But having some unworthy proved,
   Makes me less trustful of the rest.

'Tis not for me to pierce the veil
   That covers social errors o'er;
Thank God that I can live apart
   From scenes that I must needs deplore!

I find this problem hard to solve,
   To tell the false ones from the true;
The counterfeit from purest gems,
   For baseness holds a power undue

I'll give it up! and keep aloof,
　　As heretofore, from pomp and strife;
Content to live as Nature's child,
　　A happy and secluded life.

TO A BRIDE.

Merry sounds, and golden sunlight,
　　Greet thee on thy bridal morn;
As thy loving friends surround thee,
　　Offerings gay to thee are borne.

Friends will with thee be in spirit,
　　Who may never cross the main;
Winds will waft thee their good wishes
　　Though ye may not meet again.

Bright as an Arcadian bower,
　　May thy future home be there;—
Sweet to thee as spring's first flower,—
　　Like the snowdrop pure and fair.

May thy Southern home be happy,
　　An Elysium be to thee;
Mid thy joys yet think of England,
　　And thy friends across the sea.

One who knew thee as a maiden—
　　Revelled in thy friendship's glow;
Sighs amid the glad rejoicings,
　　That we must be parted now.

Like two streamlets in the woodlands,
　　For a time run side by side;
Then each separate course diverges,
　　Till at last they're sever'd wide.

So two lives may run together,—
　　Know each other's hopes and fears:
For a time, then at an angle,
　　Drift apart with smiles and tears.

Oft we see that winsome Cupid,
  Turns life's streamlet by and bye
While his soft electric glances,
  Dart across from eye to eye.

Friends who cannot here salute thee,
  Fondly wish though far away;
That a thousand blessings crown thee,
  On thy glorious nuptial day.

AN OPTIMISTIC PROPHECY.

It is coming, it is coming, I can see it from afar,
With a gloriole around it, in a grand triumphal car!
Superstition mars its progress, but that crumbles to decay,
And as light falls on the Nations, then will Wisdom clear the way.
It is coming in the distance, just a speck beyond the bars:
It is mirrored in the future, it is whispered by the stars.
It will stifle brutal instincts, give the soul a wider scope,
For it even through the present weaves a golden thread of hope.
Then in that bright Utopia, Peace's banner being unfurled,
Oh, a better type of manhood, will rise up to grace the world.
It will rule the mighty Rulers, to an epoch new give birth;
And the arch-fiends, War, and Carnage, it will sweep from off the earth!
Make those hideous cruel monsters all their awful fangs release,
And no gore-taint stain the glory 'neath the benison of Peace.
It will win us bloodless vict'ries, when it sways the Empires vast;
All that tarnished old-time glory will be buried with the past.

For the World we know is waiting for the mighty grand
    reform,
That will tranquillize all rancour, nor with war-drum's
    fierce alarm.
Though this century be closing to the sound of war-
    whoops wild,
In the next one, Federation, will be nursed a precious
    child :—
That will prove an untold blessing, as the century rolls
    along,
And its birth be kept by millions, in a grand triumphant
    song !
As the century advances, it will hold a foremost place ;
It will glorify the Universe,—ennoble every race.
Then the cannon shall be rusty, and the sword lie in its
    sheath :
And for ghastly deeds of slaughter, man shall wear no
    glory wreath :
Nor for heaping mangled bodies upon fields of reeking
    gore ;
All war's horrors, and its tortures, shall belong to days
    of yore !
For behold ! a vital atom has by God's grace now been
    sown,
And an Universal Brotherhood, will the world in future
    own !
And the life-germ now upspringing, will arise a beateous
    flower,
Ere the century before us has attained its noon-tide's
    power.
All the future is resplendent, with a bright auriferous
    light,
Till this age but seems by contrast, just emerging from
    the night :
It invests the living present with a clear prophetic glow,
Like the flush before the sunrise, and the light from new-
    dropt snow.
The World-chosen Mediators, will all Nations' rights
    secure,
And a Court of Arbitration, will maintain our honour
    pure.

For behold! this Federation shall the World with new
    life tinge,
When the gates of Peace's Temple shall swing wide on
    golden hinge!
For the Universe 'twill girdle, - all the Nations bind in
    love,
And to seal the mighty compact, 'twill be blest by God
    Above!

VALEDICTION.

I thank you all, my dearest friends,
    For list'ning to my lays;
Some penn'd in grief, and some in mirth,
    The fruit of early days,
And culled from little incidents,
    That crossed my daily life,
And called up vivid pictures,
    Of outside worldly strife.
And from my youth's aspiring thoughts
    Romantic though they were;
Born in the morning-time of life,
    When all the world seems fair,
And more than all, from nature sweet,
    In all its forms and ways;
'Twas it that first inspired my muse
    In those my early days.
It struck a chord within my soul,
    Laid dormant until then;
It stirred a latent power within,
    And bade me wield my pen!
And therefore I present to you,
    These simple, little poems;
I feel I have your sympathy—
    Each one in friendship joins.
I hope that when you read them o'er,
    You'll read them once again;
They may perchance, cheer some dull hour
    Of those who are in pain.

And those who do not know me well,
   Shall know me through this book;
Ah, e'en as well as though they knew,
   My ev'ry word and look.
I wish it were more worthy of
   The kindness that you show:
I hope its merit will repay,
   The labour you bestow,
In taking this my humble work,
   To at your leisure read;
But I have done my best to please,
   The will take for the deed.
Perchance, I'll tune the lyre again
   For you in future years—
Or I may then have passed away,
   Amid your friendly tears.
And now good-bye—my dearest friends,
   To you this book I've given—
And if I see you not on earth,
   We all may meet in Heaven.

LIST OF PATRONS.

Those with an asterisk appended take more than one copy

THE MOST NOBLE THE MARQUIS OF RIPON
*THE RIGHT HON. THE EARL OF CRANBROOK.
THE RIGHT HON. THE EARL OF WHARNCLIFFE.
THE RIGHT HON. THE EARL OF CREWE.
LADY COOK, VISCOUNTESS DE MONTSERRAT

*Armitage, Mrs. M. A.
Alderson, The Misses
Angless, James
Angless, Miss M
Asquith, Bentley, C E
Atkinson, Miss

Billson, Alfred, M P.
Batt, Rev. Wm.
*Bickerstaffe, Robert
*Bottomley, Mrs M
*Bayes, A. B
Bannister, Thos.
Briggs, Miss Edith
Bottomley, Mrs. W
Bancroft, Mrs.
Barraclough, Gathorne
Bent, Miss
Bartle, Mrs
Barraclough, Samuel
Baxter, Miss
Bywater, Matthias
Bywater, G. H
Baines, Rufus
Barraclough, Mrs E.
Brook, Mrs
Bailey, Mrs W.
Boyes, Joseph
Bartle, Miss L.

Briggs, Peter
Belfield, John
Brook, William
Briggs, Miss Emma
Bartle, Miss A
Barraclough, J. H
Blackburn, Mrs
Beaumont, John
Bryden, William
Booth, Miss H
Barraclough, Mrs. H
Blamires, William
Breaks, W T
Buckley, Mrs.
Barraclough, Miss E
Birkbeck, Mrs J.
Blackburn, Mrs C
Brook, Mrs A
Brown, Mrs
Butterworth, Mrs. J
Barraclough, Edwin
Broadley, Mrs.
Blackburn, Miss
Barmby, Mrs M
*Bradford Public Free Libra
    B Wood Chief Librar
Bradford Library and L.
    Society (per W M
    Hon Sec)

LIST OF PATRONS.

*Craven, Rev. A.
*Clay, Arthur, T., C C
Carter, J. B., J.P.
*Clough, C. S.
*Cordingley, Miss E. M.
Childe, J. B.
Christie, Miss
Clough, W. H.
Casson, Mrs. J.
Clayton, Joseph
Collins, Mrs.
Collins, Campbell
Collins, Vernal
Crossley, Mrs.
Cass, Miss
Cockroft, Miss
Crowther, Mrs. C.
Charnock, Mrs.

Dearden, Dr. C.
Denbeigh, John
Dickinson, Miss
Dobell, James

*Ellis, Lewis
Ellis, Mrs. A.
Ellis, Miss E.
Edmondson, Mrs. J.
Ellis, Mrs. J.

Flannnery, Fortescue, M.P.
*France, Mrs.
*Farrar, Harry
*Firth, John
*Fearnley, George
Fearnley, Mrs. G.
Fearnley, Mrs. B.
Flynn, Miss E. C.
Foster, Mrs.
Fairburn, Mrs. H.
Frankland, Mrs. F.
Fowler, Charles
Fearnley, Mrs. J.
Fenton, R. J.
Farrar, Mrs.

*Greenwood, Mrs. A. R.
Gill, Miss
Greenwood, Harry

Hardy, Laurence, M.P.
Holdsworth, Ald. Wm., J.P
Hilliam, Dr. W. P.
Hainsworth, Lewis
Hardwick, Mrs. J.
Hardy, Richard
Hind, Mrs. I
Hind, Fred
Hodgson, Mrs. S.
Henshaw, Miss
Henshaw, Miss H.
Hanson, Miss
Henderson, Thomas
Hitchin, Edmund
Hoyle, Mrs.
Hodgson, Jeremiah
Hodgson, Miss F.
Hartley, Miss E
Harper, John
Hall, Mrs. W.
Hudson, Joseph
Hilton, Mrs.
Hirst, Miss E.
Holdsworth, Mrs.
Halstead, Mrs.
Hargreaves, Mrs.
Hirst, Mrs. M.
Hanson, Mrs.
Holden, Mrs.
Haigh, Ben
Halifax Public Free Library (per J. Whiteley, Chief Librarian)
Harold Club, Low Moor (per T. W. Whiteley, Librarian)

Illingworth, William

Jowett, J. H.
Jackson, Mrs.

Kellett, Mrs. S.
Keighley, Miss H. A.
Knowles, Arthur
Kellett, D.
Kellett, E.
Kefford, Thomas
Kay, Mrs. W. H

Logan, Dr. T., M D.
Lister, Wm. C. C

LIST OF PATRONS

Laycock, Henry
Lightowler, Miss S.
Lund, Henry

Milligan, F. W.
Moorhouse, J. B.
Mallinson, Hanson
Maude, John
Mitchell, Miss M
Myers, John

Naylor, Dr J. H
North, Mrs. J. S.
Naylor, Mrs.
North, Mrs.

Oates, J W.
Ollerenshaw, Mrs. H
Oddy, Herbert
Oates, Benjamin
*Oates, Miss S. E
Oates, Herbert
Oates, Ernest
Orrell, Wm.

Poynton, Rev. J
Priestley, Enoch, J. P
Pyrah, James
Potter, Miss E.
Paget, Mrs.
Priestley, M. A

Robinson, Dr. A H
Rushworth, Mrs.
Rhodes, Richard
Rhodes, Bethel
Rhodes, Fred
Rayner, Mrs.
Ramsden, Miss
Robertshaw, Richard
Robinson, Joseph
Rhodes, Mrs T
Rayner, Godfrey
Rushworth, Miss

*Smith, Enoch, J.I
*Sharp, James
Smyth, Mrs. N
*Snowball, Thomas
Stakes, Jesse

Smith, Ald. W
*Sharp, Mrs. J.
Sutcliffe, Mrs.
Simpson, Mrs
*Smith, Edmund
Sharp, Mrs Jno.
Schofield, Miss
Seed, Benjamin
Smith, Tom
Seaton, Moses
Sucksmith, Miss S
Sugden, Mrs
Smith, Mrs.
Shaw, Thomas
Scott, J. P
Spencer, Miss
Surbuts, W. H
Sucksmith, Miss M
Shaw, Mrs
Smith, Miss
Sugden, J. W
Siddal, Mrs.
Spencer, Mrs.
Schofield, Mrs.

*Tordoff, Jonathan
Turnbull, Mrs. M.
Thornton, Joseph
Thompson, Mrs.
Tordoff, Mrs. J.

*Uttley, Thos F.

*Whittaker, T. P., M I
Wayman, Thos., M P
*Wickham, R. W.
*Wright, Samuel
*Woodcock, H B.
Whiteley, Geo., C.C
Ward, Coun. J
Weeder, Wm, L D S
Weeder, Mrs J
Wavell, E. M.
Woodhead, Alfred
Wilson, Mrs
Whitteron, Mrs
Willans, J. W
Warburton, Mrs
Whittaker, Joseph

LIST OF PATRONS.

Wilson, Miss
Whitley, Miss C.
Worsnop, R. W.
Woodcock, J. M.
White, Edwin
Woodhead, Miss
Wright, Mrs. D.
Wood, Mrs. H.
Wood, D.
Wilson, William
Woodhead, Mrs. R.
Wells, Miss
Wright, Mrs.
Womersley, John

Wilks, Miss
Woodcock, Smith
Worsnop, Miss M. J.
Whittaker, Mrs.
Womersley, Miss
Wilson, Miss E.
Wood, John
Wells, Mrs. F.
Woodhead, Miss L.
Wrigglesworth, John
Womersley, Mrs. F.
Warbrick, Miss
Wilson, Miss H.
Woodcock, T. W.